Barren States

The Population "Implosion" in Europe

Edited by
Carrie B. Douglass

BERG

Oxford • New York

English edition
First published in 2005 by
Berg
Editorial offices:
First Floor, Angel Court, 81 St Clements Street, Oxford OX4 1AW, UK
175 Fifth Avenue, New York, NY 10010, USA

Berg is the imprint of Oxford International Publishers Ltd.

Library of Congress Cataloging-in-Publication Data
A catalogue record for this book is available from the Library of Congress.

British Library Cataloguing-in-Publication Data
A catalogue record for this book is available from the British Library.

ISBN-13   978 1 84520 048 0 (cloth)
          978 1 84520 049 0 (paperback)

ISBN-10   1 84520 048 9 (cloth)
          1 84520 049 7 (paperback)

Typeset by Avocet Typeset, Chilton, Aylesbury, Bucks
Printed in the United Kingdom by Biddles Ltd, King's Lynn

www.bergpublishers.com

Contents

Illustrations

Figures

Tables

Notes on Contributors

Carrie B. Douglass is Associate Professor of Anthropology and Spanish in the Foreign Languages, Literatures and Cultures Department at Mary Baldwin College, Staunton, Virginia. Most of her work has been on identity and Spain. She is author of *Bulls, Bullfighting and Spanish Identities* (University of Arizona Press, 1999).

Susan L. Erikson is a medical anthropologist interested in how state and market forces shape women's reproductive health experiences. Most recently, she has published on how the historical geopolitical division of Germany continues to shape contemporary German women's experiences of prenatal diagnostic technology use. She is currently working on a book addressing the global flows of medical knowledge and technology, *Engendering the Global*. She directs Global Health Affairs at the Graduate School of International Studies at the University of Denver.

Cynthia Gabriel is a Research Fellow at the Population Studies Institute, University of Michigan. She received her doctorate in medical anthropology from University of California, Santa Cruz, and is currently working on a book about reproductive medicine in Russia.

Gail Kligman is Professor of Sociology at the University of California, Los Angeles. She has written widely on gender, culture and politics in Central and Eastern Europe, both during and after socialism. Among her books are *The Politics of Duplicity: Controlling Reproduction in Ceausescu's Romania* (University of California Press, 1998); co-authored with Susan Gal, *The Politics of Gender after Socialism* (Princeton University Press, 2000); and co-edited with Susan Gal, *Reproducing Gender: Politics, Publics and Everyday Life after Socialism* (Princeton University Press, 2000).

Elizabeth L. Krause is Assistant Professor in the Department of Anthropology at the University of Massachusetts, Amherst. She has published *A Crisis of Births: Population Politics and Family-Making in Italy* (Thompson/Wadsworth, 2005), and articles in *Cultural Anthropology, Journal of Historical Anthropology, Transforming Anthropology, Journal of Modern Italian Studies, Human*

Organization as well as *Newsday*. She has received grants from the Council for European Studies, Fulbright Program and, most recently, Wenner-Gren Foundation for Anthropological Research.

Anna Lim is a PhD student in social and cultural anthropology at the University of Virginia and the Ecole des hautes études en sciences sociales (EHESS) in Paris, France. She is currently completing her dissertation on family policy, motherhood and social membership in France and the French Antilles.

Jo Murphy-Lawless is a sociologist who has published extensively on issues of women and reproductive health in the Irish and international contexts. Currently in the School of Nursing and Midwifery Studies, Trinity College Dublin, she is the author of *Reading Birth and Death: A History of Obstetric Thinking* (Indiana University Press, 1998).

Rebecca Nash received her PhD in sociocultural anthropology from the University of Virginia in 2003. She is currently a research associate in the Department of Primary Care and Social Medicine, Imperial College London. Her current research focus includes sex work markets in the UK and sexual and reproductive health.

Malin Noem Ravn currently works as a post-doctoral researcher in the Department of Interdisciplinary Studies of Culture at the Norwegian University of Science and Technology. Her most recent work is her doctoral thesis "One Body: Two Lives: Pregnancy, the Fetus and the Pregnant Body – An Anthropological Analysis."

Heather Paxson teaches anthropology and gender studies at the Massachusetts Institute of Technology and received a PhD from Stanford University, California. Her book, *Making Modern Mothers: Ethics and Family Planning in Urban Greece* (University of California Press, 2004), was based on two years' ethnographic research into fertility control and motherhood in Athens.

Maria Stoilkova received her PhD in cultural anthropology from the University of California at Berkeley and is currently a post-doctoral fellow at the Harriman Institute, Columbia University. Publications include "A New Generation of the Bulgarian Transition: In Search of a 'Brighter Future'," in R. Stryker and J. Patico (eds) *The Paradoxes of Progress* (Kroeber Anthropological Society, 2001).

Introduction

Carrie B. Douglass
(with Rebecca Nash, Susan L. Erikson
and Anna Lim)

> It is the case that reality, like landscape, has infinite perspectives, all of them equally
> true and authentic. The only false perspective is the one that claims to be the only one.
>
> José Ortega y Gasset, *The Theme of our Time*

Barren States

- In 2003 there were just four new mothers in a population of 1600. That compares with 70 babies born in 1970, when Laviano [Italy] had around 3,000 residents. In a bid to reverse the trend Mayor Rocco Falivena is digging deep into town coffers and offering couples 10,000 euros ($11,900) for every newborn baby. "It's a lot of money but this is our top priority," said Falivena. "We are talking about the very survival of our town." (Reuters, MSNBC News, 2003)
- "Scotland's baby bust is echoing nosily in the political system. For five years running, Scotland has recorded more deaths than births and now has the lowest birthrate in Britain. Scotland is debating whether it should offer would-be parents large tax breaks." (Alvarez, *New York Times*, 2003)
- In November 2002, in an historical speech before the Italian parliament in Rome, Pope John Paul referred to what he called "the crisis" of the country's declining birthrate and urged Italians to have more children in order to reverse "this grave threat that bears upon the future of the country." (Bruni, *New York Times*, 2002)
- In May 2004, a member of the Australian government, Peter Costello, outlined a federal budget that promised $2000 for every baby born after June. In an aging nation of 20 million, two children per couple was not enough, he said. "You go home and do your patriotic duty. You should have one for your husband, one for your wife, and one for your country." (Reuters, *New York Times*, 2004).

The above comments come from newspaper articles and are reactions to the results, seen on a mass scale, of very personal decisions: the birthrates of imagined collectivities – cities or countries. These responses, recorded by the media, are by public figures or officials who want public policy to encourage more births. But what do the people who are "responsible" for the low birthrates say? What do low birthrates mean to them? Below are snippets of conversations, recorded by the authors of this book, that express the diverse and contrasting values and situations about having children, or how these individuals understand "low fertility." The first set of comments (above) is by all men. The second set of comments (below) is by almost all women.

- "The man I live with wants children and says that he is prepared to share the responsibility, but I still suspect that most of the responsibility would fall on me. Because of this I still want to wait many years [to have children]." (Norway)
- "We discussed it [to have children] as if it were a choice, but you cannot choose the *wish* to have children in itself." (Norway)
- "We were 20 when re-unification happened. Usually you would have married at 18 or 20 and had children then. It was a prerequisite to be married in order to get an apartment. You married and had a child first, and then you built your own life. Now it's completely the other way around. First you live your life and then you have children when you are about 30." (Germany)
- "He was worried that we couldn't afford a second child. I was worried that we had no room." (Russia)
- "The demographers yell that low numbers of children are born, but Marcela's generation realizes that life is more than children, more than sitting home and staying with kids." (Czech Republic)
- "There was a lot of catch up to do to compensate for the time we missed living in a closed state during socialism. Many people decided to continue their education abroad. The parents in fact were very encouraging of all this. What bothers me most about the culture of marriage here in Bulgaria is that people get married and they simply stop growing. With a child in your hand, you no longer can experiment with choices." (Bulgaria)
- "But it's difficult because I'm working and because now we want to have everything for our children." (Greece)
- "I believe all women want to become mothers. How can I tell you? It completes them." (Greece)
- "I think especially here in Athens, in the cities, they accept you if you don't have a child, but they admire you more, they accept you more if you are a working mom and have your husband, your family, your house, *and* your children." (Greece)

- "What trade do you do?" "The craft of motherhood," replied Anna, a mother who worked in the giftshop trade. (Italy)
- "Why would I leave home? I live in a five star hotel!" (Spain)
- "We want freedom, but it's a comfortable freedom." (Spain)
- "We are all children of immigrants." (France)
- "But the fact is the option isn't there to do what my mother did, to give us a good quality of life on one salary." (Ireland)

Most of what we hear about low birthrates comes from the top down: from the viewpoint of large populations – states, cities, ethnic groups. This book, *Barren States: The Population "Implosion" in Europe*, explores the culture of low fertility in Europe from the bottom up: from the viewpoint of individuals and citizens of those states. Averages conceal an astonishing diversity.

The situation of European countries with extremely low birthrates will cause changes in the demographic landscape but it certainly does not evoke barrenness. The vast majority of women, and couples, still say they want children and are having children, at least one. Anthropologists have shown that, despite what Western demographers have thought, women have always had some rational control over the number of their offspring (through abstention, infanticide, abandonment, adoption and now reproductive technologies). If in postmodernity, rational control of fertility means fewer children than needed for population replacement are produced, it behooves us to look at the society these women live in, to look at the meaning of children, and to look at exactly what is being reproduced and replaced, in order to understand this phenomenon.

By playing provocatively with the expression "Barren States" in the title of this volume, we also want to question the social construction of the state as a reified entity. Just how does the population of the state get constructed? Who counts? Who is included in this imagined community? Furthermore, by including the media's favorite (rather alarmist) description of low fertility as an implosion, we want to call attention to the nuances of negative implications in the term "implosion." If there is a population implosion about to happen in Europe, who or what will implode? By imploding, will something, something valuable, be destroyed? If so, is there something we should do to avoid implosion? Does using this term – implosion – imply blame? Are women to blame for not having "enough" children? Is society to blame? Or the cultural milieu? Or an economic system? Or a political context? Do below replacement level birthrates really matter?

Since the late 1950s, visions of a population explosion have dominated the popular demographic imagination. By the mid-twentieth century, with increased control of many high-mortality diseases of both infants and adults, people began to survive and live longer. The world's population began increasing dramatically. By the year 2000 the earth's human population passed 6 billion. In many parts of the world, population growth seemed to be producing poverty and outpacing resources. Many people, especially in the developed world, wondered whether the earth could sustain continued population growth. It seemed "obvious" that if people in the developed world did not begin to limit their fertility, or the number of children they had, they would never escape poverty and "miserable" living conditions. Moreover, it was feared they would use up the earth's resources of water, fuel and food. This argument persists despite the fact that the richest quarter of the world's population accounts for more than three-quarters of the consumption of the world's natural resources. Family planning policies became the solution to the "population bomb" of international overpopulation.

Since 2000, however, a new message has begun to emerge. Rather than trumpeting a population explosion, headlines now announce a population *implosion*.[1] The general public is now being told what demographers have been tracking for decades: fertility levels are dropping all over the earth.[2] Beginning in Europe, and then several countries in Asia, Canada, Australia and the Caribbean, a "baby bust" is replacing the boom. Although a low-fertility trend was first noted in countries with highly developed market economies, now fertility is declining even in developing nations.[3] In many places the drop in fertility has now reached below replacement levels. In other words, couples are having so few children over their lifetimes that they are not replacing themselves. This demographic trend was not predicted. The number of countries with below replacement fertility increased from five in 1960 to sixty-four in 2000, encompassing 34 percent of the world's population. Populations are growing old with no one to replace them. Soon, according to the United Nations Population Division, some countries are going to start losing population. The United States is the only developed country with fertility close to replacement level.

In the discourse of demographers, replacement level fertility is defined as "the level at which a cohort of women, on the average, have only enough daughters to 'replace' themselves in the population" (Haupt and Kane 1978: 22). The total fertility rate (TFR) is "the average number of children that would be born alive to a woman (or group of women) during her lifetime if she were to pass through all her childbearing years (fifteen to forty-nine years old) conforming to the age fertility rates of a given year" (Haupt and Kane 1978: 19). It is the average of the number of children that women have in their reproductive lifetimes. A replacement level total fertility rate in a healthy population is usually calculated at 2.1 children per woman (which allows for a normal sex ratio at birth, and takes into account some early maternal deaths).[4]

When the fertility rate of a population drops below 2.1, it is described as non-replacement fertility. Fertility has always dropped in response to war, natural catastrophes, famine, economic depression and instability. Once these uncertainties disappear, fertility typically rises again. Sustained below replacement level fertility in the present context of the developed world is something new. In this book we look at this phenomenon in Europe, the continent where it was first recorded. In 2003 the total fertility rate of Europe was 1.4 (Population Reference Bureau 2003); the TFR of the European Union was 1.47 (Eurostat 2003) – significantly below replacement level.

To examine the significance of this change, we propose to put reproduction at the center of our social, cultural and political-economic analysis. The authors of this book are not social demographers, but rather anthropologists and ethnographers of reproduction. We follow in the footsteps of others who have used reproduction – both physical and societal – to serve as a vehicle for discovering many other social concerns (Ginsberg and Rapp 1995; Davis-Floyd and Sargent 1996; Inhorn and Van Balen 2002; Greenhalgh 1995; Franklin and Ragone 1998; Strathern 1993). Reproduction can be seen as a kind of collective representation, the "shared images and symbols through which a society represents itself to itself" (Delaney 2004: 14). In this sense, the anthropologist, Rayna Rapp, has said: "Reproduction lies at the heart of a culture's representations of itself: it is in large measure through imagining reproduction that individual families, and social groups conceive of the future towards which they aspire for themselves and the next generation" (Rapp 1999: 317).

What do people in their everyday lives make of reproduction, both with respect to their personal lives and social worlds? What does it mean that certain social groups are not reproducing themselves? Is it a kind of social suicide?[5] Or does it say something about our imagined future? Do we see the future with optimism or with pessimism? Or, at the micro level, as individuals, do we feel we *are* reproducing ourselves?

This introduction contextualizes the phenomenon of sustained low fertility for the non-specialist reader – from a consideration of the possible demographic repercussions of low fertility to the history of the (two) great demographic declines in Europe, with a discussion of the convergences and divergences in reproductive patterns and behavior across Europe at the beginning of the twenty-first century. It is into this demographic conversation that the authors of this volume insert their ethnographic snapshots of fertility experiences in Europe, illuminating the differences between statistical averages and the diverse, lived realities. Ours is perhaps a more narrow perspective, certainly a deeper perspective, of European reproduction than that of the state. Rather than a review of the abundant literature dealing with reproduction and fertility, this introduction proposes to provide the reader with a broader framework in which to place the chapters that follow, each dedicated to a particular European country.

Why Countries are Worried: Repercussions of Below Replacement Level Fertility

Several topics dominate media coverage of fertility decline. In an attempt to grab public attention, most of this coverage tends to be alarmist and emphasizes perceived "problems" caused by low fertility, thus, the use of the term "implosion." Note that these problems are almost always seen from the vantage point of a collective population or the state. Here I review these "problems," which include shrinking populations, national decline, population aging, immigration and policy response.

"Shrinking" populations, or negative population growth, is one expected consequence of low fertility. After twenty or more years of below replacement level fertility, deaths now exceed births. With no recuperation in sight, many European countries are expected to begin to lose population. The United Nations Population Division has projected steep population declines in most of the forty-seven European countries by 2050. Spain will lose one-quarter of its current population, Greece one-fifth. Estonia's population will have dropped by 36 percent; Italy will be 22 percent smaller; Russia 28 percent; and Bulgaria, Estonia, Georgia, Latvia, and Ukraine will be between 30 and 50 percent smaller. In 1995 the European Union population was 100 million people larger than that of the United States. By 2050 it may be smaller than the United States by 20 million.

Fears of low fertility and population loss often become metaphors for fears about national decline, and as such, have a long history throughout the twentieth century in Europe (see the cases of Germany, the Czech Republic and France, Chapters 3, 5 and 10 in this volume). Frequently these fears are framed not only at the national level, as noted above, but also at the sub-national level. Certain ethnic groups or linguistic groups view the low birthrate of their "group" as an ominous sign of their loss of power or privilege, or even their literal physical and cultural disappearance (i.e. the Basques in Spain, Bretons in France). Other groups defined by "race," religion, or language are looked upon with concern by dominant groups and feared for their higher-than-average birthrate (i.e. above replacement level, for example, Arab immigrants in France, Roma throughout East Central Europe). As one demographer has said, "there are no shortages of humans, only perceived or relative shortages of particular kinds of humans" (Teitelbaum 2000: 162). Thus, concerns about population loss and low fertility evoke many social and political questions and have provoked responses from both the political left and political right. Curiously, population decline is primarily perceived as a threat rather than as a relief – a relief from the stress that rising population numbers put on the environment and society (Woollacott 2003).

Population aging is another expected consequence of fertility decline in Europe. With fewer children being born and people living longer than ever,[6] the age pyramid is changing. Older people (over 65) already make up a large percentage of the population in Europe, and this group will only get proportionally larger. By 2050 in Southern Europe, for example, the UN calculates that the percentage of the population above age 60 will rise from about 22 percent in 2004 to an unprecedented 40 percent in 2050. This could pose major challenges as well as potentially beneficial economic social and political opportunities. The graying of the population will strain current pension and health care systems because there will be fewer people/workers to support older and retired citizens (the so-called support ratio) (see the case of the Czech Republic, Chapter 5 in this volume), thus calling into question intergenerational compacts and affecting such things as government finances and public debt. The diminished supply of young labor may require rethinking retirement criteria (moving up the age of retirement; less social security and pension benefits). Demands for goods and services could also change as the percentage of older citizens increases (i.e. schooling, housing, entertainment and health care). Another solution to the labor supply for the support ratio, and the one urged by a UN report in 2000, is to increase the number of workers through immigration.

International immigration is another issue associated with concerns about low fertility. Significantly, the figures above of projected population loss ignore the phenomenon of international migration, an issue almost all European countries are dealing with, as people from the developing world strive to enter "Fortress Europe" for economic, social and cultural benefits. As noted above, the United Nations' Department of Economic and Social Affairs/Population Division (ESA/P 2001) proposes what it calls Replacement Migration as a solution to declining and aging populations. The total population of EU countries is projected to be reduced by twenty to 20–25 percent by 2050. The UN suggests that population loss could be avoided if 1 million immigrants moved into Western Europe every year for the first half of the twenty-first century (ESA/P 2001: 11), or fifteen times more than during the 1990s. However, experts admit this is not a likely scenario, although not because of the lack of potential immigrants. In fact, much illicit immigration (often from high fertility countries) manages to enter Europe every day. Small boats full of aspiring immigrants sailing from north Africa are intercepted daily off the shores of Mediterranean Europe. Rather, it is an unlikely scenario because, unlike the United States or Australia, no European nation defines itself as an immigrant society. Residing in the same place throughout one's life is considered normal according to the European Observatory on the Social Situation, Demography and Family (EOSSDF 2002). So far, although European public opinion wants humanitarian responses to individual cases, it does not support open immigration. Moreover, most of the European governments and the EU administration have recently crafted more restrictive immigration policies, rather than the reverse.

As noted above, national and sub-national populations are defined culturally. When immigrants come from "other" racial, linguistic, religious, or cultural groups, they often raise "deep-seated fears of losing national or ethnic identity and/or control" (Teitelbaum 2000: 178). Tension with, and political violence against, immigrant groups characterize several European societies and anti-immigration discourse is often blatantly racist. Furthermore, several EU member states are slowly working on ending even the right to asylum.

It is a demographic fiction that all national populations are closed (Kreager 1997). Thus, the very issue of how national populations are counted is the subject of three contributions to this book (see the cases of Bulgaria, France and Ireland, Chapters 6, 10 and 11 in this volume). How are birthrates calculated by country? Are all babies born within the territorial boundaries of the states considered in the total fertility rate, including babies of immigrants and undocumented workers? Or are only the newborns of citizens counted? Who gets to be a citizen? And what about citizens who reside abroad, outside the country? Are their offspring included in national statistics?

If Europe's leaders are not welcoming immigrants to replace projected (labor) losses and to maintain populations (and power/place in the world community), have there been any other policy responses, specifically pronatalist policies, to very low fertility on the part of European governments since the early 1980s? During the Socialist era in Eastern Europe, pronatalist policies were more common than in the West. In some cases, notably Romania, the state banned abortion and made access to birth control virtually impossible in the interest of forcing increased birthrates (Kligman 1998). There and elsewhere economic incentives were offered to encourage couples to have children. But these pronatalist polices have been curtailed as part of the large-scale downsizing of public provisions since the early 1990s. In liberalizing democracies, any restriction or pressure on individual liberty or autonomy seems inappropriate. Moreover, in the countries that experienced fascist pronatalist policies (Germany, Italy and Spain) and socialist pronatalist policies (Eastern Europe), governments, although often concerned about low fertility for the reasons discussed above, would not consider reintroducing policies that recall their undemocratic pasts (see the cases of Germany, Russia, the Czech Republic, Bulgaria, Italy and Spain, Chapters 3, 4, 5, 6, 8 and 9 in this volume).

Among Western European countries only France and Greece "have adopted explicit pronatalist policies" (Teitelbaum 2000: 178). France, in fact, has the longest history of political concern about low fertility and offers many economic incentives and social services to encourage explicitly fertility and support large families (see the cases of Greece and France, Chapters 7 and 10 in this volume). Other countries recognize that their family policies, originally put in place as part of an extension of their welfare systems, may also help encourage fertility (see the cases of Norway and Germany, Chapters 2 and 3 in this volume). However, it is not clear whether these pronatalist policies actually affect fertility levels (Gautier 1994: 234). European governments, in general, have not instituted pronatalist policies. This may be so because at the end of the twentieth century Western governments re-emphasized the limits of the role of the state on the lives of its citizens. Another factor may have been that measures to increase fertility would have been "too costly in economic terms or in losses of individual freedoms" (Teitelbaum 2000: 181). Several of the studies in this volume take a closer look at what people are actually saying about these issues and how that merges or conflicts with what people actually do.

While not wanting to negate the importance and reality of the above issues and the need for governments to understand their possible repercussions and to plan for them, in this book we reframe these matters and look at them from a different perspective. We investigate how individual Europeans, not demographers, understand low fertility and make sense of it within their systems of meaning. The "problems" taken up by the media may not be so problematic for individuals. As shown by the authors of this volume, low fertility is often understood positively in Europe, and can even be understood as a means to "freedom" and self-empowerment.

Shaping Population Discourses: History of Demographic Perspectives

The First Demographic Transition

Before considering the contemporary moment, it is necessary to contextualize European demography historically. Even amid talk of population explosions in the late twentieth century, demographers knew that one part of the world had seen its fertility drop to sustainable levels (when the population was merely replacing itself rather than growing). Although lower trends in Europe had begun by the sixteenth century, almost all European countries between 1870 and 1930 had seen their birthrates drop rather drastically.[7] This process was called the demographic transition (Notestein 1945). With the looming "population explosion" in the second half of the twentieth century, demographers had sought to understand the causes of the demographic transition in Europe and then apply demographic transition theory to other parts of the globe in order to bring those populations "under control."

Investigation into the causes of the demographic transition brought to light several characteristics of European fertility. According to demographers, there were two main components of the decline. One, called the Malthusian transition after Thomas Malthus, was delay and/or curtailment of marriage (Coale 1973). This transition spread the European marriage pattern (Hajnal 1965), where women's first marriage occurs at an older age (middle or late twenties) and with many women never marrying (10 percent or more). This system contrasts with early and universal marriage of females, common in non-Western societies where many anthropologists work. After the Middle Ages, this marriage form spread through Western Europe and much later to Eastern Europe.

A second component of the fertility decline in Europe was the decline in marital fertility, or a decline in childbearing among married women, which is called the neo-Malthusian component. This was a change from what demographers called natural fertility (Henry 1968) to family-size limitation.[8] Natural fertility refers to couples who do not try to end childbearing before the end of their reproductive career.[9] Limiting family size occurs when couples stop having children when they have produced the number of children they desire, generally using contraceptive methods and/or abortion to control their fertility (Van de Walle and Knodel 1980).

Demographic transition theory claims to explain which social and cultural factors made Europeans start to control births in the late nineteenth century. From the beginning these answers were entwined with modernization theory, a unilineal view of societal development whereby history is collapsed simply into a traditional or a modern phase. The modern phase equaled "Westernization." The parallel demographic project was the transition from high to low fertility. Despite the demise of modernization theory in the social sciences in the late twentieth century (Greenhalgh 1996), low birthrates and modernity continue to be linked in the popular mind, as will be seen in several of the chapters here (see the cases of Russia, the Czech Republic and Bulgaria, Chapters 4, 5 and 6 in this volume).

Much demographic literature on European birthrates is devoted to a discussion of which factors account most significantly for the decline because so many processes were supposedly taking place at the same time: urbanization, industrialization, secularization, individualization, economic rationalization and improvement in sanitation (mortality decline). Two areas seemed most important: the changing role of children and the changing role of women. Since more and more children survived infancy and childhood, families could be more sure of their children living to adulthood with fewer births. Moreover, Caldwell (1976) postulated that the value of children to parents changed with industrialization. Children supply labor in agricultural and pre-industrial societies. But with urbanization and industrialization (and child labor laws), where work takes place outside the household, children become dependent for longer periods of time. Furthermore, they must be formally educated in order to leave dependence to become independent and compete in the marketplace. Thus, children lose their economic value to parents. Parents must now be motivated to have children for non-economic reasons, such as love and affection. For Caldwell (1976), the moment when wealth (in the form of labor) stopped flowing from children (younger generations) to parents (older generations) and began flowing from the older generations to children (in the form of longer dependent care) characterizes the first demographic transition as having essentially economic roots.[10]

Others emphasize the changing role of women, itself probably a result of the coherence of many factors: democratization, individualization, urbanization, industrialization, secularization, economic rationalization, after which appears universal education and fewer numbers of children (long periods of post-mothering). All of these social factors seem to conjoin, along with birth control techniques and technology, to produce women who often desire fewer children. The correlation between women's educational levels and low fertility is especially strong. Thus, particularly since the UN-sponsored International Conference on Population and Development in Cairo (1994) and World Conference on Women in Beijing (1995), fertility reduction programs in less-developed countries assertively promote women's education.

For twenty years starting in 1963, Ansley Coale, an economic demographer, headed an ambitious research project at Princeton, New Jersey to test the model of demographic transition theory in Western Europe. Coale led a team of collaborators who collected social, economic and demographic data at the level of provinces (rather than at the level of the state) throughout Western Europe for a period of more than a hundred years. To the shock of many, the Princeton team proved that demographic transition theory did not match the data. Urbanization, industrialization, infant mortality and education did not "explain" the historic decline in fertility. For example, fertility in many provinces began to drop before urbanization or industrialization. The project found that cultural factors seemed to influence the decline more than "modernization." Cultural setting affects the onset and spread of fertility decline independently of socio-economic conditions. The research project concluded, "Areas next to each other with similar socio-economic conditions entered the transition period at different times, whereas areas differing in the level of socio-economic development but with similar cultures and languages entered the transition at similar times" (Knodel and Van de Walle 1986: 412). "The spread of knowledge and ideas seems to offer a better explanation for the observed pattern than structural determinism" (Cleland and Wilson 1987: 20).

When culture was recognized as one explanatory factor of fertility decline, demographers added to their conceptual framework the life course approach, a framework that integrates the "micro level of behavior and the macro level of institutional and cultural influences on behavior" (see Van Wissen and Dykstra 1999: 5). Anthropologists also began research on population issues. It was this space that anthropologists of reproduction came to share with others working on these matters.

Meanwhile, however, some demographers had taken their demographic transition theory and applied it in the form of policies to other parts of the world, which they deemed at risk due to overpopulation. The goal was to "rationalize" fertility in these usually non-Western countries based on the somewhat ethnocentric assumption that people in these countries were stuck in mindless cycles of reproduction. In response, much anthropological demography has since been dedicated to explicating the culturally specific rationality of people's fertility careers (Bledsoe *et al.* 1994; Renne 1995).

Changing the Life Cycle in Europe: The Second Demographic Transition:

The second demographic transition was the label demographers gave to the phenomenon of "continuing fertility decline beyond the end of the (first) demographic transition to levels below replacement" (ESA/P 2003; Lesthaeghe 1995). Although all European countries had achieved low birthrates by the 1930s, fertility rates rose after the Second World War and stayed high until the 1970s. Then beginning in Northern and Western Europe, birthrates began to drop below replacement levels. Southern Europe followed a bit later. Following the end of Communist rule in the late 1980s and early 1990s, the countries of Eastern Europe also saw their birthrates plummet. During the 1990s, Spain and Italy vied for the lowest birthrates in the world (at TFR 1.1–1.3), stunning those who still held stereotypes of those Catholic countries as full of large "traditional families." By 2000, several countries of the former Socialist bloc (Czech Republic, Bulgaria, Russia, Bosnia-Herzegovina and the Ukraine) had birthrates even lower than Southern Europe (see Table 1.1).

As these patterns began to emerge in Europe (and later elsewhere in the world), demographers strove to explain them. Most scholars had held the unproven assumption that the (first) demographic transition would spread (albeit slowly) to the rest of the world with "modernization" or market economies, but that with low mortality and with replacement level fertility a kind of population equilibrium would be reached leading to stationary population. No one had really foreseen that birthrates would continue to decline below TFR 2.1. How far would they go down? It is no longer expected that low fertility countries will return to sustained fertility levels of above two children per woman (ESA/P 2003). Given the consequences of low fertility for the nation-state, deep population decline and population aging (as discussed above), much research has been aimed at explaining this phenomenon so as to affect family policy and ameliorate economic disruption. The United Nations calculates that the population of the earth will stop growing soon after 2050, leveling off at about 9 billion people, a significant reduction from the 12 billion projected in the early 1990s. It is, of course, unclear whether the earth's population will decline after that, and if this would be a good or a bad thing for humanity. Even small differences in fertility rates have significant economic, social and, therefore, political implications.[11]

Although demographers had taken the European marriage pattern (late female age at marriage and many women never marrying) into consideration when explaining the first demographic transition, in general they emphasized reproductive

Table 1.1 Total Fertility Rate: Ten European Countries, 1960–2002

	Norway	Germany	Czech Republic	Russia	Bulgaria	Greece	Italy	Spain	France	Ireland
1960	2.91	2.37	2.11	2.56	2.31	2.26	2.41	2.86	2.73	3.76
1961	2.94	2.44	2.13	2.47	2.28	2.19	2.41	2.76	2.81	3.79
1962	2.91	2.44	2.14	2.36	2.22	2.24	2.46	2.80	2.79	3.92
1963	2.93	2.51	2.35	2.31	2.19	2.22	2.54	2.88	2.89	4.01
1964	2.98	2.53	2.36	2.19	2.17	2.31	2.70	3.01	2.91	4.07
1965	2.94	2.50	2.18	2.12	2.08	2.30	2.66	2.94	2.84	4.03
1966	2.90	2.51	2.01	2.13	2.02	2.38	2.62	2.99	2.79	3.95
1967	2.81	2.45	1.90	2.04	2.03	2.55	2.53	3.03	2.66	3.84
1968	2.75	2.36	1.83	1.99	2.28	2.56	2.49	2.96	2.58	3.78
1969	2.69	**2.21**	1.86	2.00	2.28	2.53	2.51	2.93	2.53	3.96
1970	2.50	2.03	1.91	2.00	2.18	2.39	2.42	2.90	2.47	3.93
1971	2.49	1.97	1.98	2.03	2.11	2.32	2.41	2.88	2.49	3.99
1972	2.38	1.74	2.07	2.03	2.04	2.32	2.37	2.86	2.41	3.89
1973	2.23	1.56	2.29	1.96	2.16	2.26	2.24	2.84	2.30	3.75
1974	**2.13**	1.53	2.43	2.00	2.30	2.37	2.33	2.89	**2.11**	3.62
1975	1.98	1.48	2.43	1.97	2.24	2.32	2.20	2.79	1.93	3.40
1976	1.86	1.51	2.36	1.96	2.25	2.35	**2.10**	2.79	1.83	3.31
1977	1.77	1.51	2.32	1.92	2.21	2.28	1.97	2.66	1.86	3.27
1978	1.77	1.50	2.32	1.90	2.15	2.29	1.87	2.53	1.82	3.24
1979	1.75	1.50	2.29	1.87	**2.15**	2.29	1.76	2.31	1.86	3.23
1980	1.72	1.56	**2.10**	1.86	...	**2.21**	1.64	**2.20**	1.95	3.25
1981	1.70	1.53	2.02	1.88	2.01	2.09	1.59	2.04	1.95	3.07
1982	1.71	1.51	2.01	1.96	2.02	2.02	1.56	1.94	1.91	2.95
1983	1.66	1.43	1.97	2.09	2.00	1.94	1.51	1.80	1.78	2.74
1984	1.66	1.39	1.97	2.05	2.00	1.82	1.46	1.73	1.80	2.57
1985	1.68	1.37	1.96	2.05	1.95	1.67	1.42	1.64	1.81	2.47
1986	1.71	1.41	1.93	2.18	2.00	1.60	1.34	1.56	1.83	2.43
1987	1.75	1.43	1.91	2.23	1.95	1.50	1.32	1.50	1.80	2.31
1988	1.84	1.46	1.94	**2.14**	1.97	1.50	1.36	1.45	1.81	2.17
1989	1.89	1.42	1.87	2.02	1.90	1.40	1.33	1.40	1.79	2.08
1990	1.93	1.45	1.89	1.90	1.81	1.39	1.33	1.36	1.78	**2.11**
1991	1.92	1.33	1.86	1.75	1.65	1.38	1.31	1.33	1.77	2.08
1992	1.88	1.30	1.72	1.56	1.54	1.38	1.31	1.32	1.73	1.99
1993	1.86	1.28	1.67	1.36	1.46	1.34	1.25	1.27	1.65	1.90
1994	1.86	1.24	1.44	1.39	1.37	1.35	1.21	1.21	1.66	1.85
1995	1.87	1.25	1.28	1.34	1.24	1.32	1.18	1.18	1.70	1.84
1996	1.89	1.32	1.18	1.28	1.24	1.30	1.20	1.17	1.72	1.89
1997	1.86	1.37	1.19	1.23	1.09	1.31	1.22	1.19	1.71	1.92
1998	1.81	1.36	1.16	1.25	1.11	1.29	1.19	1.15	1.75	1.93
1999	1.84	1.36	1.13	1.17	1.23	1.28	1.23	1.20	1.79	1.88
2000	1.85	1.36	1.14	1.21	1.30	1.29	1.24	1.23	1.88	1.89
2001	1.85	1.29	1.14	1.30	1.20	1.29	1.24	1.25	1.90	1.98
2002	1.80	1.40	1.20	1.10	1.14	1.30	1.20	1.20	1.90	1.90

Sources: Eurostat/Population and Social Conditions/Demography/Fertility/ 1/29/03; Council on Europe/Social Cohesion/Population/Demographic Year Book/2002; Population Reference Bureau, World Population, 2002.

choice (choosing to stop having children after the desired number was reached). Of course, modern contraceptives, which did not appear until the 1960s, have played a central role in this process. Analysis of the second demographic transition, however, has focused on changes in the family as a social institution, and, in particular, on patterns of partnerships and reproductive behaviors in the last decades of the twentieth century (ESA/P 2003: 5). An equally important repercussion of the widespread distribution of reliable contraception has been the uncoupling of sex, marriage and childbearing, leading to the changed values of young adults about family formation (Cook 2004).

Most literature assumes it is these transformations that account for the current surprisingly low fertility levels. For example, obligation to marry seems to have weakened in general. The reduction in the number of marriages has been universal in Europe. Other changes have been a greater preference for cohabitation, dramatic increases in the divorce rate, and an increase in births outside marriage. Informal partnerships (cohabitation) may or may not involve childbearing. "Marriages and parenthood are drifting apart" (ESA/P 2003: xi) and marriage no longer necessarily entails children. Age at marriage has increased by two to three years, in some European countries approaching 30 years for females. Moreover, high proportions of European women are never marrying.[12] More people are choosing and are content to be partnerless (and thus childfree). In other words, previously strict norms about the paths to adulthood have been relaxed.

An important development is a growing emphasis on individualization and individuating. Many young Europeans have added a new stage in the life cycle devoted to individuating, or creating a Self, during which they aspire to study, travel and socialize before they feel ready to "settle down" (see the cases of Norway, the Czech Republic and Spain, Chapters 2, 5 and 9 in this volume). Individual autonomy is highly valued (over relational interdependence and social obligation) (Budgeon 2003; Giddens 1992).[13] The adoption of these so-called post-materialist values of autonomy and self-fulfillment has also changed the emphasis in marriage from children to an emphasis on the quality of the partner relationship (Lesthaeghe 1995).[14] Often the search for a suitable partner, equally self-actualized, postpones marriage or results in cohabitation as a form of prolonged dating (see the case of Norway, Chapter 2 in this volume). The creation of Self is often perceived to be generated by the competitive job market. During this time young people position themselves for the market, especially through extended education such as university and postgraduate study, workshops, language learning, internships and peripheral work experience. At the same time, the young have rising consumption aspirations, of both commodities and experience (Easterlin 1976). The pursuit of such goals as self-fulfillment, consumerism and hedonism seem to characterize postmodern youth (Lifbroer 2001) (see the cases of the Czech Republic and Bulgaria, Chapters 5 and 6 in this volume).

Women's roles in society and the family have also dovetailed into the partnership changes. As in the first demographic transition, women are pivotal. Steps toward gender equality and women's empowerment in Western Europe (known as "second wave feminism") have changed the family from the male breadwinner/female caregiver model to one of two breadwinners. As women moved massively into the labor market in the 1970s, they also spent more time in educational pursuits preparing for careers. Female economic independence is associated with higher divorce rates, as well as postponement of marriage and children. In some areas women's roles have changed so radically and rapidly among the young that it is easy for many people to blame low fertility on women's new career-mindedness. Women's efforts to individuate themselves through work and careers bring charges that they are too "selfish" to have children (see the cases of Greece and Italy, Chapters 7 and 8 in this volume).

However, women in Eastern Europe under communism had always worked alongside men. The state encouraged having children by offering free childcare and other direct payments for families. The "transition" to market economies, however, has been accompanied by the curtailment of family services which were widely available during the socialist era. At the same time as those prior benefits have been withdrawn, fertility rates have plummeted. Meanwhile a newly discovered consumerism, the hallmark of modernity for many, has emerged in certain parts of these countries. So there is debate about whether the low birthrates are a result of economic insecurities and instabilities, or whether they are simply a sign of the "modernity" of these postsocialist countries that now have family forms resembling those in Western Europe (see the cases of Germany, Russia, the Czech Republic and Bulgaria, Chapters 3, 4, 5 and 6 in this volume).

Moreover, if in this two breadwinner family childbearing implies withdrawal from the workforce (and a lack of income), the so-called opportunity costs of childbearing seem, thus, too high (unless the state subsidizes the loss of income and/or career progress).[15] Ironically, in the richest countries in the world, many couples say they cannot afford to have children. On close examination, they are not "describing a change in the costs of children as much as a change in their own definition of appropriate childrearing" (Alter 1992: 16). In the highly insecure market economy since the late 1970s, young people try to avoid risk, which having children seems to represent. Individuals want to enjoy life and concentrate on security (education, career), rather than risk the insecurities of childbearing (with its unknown psychological benefits, loss of job income if one stays home to care for a child and economic dependencies) (Chesnais 2000) (see the cases of Norway, Germany, the Czech Republic, Bulgaria, Spain and Ireland, Chapters 2, 3, 5, 6, 9 and 11 in this volume).

Thus, in these European countries there is no longer an idealized (albeit culturally specific) sequence of events in an individual's life cycle. The only part of the sequence that has been preserved and is typical throughout all the countries studied here is that childbearing is the last step taken (if at all), only after all the others. It rarely precedes leaving home, completing education, finding a job, finding a partner, securing a home or experiencing the world.[16] The result of all these changes in the family and forming partnerships is to postpone child-bearing.[17] Although polls and surveys all over Europe show that people say they want to have two children (ESA/P 2003: 81), the TFR at 1.4 may mean that couples who postpone childbearing until their thirties do not have enough time (biologi-cally) to reach their "desired" number. To begin childbearing ten years older than in the mid-1950s lowers the ability to conceive and coincides with the appearance of health problems that manifest themselves later in life and impede conception (but see the case of Russia, Chapter 4 of this volume). This does not mean that couples, and specifically women, do not want to have children. On the contrary, researchers are finding that most couples are satisfying their desires for parenthood with one child, rather than more (Chesnais 2000; also the case of Greece, Chapter 7 in this volume). The demographic term "replacement level fertility," thus, has no meaning to couples living their lives and building their families. They are having children "consistent with their goals, resources and constraints" (ESA/P 2003: 80).

Divergences

Although it is true that there has been a broad convergence of at least some repro-ductive characteristics and behavior all across Europe (and the world), in this volume we are more fascinated by the particularities of fertility decline in each country. In other words, what are the divergences within the generalized decline? Some scholars believe that the family forms and partnership patterns that emerged in Northern (or northwestern) Europe in the late 1960s or 1970s will diffuse, in time, not only to the rest of Europe but also to the rest of the world along with low fertility. Others, including the authors of this book, want to emphasize how deeply rooted national and regional cultural practices reflect continuities, as well as changes, in distinct aspects of family forms, partnership and reproduction. As the demographic anthropologist Philip Kreager has said:

> Some have come to view the continuing pluralization of household and community demographics as a more significant feature of modern demographic change than con-vergence of fertility and mortality trends at higher levels of aggregation and the processes hypothesized to lie behind them. (Kreager 1997: 141)

The many European nations have effectively arrived at below replacement fertility (TFR around 1.4) through different means, or along different paths, and at dif-ferent times.

Despite the extremely low birthrates in all of Europe, European demography itself is not homogeneous. Averages, such as fertility rates, tend to hide diversity. Within states fertility varies along an urban–rural axis (rural fertility is higher than urban). It also varies by the level of a woman's education (the lowest rates correspond to women with post-secondary education) and religious beliefs (secularists have the lowest fertility). It may further differ by political affiliation, social and economic class and ethnicity. Different provinces within countries can vary radically (for example, the north–south variation in the Mediterranean countries). Europe, of course, is divided into political states, and although all of Europe has below replacement level fertility, some countries are lower than others (see Table 1.1). Why?

Sociologists and demographers have recognized that similarities in reproductive behavior exist among countries that share other important social, cultural, economic and political characteristics. These groups of countries typically correspond to conventional geographic regions or socio-economic systems. Sociologists of the family have grouped Western European countries into several broad categories that share many family, as well as political and cultural, characteristics. These are the Nordic or Scandinavian countries, associated with socialist or social democratic welfare regimes; Anglo-Saxon countries associated with liberal welfare regimes; the German- and French-speaking countries, with conservative welfare regimes; the Mediterranean countries, identified with a Southern European welfare regime (Esping-Anderson 1990; Breen and Buchmann 2002); and postsocialist Eastern European countries, at present in various stages of transition to market capitalism (Gal and Kligman 2000). Currently, the United Nations Population Division uses only four categories: Northern, Western, Southern and Eastern Europe. The categories are social constructions and different countries are put into different categories according to the author's interest.[18] The point is that when we look at low fertility, neighboring countries, or countries that share certain features (economic, religious, linguistic), also share certain demographic characteristics. However, the wide variations in these distinct patterns of demographic behavior have surprised many demographers, who assumed one pattern for the second demographic transition would suffice (the Out of Scandinavia model).

The direction of the second demographic transition in Europe from its appearance in northwest Europe (Scandinavian countries) (see the case of Norway, Chapter 2 in this volume) to southeastern Europe coincides with political and economic liberalization. It arrived in Southern Europe (Portugal, Spain and Greece) when those countries were released from conservative dictatorships in the mid-1970s (see the cases of Greece and Spain, Chapters 7 and 9 in this volume), and lastly, to Eastern Europe, after the fall of communism in 1989 and the transition to market democracies (see the cases of Russia, the Czech Republic and Bulgaria, Chapters 4, 5 and 6 in this volume). As in all patterns, not every country fits where it "should." Ireland, in Western Europe, has always had the highest fertility, and many commentators refer to its Catholic heritage to explain its high TFR.[19]

Others insist that the social services and subsidies provided by the state to families and working mothers ultimately influence whether women and/or couples have children and the number of children they have. These scholars note that when childcare and family allowances are government sponsored, fertility rates remain relatively high, such as in the northern social democratic welfare regimes of Scandinavia, France in the 1980s and Ireland in the 1990s (Pinnelli 1995) (see the cases of Norway, France and Ireland, Chapters 2, 10 and 11 in this volume). On the other hand, where social transfers to families with children are lowest (i.e. Mediterranean Europe), fertility is lower (see the cases of Greece, Italy and Spain, Chapters 7, 8 and 9 in this volume).

By the same token, it is unclear whether social policy on the part of the state should or could be used to influence fertility levels. Theoretically, family subsidies, tax breaks and state-sponsored childcare would relieve voiced anxieties and eliminate burdens that informants say keep them from wanting and having children. Yet, despite such policies being in place in Scandinavia and France for decades, no country has returned permanently to above replacement level fertility.[20]

Cultural characteristics in the various European countries also shape when and how birthrates drop below replacement level. Cultural traditions, too, affect ideas about the appropriate paths of the life cycle (i.e. partnership and reproductive behavior): when one leaves home; the timing of education; when one achieves economic independence; housing practices; the function and meaning of marriage; age at marriage; the popularity of alternative forms of partnership unions and same-sex unions; the acceptability of cohabitation; the prevalence of birth outside marriage; the timing of motherhood (age at first birth); birth spacing practices; issues surrounding motherhood and work; appropriate childcare (parent, grandparent, or institutional); the gender division of labor; acceptability of childlessness; social acceptance of abortion; and attitudes towards divorce. These are issues whose norms differ from country to country, or region to region and which we describe in the following chapters. It is important to unpack the meanings attached to such institutions and practices. The combinations of these key parameters can lead to particularly low fertility, or not.

These combinations produce many counterintuitive situations. For example, counties with the lowest age of mothers at first birth have the lowest fertility (Eastern Europe); countries with the lowest percent of women in the workforce have lower fertility than countries with a higher percentage of women working; some Catholic countries have lower fertility than Protestant countries; countries with higher marriage rates and lower divorce rates have lower fertility than countries with high incidences of cohabitation and high divorce rates. Most characteristics of Eastern European reproductive patterns (low age of marriage and prefer- ence for formal marriage over cohabitation) should promote fertility, yet Eastern European levels are currently the lowest in the world. Obviously, there is no single pattern that leads to below replacement level fertility.

Thus, although all of Europe may share the same low fertility statistics, this fact does not necessarily imply homogenization of family forms and behavior. To the contrary, shared statistics mask the many differences, both within and between countries. It is the divergences that characterize the second demographic transition rather than the convergences.

Contributions

There are many valid approaches for examining low fertility. Demographers, economists, historians, sociologists, political scientists and journalists all offer their own perspectives on the issue. The collaborators of this book are all anthro- pologists and have explored these questions ethnographically. Now that the media have discovered the demographers' message about the European fertility decline and its repercussions, how have individuals responded? In this volume we want to consider fertility from the "ground up." We are interested in what the lived expe- riences of people are. How do they speak about, how do they live, what is called, at the country level, low fertility? On the individual level, is there such a thing as low fertility? How do people understand and talk about their choices and the per- ceived limitations on their lives? What is the meaning of motherhood for women today? How has the definition of "family" changed? How has policy figured into, or not, people's understanding of fertility? How do people resist, reinterpret or collude with policy?

The methodology of anthropologists, the way we get our data, is based on field- work. Fieldwork requires that researchers live among the group they are studying for an extended period of time, learning (if necessary) and speaking the language, participating in the culture, all the while collecting and evoking data. Usually the ultimate goal of an anthropologist is to "see the culture," or "understand life" from the informants'' "point of view"; to understand the other's "logic."[21] Although the researcher seeks out quantitative data (in our case, population and demographic statistics, TFRs, etc.), cultural anthropology's defining feature is the qualitative data it provides. How does the person on the ground understand his or her world? What moves the individual? What are the norms and behaviors and ways of under- standing the world that individuals bring to their specific institutions and social structures? How do people "make sense" of their "world"? Cultural anthropology offers new readings of low birthrates, which many analysts to date have approached only quantitatively and from the level of the state. Here we add the voices of everyday people to the previous state-centered studies.

Thus, in this book, our aim is not to explain why fertility has dropped "so low" in Europe. Nor is our goal to explain how birthrates could be increased. Rather, we explore how low fertility is lived or experienced and what tendencies toward fewer births means to the women and men who ultimately become demographic statistics. The considerable public interest in the technical aspects of fertility (contraception, abortion, in vitro fertilization, surrogate mothers) has been noted by many, but until now, there has been little interest about the child-making decision (whether to have children, if so, how many and when to have children) (Rees 1997: 389).

In the interest of capturing the breadth of variation, each chapter in this volume studies one country. We begin with Chapter 2 on Norway, located in Northern Europe, the first region to go through the second demographic transition. The author, Malin Noem Ravn, describes how, despite many years dedicated to individual fulfillment and long postponements of parenthood, the concept of the "good life" in Norway must eventually include children. Voluntary childlessness is not really a "choice," according to Noem Ravn. In Chapter 3, Susan L. Erikson writes of the lingering differences in perception about fertility decisions between eastern Germany (formerly East Germany) and western Germany (formerly West Germany). Older women in eastern Germany remember a state where working women and motherhood were coterminous. Now these same women see a world turned the other way around, where one works first and then has children.

In Cynthia Gabriel's Chapter 4, Russia's low birthrate is depicted as having two characteristics that distinguish it from the rest of low fertility Europe: the young age at which Russian women give birth (between 18 and 24 years old) and the concomitant increase in adult mortality. Gabriel suggests four interrelated cultural reasons for the low birthrates: the socio-medical practice of defining women over the age of 28 as "older mothers," limited childcare options, male alcoholism and housing problems. In Chapter 5 Rebecca Nash portrays the continuity of a birthrate "crisis" and the varying metaphors used to describe it in socialist and postsocialist Czech Republic. Nevertheless, many Czechs respect the current decisions of young Czech people not to have children as reasonable and contributing to the transition out of socialism and into postsocialism and a return to "Europe." Maria Stoilkova proposes in Chapter 6 on Bulgaria that the extremely low fertility in Bulgaria is connected to the massive rates of emigration from Bulgaria since 1989. Over 10 percent of the population, mostly young, has left Bulgaria due to dashed expectations and disappointments about the moral climate in Bulgaria. Those who have stayed in Bulgaria are not reproducing, yet anecdotal evidence implies that Bulgarian émigrés are having children. Stoilkova, while challenging conventional understandings of bounded countries, also explains how shifts in demographic patterns are precipitated by cultural struggles.

The sense that Greece "is getting smaller" (especially vis-à-vis the neighboring

Turks) has led to recriminations that "modern" Greek women are to blame for Greece's low birthrate because they are selfishly "refusing" to have traditionally large families. In Chapter 7, Heather Paxson contends that middle-class Athenian women depict limiting family size as responsible behavior. Paxson discusses the economic and cultural factors that impede Greek couples from realizing their desires for larger families. Although Greeks say motherhood completes a woman, birthing and raising just one child is now sufficient to transform a woman into a mother. In Chapter 8, Elizabeth L. Krause also looks at the demands of middle-class motherhood but this time in Italy. Italian mothers have on average only one child, not because juggling work with family has caused them to "give up on children," but rather because the so-called culture of responsibility dictates a demanding set of expectations for Italian mothers. The new middle-class mothering is so labor intensive and economically demanding that often more than one child is impossible to have. In Spain, young people postpone marriage until they are on average almost 30 years old. However, unlike their peers in Northern European countries, Spanish youth (like Italian youth) stay in their natal homes until marriage. In Chapter 9, Carrie B. Douglass explores the dynamic of young adults who are still living in their parents' houses. Although sociologists and demographers assume that these young people would leave home if they could (that they are impeded by lack of jobs and housing prices), young people contradict those experts by insisting that they are "fine" at home. They purport to value "freedom" more than "independence." Their culturally defined freedom negates parenthood.

Anna Lim, in Chapter 10 on France, examines the development of French family policy. At the same time that family policy was being reinforced to encourage higher birthrates, legislation on foreign immigration became more restrictive. Moreover, certain members of the French population were excluded from definitions of the French family, such as the populations in several of the overseas departments, namely the islands of Martinique and Guadeloupe. Of interest in this chapter is which families were used to define French society. Finally, Ireland was the last European country to arrive to below replacement level fertility. The speed and scope of the Irish demographic transition surprised many. It is also the last EU country to become a multiethnic society. In Chapter 11, Jo Murphy-Lawless describes the postmodern aspects of women's decision making on childbearing, which reflect a diversity of needs and identities.

In her short afterword, Gail Kligman reflects on the demographic paradoxes of consumer capitalism, noting common themes running throughout all the chapters. She reminds the reader that demographic crises are determined not only by numbers but also by the social constitution of these statistics. Views about who "should" bear children are often in opposition to who is bearing them. It is in this context that anxieties about the demise of "the nation" emerge. Kligman proposes that the title *Barren Nations* may better capture the underlying issues referenced in this volume.

With these contributions, we hope to enrich the discussion of below replacement level fertility in Europe. We want to call attention to certain perspectives on reproduction and reproductive choices that the alarmist headlines ignore. The next step will be to widen the discussion to include ethnographic description of this phenomenon from other parts of the world where fertility is declining. It will be intriguing to find out what the many different societies share in common and what such low fertility means in other places in the world.

We who live in such societies today often see our reproductive choices as eminently rational and practical. We normalize them. But from an anthropological point of view, they are exceptional. As far as we know, for the first time in human history (in the absence of war, economic decline or natural disasters), large groups of people (34 percent of the world's population in sixty-four countries) are not reproducing themselves in terms of aggregate numbers. It is important to historicize the contemporary moment and realize how novel it is (versus how "natural" it is). The ideas of individual autonomy and the individual right to choose have triumphed over religious and political institutional control. Equality, specifically gender equality, seems a self-evidently "natural" truth. What is more, these ideas are couched within an economic structure, based on consumerism that, among other things, requires long socialization and training/education of youth before they can access the workforce. Adulthood is postponed as perhaps never before. Below replacement level fertility is embedded in these modern revolutions. If this phenomenon continues to spread to other societies, it will be instructive to track how new kinds of relationships between women and men, between children and parents, between education and work and between self-realization and the demands of the market weave tightly or loosely with cultural particulars.

Notes

1. Note these North American newspaper headlines: "The Population Vacuum" (McGovern 2000); "The End of World Population Growth" (Lutz, Sanderson and Scherbov 2001); "Fertility Revolution Lowers Birthrates" (Naik *et al.* 2003); "Population Implosion Worries Graying Europe" (Specter 1998). Newspaper headlines from the European countries included in this book are noted in the various chapters.
2. Fertility is not to be confused with fecundity. Fertility is defined as "the frequency with which birth occurs in a population," while fecundity is "the biological capacity of a man, a woman, or a couple to produce live birth" (Yaukey 1990: 334)

3. Declining fertility worldwide does not negate the fact that in some areas of the world population increase is still occurring and is seen as a major problem by some global organizations.

4. Demographers grapple with the best way of calculating (and projecting) fertility rates and their relation to generation replacement. Calculating the annual number of births or calculating the crude birthrate (when population size is controlled for) provides only the reproductive behavior of entire populations, rather than that of women of reproductive age. Another contrast is period age-specific fertility rates with cohort indicators. Cohort indicators measure the level of fertility of real versus hypothetical cohorts. Period rates may yield a biased picture of fertility since hypothetical cohorts may not behave the way real cohorts do (who may postpone or change their timing of childbearing). The tempo-adjusted fertility rate has been proposed as a rough solution to the above problems (see ESA/P 2003: 9–11). In this book we refer to TFR (which fertility projections rely upon) as more of a long-term indicator and for the sake of comparison rather than any touchstone of reality.

5. Within evolutionary biology, there has been much rich discussion, although no real consensus, about the evolutionary advantages, or disadvantages, of low fertility. Evolutionary biology, or sociobiology, assumes the maximization of one's genes. Although in many species females may "rationalize" births (or commit infanticide) in order to protect their own health and well-being and that of other offspring (and potential offspring), evolutionary biology does assume reproduction of populations and/or species (i.e. replacement level fertility at least). Historically there has been a long-standing positive correlation between wealth (resources)/status and fertility. But many evolutionary biologists agree that "for humans, it looks increasingly as though the decline in fertility that has accompanied industrialization and shifts in education and labor markets has been driven by within-population competitiveness but has gone so far as to become suboptimal from a reproductive point of view" (Clarke and Low 2001: 649; see also Pérusse 1993, 1994; Borgerhoff Mulder 1998; Low, Simon and Anderson 2002). Others argue that "low fertility in post-transitional societies is unlikely to fall any lower because women have a biologically based predisposition towards nurturing or maternal behavior that interacts with environmental stimuli, resulting, in most cases, in a conscious motivation for bearing at least one child" (Foster 2000: 214).

6. Some of the countries with the lowest fertility are also the longest living populations in the world.

7. France was the first country to notice its population decline, and that has been a source of French governmental worry since the nineteenth century.

8. Fertility is never "natural." The noted ethnographer, Bronislaw Malinowski

(1967: 74), said, "There is not one single instance on record of a primitive culture in which the process of gestation is left to nature alone."

9. The most fertile population of which we have records is the Hutterites of the 1950s (TFR 10.9) (Eaton and Mayer 1954).

10. "Economic terminology like 'costs' and 'wealth' are used to describe changes in preferences and life-style that are fundamentally non-economic in origin" (Alter 1992: 16).

11. Theoretically, if humanity didn't reproduce itself, we could, in time, face extinction (see Foster 2000: 209).

12. In the western countries of Europe childlessness in women at age 40 varies from 2 percent in Ireland to 30 percent in Germany (ESA/P 2003: xii).

13. Or social obligation is being redefined.

14. Post-materialism refers to non-material needs such as personality development, individual autonomy, self-fulfillment and recognition. It supposes that the basic economic and security needs have already been met by society (Inglehart 1990).

15. As others have noted, the discussion of opportunity costs and fertility assume two things: that only mothers bear the burden of the time costs of children and that these women are working in a wage labor market economy (see Townsend 1997: 99). Thus opportunity costs are culture specific. Anthropologists have studied many other economic systems where childcare is shared in different ways and where women work in other forms of productive labor.

16. Teenage pregnancy is of marginal concern in the countries represented in this book. However, England (like the United States) has high rates of teenage pregnancy.

17. The choice to postpone or skip childbearing is strongly class related. Those who complete their education are generally from higher social class backgrounds, while those young women experiencing social exclusion with in their own society do have babies possibly because they have so little to gain from the skilled worker/consumer paradigm compared with their better-off sisters in the different class locations (Jo Murphy-Lawless, personal communication).

18. For example, Latvia (in the north) is considered Eastern Europe, while France is rarely considered Southern Europe.

19. Spain and Italy are also Catholic counties but have some of the lowest TFRS in Europe.

20. Sweden did return to above replacement level fertility for two years in the 1990s and then went back down.

21. The authors of all the contributions to this book are socially located beings. Despite an anthropologist's attempt to understand the "Other," an alert reader may notice subtle positions with respect to low fertility on the part of the

authors: indignation that the state does not step in and help defray the opportunity costs of having children and/or dismay at the evolution of market-oriented individualism.

References

Alter, G. (1992), "Theories of Fertility Decline: A Nonspecialist's Guide to the Current Debate," in J.R. Gillis, L.A. Tilly and D. Levine (eds), *The European Experience of Declining Fertility, 1850–1970: The Quiet Revolution*, Oxford: Blackwell.

Alvarez, L. (2003), "Scotland Takes Action to Halt Drop in Population," *New York Times*, International pages, November 30.

Bledsoe, C.H., Hill, A.G., D'Alessandro, U. and Langerock, P. (1994), "Constructing Natural Fertility: The Use of Western Contraceptive Technologies in Rural Gambia," *Population and Development Review*, 20(1): 81–113.

Borgerhoff Mulder, M. (1998), "The Demographic Transition: Are We any Closer to an Evolutionary Explanation?," *Trends in Ecology and Evolution*, 13: 266–270.

Breen, R. and Buchmann, M. (2002), "Institutional Variation and the Position of Young People: A Comparative Perspective," in F. Furstenberg (ed.), *Early Adulthood in Cross-National Perspective, Special Edition of The Annals* (A. Heston, ed.), vol. 580, March, London: Sage.

Bruni, F. (2002), "John Paul Makes First Papal Address to Italy's Parliament," *New York Times*, International pages, November 15: A3, col. 1.

Budgeon, S. (2003), *Choosing a Self: Young Women and the Individualization of Identity*, London: Praeger.

Caldwell, J.C. (1976), "Toward a Restatement of Demographic Transition Theory," *Population and Development Review*, 2(3/4): 321–366.

Chesnais, J-C. (2000), "Determinants of Below-Replacement Fertility," in Department of Economic and Social Affairs/Population Division (eds), *Population Bulletin of the United Nations: Below Replacement Fertility*, special issue 40–41 1999, New York: United Nations.

Clarke, A.L. and Low, B.S. (2001), "Testing Evolutionary Hypothesis with Demographic Data," *Population and Development Review*, 27(4): 633–660.

Cleland, J. and Wilson, C. (1987), "Demand Theories of the Fertility Transition: An Iconoclastic View," *Population Studies*, 41: 5–30.

Coale, A. (1973), "The Demographic Transition," *Proceedings of the International Population Conference, Liege*, vol. 1, Liege: IUSSP.

Cook, H. (2004), *The Long Sexual Revolution: English Women, Sex, and Contraception, 1800–1975*, Oxford: Oxford University Press.

Davis-Floyd, R.E. and Sargent, C. (eds) (1996), *Childbirth and Authoritative*

Knowledge: Cross-Cultural Perspectives, Berkeley, CA: University of California Press.

Delaney, C. (2004), *Investigating Culture: An Experiential Introduction to Anthropology*, Oxford: Blackwell.

Easterlin, R.A. (1976), "The Conflict between Aspirations and Resources," *Population and Development Review*, 2(3/4): 417–425.

Eaton, J.W. and Mayer, A. (1954), *Man's Capacity to Reproduce*, Glencoe, IL: The Free Press.

EOSSDF (European Observatory on the Social Situation, Demography and Family) (2002), *Annual Seminar 2002: Immigration and Family*, Helsinki: EOSSDF.

ESA/P (Department of Economic and Social Affairs/Population Division) (2000), *Population Bulletin of the United Nations: Below Replacement Fertility*, special issue 40–41 1999, ST/ESA/SER. N/40–41, New York: United Nations.

—— (2001), *Replacement Migration: Is It a Solution to Declining and Ageing Populations?*, ST/ESA/SER.A/206, New York: United Nations.

—— (2003), *Partnership and Reproductive Behavior in Low-Fertility Countries,* ESA/P/WP. 177, revised version for the Web, May.

Esping-Anderson, G. (1990), *The Three Worlds of Welfare Capitalism*, Cambridge, MA: Polity.

Eurostat (2003), *Statistics in Focus: Population and Social Conditions*, Theme 3–20/2003, http://europa.eu.int/comm/eurostat/Public/datashop/print-product/, May 7.

Foster, C. (2000), "The Limits to Low Fertility: A Biosocial Approach," *Population and Development Review*, 26(2): 209–234.

Franklin, S. and Ragone, H. (eds) (1998), *Reproducing Reproduction: Kinship, Power and Technological Innovation*, Philadelphia, PA: University of Pennsylvania Press.

Gal, S. and Kligman, G. (eds) (2000), *Reproducing Gender: Politics, Publics, and Everyday Life after Socialism*, Princeton, NJ: University of Princeton Press.

Gautier, A.H. (1994), "Population and Family Policies in Low Fertility Countries: Western Europe, North America, Austrasia," in Korea Institute for Health and Social Affairs (eds), *Low Fertility in East and Southeast Asia: Issues and Policies* (Seoul), vol. III, no. 8, Seoul: Korea Institute for Health and Social Affairs.

Giddens, A. (1992), *The Transformation of Intimacy*, Cambridge: Polity.

Ginsburg, F. and Rapp, R. (eds) (1995), *Conceiving the New World Order: The Global Politics of Reproduction*, Berkeley, CA: University of California Press.

Greenhalgh, S. (1995), *Situating Fertility: Anthropology and Demographic Inquiry*, Cambridge: Cambridge University Press.

—— (1996), "The Social Construction of Population Science: An Intellectual,

Institutional, and Political History of Twentieth-Century Demography," *Comparative Studies in Society and History*, 38(1): 26–66.

Hajnal, J. (1965), "European Marriage Patterns in Perspective," in D.V. Glass and D.E.C. Eversley (eds), *Population in History*, London: Arnold.

Haupt, A. and Kane, T. (1978), *The Population Reference Bureau's Population Handbook*, Washington, DC: Population Reference Bureau.

Henry, L. (1968), "Historical Demography," *Daedalus*, 97(2): 385–396.

Inglehart, R. (1990), *Culture Shift in Advanced Industrial Society*, Princeton, NJ: Princeton University Press.

Inhorn, M.C. and Van Balen, F. (eds) (2002), *Infertility around the Globe: New Thinking on Childlessness, Gender, and Reproductive Technologies*, Berkeley, CA: University of California Press.

Kligman, G. (1998), *The Politics of Duplicity: Controlling Reproduction in Ceausescu's Romania*, Berkeley, CA: University of California Press.

Knodel, J. and Van de Walle, E. (1986), "Lessons from the Past: Policy Implications of Historical Fertility Studies," in A. Coale and S. Watkins (eds), *The Decline of Fertility in Europe*, Princeton, NJ: University of Princeton Press.

Kreager, P. (1997), "Population and Identity," in D. Kertzer and T. Fricke (eds), *Anthropological Demography: Toward a New Synthesis*, Chicago: University of Chicago Press.

Lesthaeghe, R. (1995), "The Second Demographic Transition in Western Countries: An Interpretation," in K. Oppenheim Mason and A. Jensen (eds), *Gender and Family in Industrialized Countries*, Oxford: Clarendon Press.

Lifbroer, A. (2001), "The Link between Values and Demographic Behavior," paper presented at the EuroConference on the Second Demographic Transition in Europe, Bad Harrenalb, June 23–28, 2000.

Low, B.S., Simon, C.P. and Anderson, K.G. (2002) "An Evolutionary Ecological Perspective on Demographic Transitions: Modeling Multiple Currencies," *American Journal of Human Biology*, 14(1): 149–167.

Lutz, W., Sanderson, W. and Scherbov, S. (2001), "The End of World Population Growth," *Nature*, 412 (August 2): 543.

McGovern, C. (2000), "The Population Vacuum," *Alberta Report*, 27(3): 42.

Malinowski, B. (1967), *Sex, Culture, and Myth*, 2nd edn, London: Dell.

Naik, G., Fuhrmans, V., Karp, J. and Millman, J. (2003), "Fertility Revolution Lowers Birthrates," Wall Street Journal-online-Jan. 24, http://online.wsj.com/arti...507264–IfheoZg16B1xJuqHupeqaAdY,00.html.

Notestein, F.W. (1945), "Population in the Long View," in E. Shultz (ed.), *Food for the World*, Chicago: University of Chicago Press.

Pérusse, D. (1993), "Cultural and Reproductive Success in Industrial Societies: Testing the Relationship at Proximate and Ultimate Levels," *Behavioral and Brain Science*, 16: 267–322.

—— (1994), "Mate Choice in Modern Societies: Testing Evolutionary Hypothesis with Behavioral Data," *Human Nature*, 5: 255–278.

Pinnelli, A. (1995), "Women's Condition, Low Fertility, and Emerging Union Patterns in Europe," in K. Oppenheim Mason and A. Jensen (eds), *Gender and Family in Industrialized Countries*, Oxford: Clarendon Press.

Population Reference Bureau (2003), *World Population Data Sheet of the Population Reference Bureau*, http://www.prb.org/pdf/WorldPopulationDS03_Eng.pdf.

Rapp, R. (1999), *Testing Women, Testing the Fetus: The Social Impact of Amniocentesis in America*, New York: Routledge.

Rees, P. (1997), "The Second Demographic Transition: What does it Mean for the Future of Europe's Population?," *Environment and Planning A*, 29(3): 381–90.

Renne, E.P. (1995), "Houses, Fertility, and the Nigerian Land Act Use," *Population and Development Review*, 21(1): 113–126.

Reuters (2003), "Italian Town Offers $11,900 per Baby," MSNBC News, http://www.msnbc.com/news/1000631, December 3.

—— (2004), "What You Can Do for your Country," *New York Times*, May 13: A6.

Specter, M. (1998), "Population Implosion Worries a Graying Europe," *New York Times*, July 10: A1.

Strathern, M. (1993), *Reproducing the Future: Anthropology, Kinship and the Reproductive Technologies*, Manchester: Manchester University Press.

Teitelbaum, M. (2000), "Sustained Below-Replacement Fertility: Realities and Responses," in Department of Economic and Social Affairs/Population Division (eds), *Population Bulletin of the United Nations: Below Replacement Fertility*, special issue 40–41 1999, New York: United Nations.

Townsend, N. (1997), "Reproduction in Anthropology and Demography," in D. Kertzer and T. Fricke (eds), *Anthropological Demography: Toward a New Synthesis*, Chicago: University of Chicago Press.

Van de Walle, E. and Knodel, J. (1980), "Europe's Fertility Transition: New Evidence and Lessons for Today's Developing World," *Population Bulletin*, 34(6), Washington, DC: Population Reference Bureau.

Van Wissen, L.J.G. and Dykstra, P.A. (1999), "Introduction: The Life Course Approach as an Interdisciplinary Framework for Population Studies," in L.J.G. van Wissen and P.A. Dykstra (eds), *Population Issues: An Interdisciplinary Focus*, New York: Kluwer Academic/Plenum.

Woollacott, M.(2003), "We Should Welcome Signs of a Shrinking Population," *Guardian*, August 14.

Yaukey, D. (1990), *Demography: The Study of Human Population*, Prospect Heights, IL: Waveland Press.

–2–

A Matter of Free Choice?
Some Structural and Cultural Influences on
the Decision to Have or Not to Have Children
in Norway

Malin Noem Ravn

Although below replacement level, the Norwegian fertility rate is quite high, and has been relatively stable compared to that of other European countries. As in the rest of Western Europe, there was a marked decrease in the fertility rates in Norway from the mid-1960s to the mid-1980s (from 2.98 in 1964 to 1.66 in 1984). At this time the fertility rates in most of Europe continued falling, while they started to rise again in the Nordic countries. After a peak in 1990 at 1.93, the fertility rate had dropped to 1.75 by 2002 (Figure 2.1).

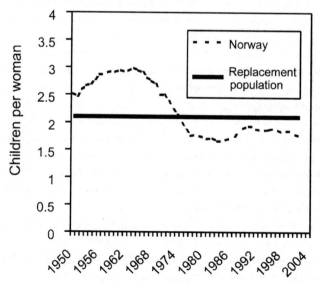

Figure 2.1 Total Fertility Rate, Norway, 1950–2004.
Source: Eurostat, Population and Social Condition, Demography, Fertility Indicators, January 29, 2003.

In this chapter my aim is to provide a context in which to read the peculiarities of the Norwegian fertility rate. I suggest that a tension in Norwegian culture between relational and individualistic values, both highly valued, constitutes an important part of this context. On the one hand, family life is culturally elaborated and also politically endorsed (Howell 2001: 205). On the other hand, Norwegian culture can be described as highly individualistic (Gullestad 1992). This chapter's core theme will be a discussion of how individual women balance these two value-systems in making choices about whether to have children, when to have children and how many children to have.

Norway is a wealthy, highly developed social democratic country on the northern fringes of Europe. The women's movement has led to a political and social focus on gender equality. A relevant characteristic is that Norway has a high female workforce participation, combined with relatively high fertility numbers, which means that a high percentage of the women with children continue with their working life.[1] Cohabitation is a socially accepted form of living, and almost half of the children born in 2001 had cohabiting parents.

This chapter is based on fieldwork I conducted in Trondheim, Norway's third largest city with approximately 150,000 inhabitants, during the years 1998–2000. I conducted in-depth interviews with eight pregnant women throughout their first pregnancies, and in the year after their children were born. In these interviews, reasons to have children emerged as important elements in these women's narratives about pregnancy.[2] Through this ethnographically based qualitative material I cannot point to any direct causality between birthrate and individual choices. My intention is rather to sketch out the argumentation these women use when they discuss what I term the child-choice (i.e. *why* they want to have children, *when* to have children and *how many* children to have). Through these women's stories I discern the tension between the relational and individualistic values, which the women themselves seemed to find relevant as a context for the child-choice, and which in turn influence the overall birthrate of Norway.

There is, however, one context noticeable for its absence in these women's stories, a context that I nevertheless believe is of importance. As opposed to women's argumentation shown for instance in the chapter by Nash (Chapter 5 in this volume) for having no children, or only one child, the women that I have spoken to rarely, if ever, use economic arguments when they discuss the child choice. Neither do they present family life as an insuperable obstacle to having a career (nor the other way around). This leads me to consider the political context of family life. Both politicians and demographers believe that the Norwegian state's encouragement of a combination of family life and participation in the workforce, for example, through state benefits for pregnant women and families with children, influences the fertility numbers. Based on my own material, I agree with this interpretation. All the women I have spoken to have jobs, and their family economies depend on their income. Therefore, I find it highly probable that the state's benefit program is a prerequisite for making the child choice.

In this text I take women's experiences as my point of departure. This choice is both grounded in my own research material, and in the fact that reproductive choices, in a Norway that takes pride in its equal rights politics, still influence women's lives the most. The women that I quote in the text are interesting in the present context as they represent the women in Norway that are likely to pull the birthrate down: they have three to six years of higher education, and statistically, women with high-level education have the highest mean age of first childbirth, the highest probability of ending up with only one child and the highest percentage of childlessness.

I will initiate my account by briefly sketching out some of the relevant structural/political contexts, which influence the "child choice," namely women's general status in Norway and the state benefit program for pregnancy, birth and childcare. Through this program, the state tries to eliminate economically based reasons not to have children. It also promotes a combination of career and family life. Still, the (partial) elimination of possible causes *not* to have children does not fully explain why Norwegian people *choose* to have children. The second section examines "making the choice." What explanations do women use as to why they choose to have children? In this section I suggest that family life is "culturally naturalized" and that the choice to have children is actually part of the individualistic endeavor. The third section deals with sequence and/or timing, important factors to account for the general trend to postpone childbirth. The fourth section is a re-evaluation of the arguments in the chapter.

Women's Position and the Structural Context of Pregnancy and Family Life in Norway

Norway, with a population of 4.5 million people,[3] has embraced and pursued the ideals of social democracy. Equality is a core concept and an important value in Norway, a value that is emphasized both in politics and in everyday cultural life. The concept of equality may need some explanation though, as it diverges somewhat from an emphasis on equality of opportunity. The Norwegian concept of equality emphasizes rather equality in outcome/result, and equality in this context can in some regards be understood to denote *sameness* (Gullestad 1992). Probably due to the cultural and political valuation of equality, the concept of class is rarely used in Norwegian official statistics or demographic research. Nevertheless, using occupational indicators approximately 74 percent of Norwegian families can be classified as "middle class" (deduced from Leiulfsrud 2004).

Norway, and the other Nordic countries, can be characterized as exemplifying a social democratic version of the welfare state, also called "the Nordic welfare model': "[T]he 'Nordic model' has a greater share of public expenditure and a higher share of social expenditure of the GDP than other [welfare] models, accompanied by higher taxation. With regards to outcomes, the ideal-typical Nordic model should achieve low income inequality, low poverty rates and small differences in levels of living and gender equality" (Kautto *et al.* 2001: 6). As this portrays an ideal-typical system, none of the Nordic states, Norway included, can be said to truly fulfill this picture. Nevertheless, this quote is a good attempt at presenting the political goals of the Nordic states. In the following section I will look more closely at some of the particularities of the Norwegian family and gender politics, to illustrate how Norway tries to reach its version of the welfare state.

The family politics in Scandinavia have been oriented towards giving social security through benefits and services, with the intention of diminishing the differences in the standard of living between families with and without children respectively. Another explicit objective is to level the differences between men and women when it comes to paid employment and work in the home (Björnberg 1999: 509). Some people would say that the Norwegian gender equality politics has been a story of success, although many claim that there still is some work to be done. Norway was, for example, the first country in the world to appoint a Gender Equality Ombud (1978), which is affiliated with the Ministry of Children and Family Affairs (established in 1991). There also exists a comprehensive legislation on gender equality in a separate Gender Equality Act (Mørkhagen 2002). The Gender Equality Ombud has among its tasks to monitor hiring in both the public and private sectors. The ombud exists to ensure that women and men are treated according to the law with regards to important life cycle events such as pregnancy, birth and childcare. It is illegal to fire an employee who is pregnant or on maternity leave. It is also illegal for an employer to make it difficult for a man to take statutory paternity leave.

Although women in Norway have achieved many high positions in politics and government posts, they remain absent in large part from positions of power in working life (Mørkhagen 2002). There are only a handful of women in leading positions in Norwegian business and industry. The picture is different on the political arena: In the mid-1990s female representation in the Norwegian Parliament (Stortinget) was 39 percent, which was the highest ever. About 60 percent of all university students are women, and women constitute almost half the workforce in Norway. There are, however, major differences between women's and men's position in the labor market. On average, women work 9.1 hours less a week than men (Mørkhagen 2002). This is explained by the fact that many women work part-time, to be able to combine paid work with the bulk of the chores in the family.

The main aim of gender equity politics in Norway is to ensure that men and women have equal opportunities, rights and duties within all areas of society. Central themes are the even distribution of power and influence between men and women; equal possibilities for economic autonomy; equal terms for women and men in the labor market; equal access to education and shared responsibility for home and children (Samuelsberg 2001).

As I have indicated, I agree with those who state that one of the probable reasons for the Norwegian birthrate being relatively high and stable is the rather generous state-provisions for pregnancy, birth and families with children (see for instance Samuelsberg 2001). In order to substantiate this claim, I will briefly sketch the most relevant elements of this support system.[4] Most of the state benefit program for pregnancy, birth and children is directed at *all* parents in Norway; that is to say that they are not subject to any testing of means.

About 35 percent of the Norwegian national budget is spent on the health and social welfare system, and parental leaves constitute part of this system. To be entitled to a parental benefit, the parent must have been employed and earned a pensionable income immediately prior to the benefit period (for at least six of the previous ten months). The parental benefit period is either 52 weeks with 80 percent pay or 42 weeks with 100 percent pay. Most of this leave can be shared between the two parents. Parental benefits are calculated on the basis of the income of the parent who takes leave of absence. There is a limit at six times the National Insurance basic amount, and if the parent's income exceeds this amount, the parental benefit will not cover the excess.[5] Women who do not qualify for a parental benefit (by not having been a wage-earner prior to the childbirth) will receive a lump sum grant.

As women through time have gained a stronger position in Norway, gender equity politics has changed since the early 1990s to focus on men's situation, especially regarding men in relation to various aspects of family life. This has resulted in changes in the parental leave legislation, where since 1993 fathers have had a statutory right to the "father's quota": a month of paid leave within the first year after birth that is reserved for the father. Mørkhagen (2002) states that when the father's quota was introduced in 1993, the percentage of new fathers who took paternity leave increased from 45 to 70 percent during the first year. The introduction of the paternity quota reflects an emphasis on shared care responsibility and on the importance of the child also spending time with the father, an emphasis that seems to be unique to the Nordic countries (Rostgaard and Lehto 2001: 162). Research from Sweden indicates that sharing of parental leave between mother and father has a positive influence on both divorce rates and final family size (Oláh 2001).

Parents furthermore have the opportunity to use the so-called time-account scheme, where they can combine parental benefits with shorter working hours. In addition to paid parental leave, each parent is entitled to up to one year's unpaid leave for each child. When they return to work after parental leave, nursing mothers are entitled to at least one hour off each day to breastfeed. About 40 percent of 1-year-old children in Norway are still nursed, and several representatives of the health care sector take pride in Norway for being a very "nursing-friendly" country.

When the children are small, parents may use the cash-benefit scheme for families with small children. In the cash-benefit scheme, parents receive a cash benefit per month for children between 1 and 3 years old, on condition that they have made no agreement for a full-time place in a daycare center that receives a state grant. This is a new arrangement that has been criticized, primarily by feminists who believe that it reinforces traditional gender roles by being an incitement for women, as opposed to men, to stay at home with small children. There are also several other financial support schemes and special tax rules for families with children. The child benefit is the most important of these. Anyone living in Norway who supports children under the age of 18 has the right to the child benefit. Single providers are entitled to additional support.

In 2001 almost half of the children born were born to cohabiting parents. The cohabitation tradition is largely socially accepted, and cohabitation is often regarded as a choice for a life partner on a par with formal marriage. Moreover, 8 percent of the children born in 2001 were born to single mothers (women who are neither married nor cohabiting). To be a single parent is, partly due to the state grants, also a financially manageable situation. Furthermore, being a single mother is, in most social milieux, socially accepted.

There are other relevant characteristics of the welfare system that influence the "cost" of having children: medical care is free for children up to 7 years; dental care is free for children up to 17 years and all public education is free up to and including the upper secondary level. Preschool care is currently the weak point in this picture, as it is rather expensive, and full coverage has not been achieved.

With this brief account of the Norwegian gender equality politics and the statutory rights of parents, I illustrate that, at least on paper, to have children represents no insurmountable economic strain, nor is it perceived to be an insuperable obstacle for a woman's career. Reality, of course, may differ from the good intentions in the legislation. In the arena of the home and family, pregnancy and childcare have been shown to represent a possible backlash for the gender equality mentality. The combination of family life and career is made possible in theory by a genuine sharing of work in the household between the man and the woman. The reality, though, is that many women have the bulk of responsibility for the household- and family related chores. Mørkhagen states: "Time studies show that even in families where both parents work, the woman spends far more time on housework and being with children than the man" (Mørkhagen 2002). Thus for many women the combination of family life and employment represents an ubiquous lack of time and of energy, in a situation where they constantly have a guilty conscience for not giving enough attention to one or both of the two arenas. This makes the choice of having children a choice that affects women the most. It can also be interpreted as a partial explanation of why many women wait quite some time to have children. For example, Kvande and Arntzen (1986) interviewed female engineering students about their visions of the future, with specific regards to career and family life. All of the students interviewed emphasized that they wished to combine motherhood with a career, and they expressed an intention to demand genuine sharing of labor with a prospective partner. All of them obviously wanted a job, but they were willing to give up a "grand" career that would take so much of their energy it would affect the quality of family life. One of the students interviewed is quoted as saying, "The man I live with wants children and says that he is prepared to share the responsibility, but I still suspect that most of the responsibility would fall on me . . . Because of all this I still want to wait many years [to have children]" (Kvande and Arntzen 1986: 5–6).

The above description presents some relevant parts of the structural and political context to the child choice. I have illustrated that the Norwegian state explicitly encourages a combination of working life and family commitment, and that economic impediments not to have children have been eliminated in part. Now, this is the context that makes it possible to choose to have children, but it doesn't explain *why* so many Norwegian women choose to have children. I will now bring in a few examples of women living in this context, women who have chosen a life with children. What does having children signify for them? Why do they choose lives as mothers?

Making the Choice

Increased level of education and labour market participation among women has reduced the economic value of childbearing (Lappegård 2002: 4). Furthermore, legal abortion on demand and access to contraceptives makes having children (at least to some degree) a matter of individual choice. To explain why people still choose to have children, economic-based theories point out that children have psychological and emotional value (see a discussion of this in for instance Jensen 2003). I would rewrite this argument in a more culture-sensitive idiom: in Norway there is a notable *cultural* emphasis on the emotional value of children. Furthermore, childbearing and family life are "culturally naturalized."

I will, by example, try to explain what I mean by "culturally naturalized." My material is in accordance with other Nordic studies, revealing that many women and men state that to have children is a "natural" continuance of a relationship of love, and that it is "natural" in the course of an individual's life (see for instance Tjørnhøj-Thomsen 1998). A "good life" implies a family life, and to have a family, you need to have children. In this line of thought, having children can hardly be construed as a choice at all; it is simply something that is supposed to happen at

some point in a couple's life together. This can be illustrated by one of my informants, Lena, a 29-year-old university-educated woman, who has been with her
partner for seven years.[6] When I ask Lena how she and her partner made the choice
to have children, she tells me that they had discussed it: they talked about all the
things they could not continue doing if they had a child; they checked out the
current rates of the parental benefits; they reflected upon what having children
would mean for their careers; they discussed what joys a life with children would
bring. Still, Lena said, the discussion was not really about whether to have children
or not, even though that was how they framed it:

> We discussed it [to have children] as if it were a choice, but you cannot choose the *wish*
> to have children in itself. The wish comes from within, and I think that for most people
> it comes naturally, given what we are, that we want to reproduce ourselves, and given
> the fact that that is how we live; we live in families. My partner and I *wanted* children,
> and deep inside we both knew that, so when we discussed whether to have children or
> not, what we *really* discussed was if it was the right time.

I will come back to the question of the right time to have children. Presently I will
deconstruct this "natural wish" that Lena indicates. Quite a few women in my
material understand, as Lena does, the "urge" to have children as partly "biological." Franklin (1997: 102) notes a similar interpretation in the narratives of invol-
untary infertile women, who naturalize "reproductive desire . . . as an inherent
human or parental drive." In the Western world there is a marked tendency to
describe and interpret ourselves through what we understand as "natural givens"
(Arrhenius 1999). Our brain structure, our genes and our hormones are portrayed
by popularized science literature and popular media as influencing – and to a
certain degree determining – who we are as individuals, especially when it comes
to gender-specific traits. This way of interpreting ourselves through the concept of
"nature" seems convincing probably because it provides easy answers to difficult
questions (Arrhenius 1999). When Lena indicates that the wish to have children is
biological, she constructs this wish as a universal by hinting at our human nature.
Still, this "nature" is – as Lena also knows – something that we can choose to listen
to or not; Lena herself has used contraceptives for a period of ten years. She quit
using the pill approximately two years before she got pregnant, but she insists that
she didn't quit *because* she wanted to get pregnant. She explains that she didn't
like the thought of feeding her body hormones, and that she preferred to use
"natural" contraceptives that didn't involve manipulating the body directly. When
she quit the pill, Lena felt that she was more in contact with her body; the body's
signals became clearer when the "false" hormones did not repress them. When in
touch with her "natural" body she believed that her body was trying to "tell" her
something. Her periods became more painful, but the most meaningful change that
Lena detected was that she could easily feel her ovulation. This may not be very

peculiar, as these are changes that often occur when one quits using the pill, but the interesting part is how Lena interprets the bodily changes. She tells me: "And then the body started to send me signals that I was ovulating. It was as if it was saying: 'Now is the time! Please get pregnant now!' It was really weird, but I think that my body *wanted* to get pregnant." Lena doesn't "give in" to what she interprets as her body's wishes right away, but she incorporates this story as an important event in her narration of how she eventually chose to get pregnant.

Lena's story gives depth to the understanding of the perceived "naturalness" of having children. Certainly not all of the women I have spoken to ascribe to their bodies the same degree of intentionality in getting pregnant as does Lena, but nevertheless I can detect in many of the narratives an understanding of pregnancy as a way of inviting "the natural" back into one's life. However, "nature" is an ambiguous concept, and what the women seem to invoke is a "romantic" image of nature, that is; nature as a repressed entity which is given value and presented as something to yearn for, something authentically human that can free us from an alienating modern life.

In Lena's narrative there is, to borrow a phrase from Franklin (1997: 103), a "seamlessness of interplay between 'social' and 'natural' facts." When Lena speaks of the wish for children as "natural" she also implies a *social* naturalness. "That is how we live, we live in families," she says. When I ask her to specify what values she associates with family life, she talks about intimacy and caring, about love, about really knowing someone and about how much she values the feeling of belonging with someone. The short version of Lena's answer is that family is about stable and good quality relationships.

Lena and her partner are not married, and she tells me that they do not intend to marry either. Marriage is, neither in Lena's story nor in Norwegian culture at large, a prerequisite for family life. As I have stated earlier, cohabitation is a socially accepted family form in Norway. Marriage is by no means unimportant for those who choose to formalize their relationship this way – for many of them marriage is an important element of both romance and founding a family – but marriage and cohabitation emerge as two possible choices one can make, the effect of which has personal, but not social, importance.

Lena has cohabited with her partner for five years. Until recently, they have led a typically "young adult" life; they have travelled a lot, they have been socially active in student activities, they have spent a lot of time at cafés, restaurants and bars. Lena says that she has appreciated this time, but that she now is ready for "another phase of life." Most of her close friends have also settled down and have recently become parents. Having a baby now is also "natural" in this regard; Lena says that she thinks her friends' choices confirm her choice of becoming a mother.

Vera, a 31-year-old teacher, tells me that her friends are "one step ahead" of her, and she laughingly says that she became pregnant out of "social pressure." On a more serious note, she says that the fact that almost all of her friends were settled with families was an important factor to make her think about having children. Vera's husband was definitely ready for family life, but Vera herself was more skeptical. She wanted children, but she was not sure whether the time was "right" yet. She says:

> But then one of my friends became pregnant, and I was practically the only one left [in our social circles] without children [laughs]. So I started to think more and more about it. Everybody around us had children so in that respect the time was right. And I came to the conclusion that we [Vera and her husband] get along so well, and our life together is so good, so I wanted to give it a try.

Having children and becoming a family is "natural" because it is "normal." Having children implies, at least while the children are small, "a different kind of everyday life" (Vera). By moving into this "different" phase of life at the same time as your friends, a notion of continuity and "normality" is reintroduced. The "difference" a life with child brings becomes the norm.

A longing to fit into this "norm" can also be extracted from infertile couples' narratives about wanting to become parents. Howell (2001) has studied transnational adoption in Norway. She argues that the dominant motivation for infertile couples to adopt a child is "a wish for significant sociality within a conventional model of the so-called normal family." She elaborates on this and writes: "Cultural expectations, across socioeconomic categories, hold that women, and increasingly men, cannot fulfill themselves without embracing motherhood, or respectively fatherhood" (Howell 2001: 204, 205). Howell stresses the cultural emphasis on family life, and the importance of relatedness in this context. She contends that child-related activities constitute an important part of Norwegian adults' life, and she states: "Meaningful sociality becomes inseparable from individual satisfaction" (Howell 2001: 205).

The last quotation from Howell is important in this context. The emphasis on relatedness, "normality" and family life coexists with a strong notion of individualism and an urge to create individually meaningful lives. One could easily construe the two values as antagonistic, but in the lives of many Norwegian women, they seem at some point in life to converge. After years of pursuing individual desires in the late teens or early twenties, a usual next step is to create a family. As Howell stresses, this can be interpreted as a social accommodation, a wish to adjust to one's immediate surroundings and to the sociality of everyday life, or it can be seen as an inner quest, spurred by a wish to realize one's personal potential as a parent.

Becoming a mother is understood by all of my informants as an enrichment of their lives. Partly it is constructed as an opposition to an individualistic life, and partly it can be understood as a constituent part of actualizing other elements of the unique Self. As such in some ways becoming a parent becomes part of the individualistic endeavor. I will illustrate this ambiguity with a couple of examples.

Åse is 27 when she becomes pregnant. She is an urban woman who spends her time in a very individualistic and artistic milieu. None of Åse's friends have chil·dren; nor do they plan to have any in the immediate future. This is a social environment where promoting one's own personal development is highly valued, and Åse is also influenced by this ideal. It is important for her to have her own projects in the world; to follow her own personal wants and needs, to have her own will and not be dictated by the norms of the society. At the same time, Åse is very critical of the milieu she belongs to and to the values it promotes. She juxtaposes those values with the values she associates with having children. Åse's pregnancy was unplanned (although she did not use contraceptives), but welcome nonetheless. I ask her if she ever had considered having children before she got pregnant, and she answers:

> [P]art of me has been thinking about it for a long time. Because I was so sick and tired of my life being centered only on me. Especially because I was in that world, you know. They are so self-absorbed, it is completely awful. I was sick of it, it didn't make sense to me whatsoever. It was just "me, me" all the time. So I yearned for something *real*, a cat, a dog, or . . . that's how it started, really. And then I realized, OK, maybe I can have a child. [Laughs] But it was not a conscious thought, not anything like "I am going to make a baby". No! 'Cause that was way too scary. I couldn't have *planned* it. But I am very happy that it happened now. I feel that it is important for my life. It's like I'm at a junction. I have to tighten up; make more decent choices. Not only stupid, unimportant choices.

In this quotation, Åse points to some important aspects of the parental role and the values associated with children. Life with children is perceived by many to represent something real, something fundamental for existence itself, almost with religious connotations. Having children gives meaning to life, both generally and specifically. Moreover, becoming a parent signifies important changes in a person's life. Parenthood is strongly associated with responsibility and maturity. Ideally, a parent must to some extent be altruistic: to be a parent is to have an important mission in life that transcends the person's individual life and self-centered desires. Åse, then, constructs becoming a mother as an alternative to a very individualistic life. By having a child she feels that she opens up to what she conceives as a more "natural" life: a life with a deeper meaning. Again, "the natural" emerges as a core value associated with family life.

But having children can also be understood to be *part of* an individualistic formation of the self. The Norwegian freelance journalist Kvamme presents an ironic and not-so-romantic view of why people choose to have children. She polemically states that people choose to have children out of cowardice and egoistic reasons, and contends that "adults use children to get on with their lives, to grow up, and to accomplish a full circle of life experiences" (Kvamme 2000: 14, my translation). Further, she states that instead of saying that parents offer children "safety and comfort," it is more correct to view the relationship between parent and child the other way around. In her view, children offer their parents the only stable and lasting relationship possible in an otherwise uncertain and all-demanding world. Disregarding her sarcastic style, I think that Kvamme points to some relevant aspects of becoming a parent. To have children is perceived as an important part of an individual life course, as an idiosyncratic happening and as a realization of certain potential resources in a given person. These are latent traits in a person that can be "activated" if the person has children. Further, to be in contact with children is regarded as something valuable for adults: spontaneity; curiosity; innocence; a sense of the importance of the small things in life. To have children is to learn something valuable about life itself and about our existential being. To become a parent can therefore be constructed as a fulfillment of the self, as a chosen endeavor that you shape in your unique way: parenthood becomes part of self-actualization.

Still, the changes that a family life implies are to some degree a matter of concern for the women I have interviewed. How will they manage to balance motherhood and the other parts of the Self? When I ask Åse how she anticipates her future as a mom, she says:

> I become two persons, in a way. I *really* want children. I am so much looking forward to it. To the intimacy, to the natural life, so to speak. But on the other hand I think: What about *me*? I think a lot about that. Because the only role models I have are self-realizing women, you see? So I keep thinking: how can I become the person I *want* to become when I am a mom? . . . In my head there are two possibilities, the only role models that I have access to, and that is either a sort of housewife or a career woman.

While Åse struggles to imagine a balance between "mother" and "Self," and anticipates that it might be problematic, Lena's strategy is to reassure her self that it is possible to maintain parts of her previous lifestyle even as a mother: "I realize that things will change, especially the first years, but I feel ready for that change. At the same time, *everything* doesn't have to change. It *is* possible to travel with children, and it *is* possible to go to cafés with a child, or at least, so I wish to believe! [laughs]." Lena, and most of the other women I have spoken to say that they "will not change radically" when they become mothers. "I hope motherhood will come in *addition* to everything else that is me," articulates one of the women, a declaration that sums up my informants' hopes for the future as mothers.

In this section I have shown that having children and becoming a family is "culturally naturalized" in Norway. Strong values are attached to family life and relatedness, and having children is seen as an important part of a "good" life. At the same time Norway is an individualistic society, and women as much as men are expected to realize themselves through a career. There are, obviously, latent conflicts between "relational" and "individualistic" values here. Still, as I have tried to show, these two value systems seem to converge at some point in individual narratives, where one at some point in life feels ready for another "phase." In this new "phase" of life, becoming a parent in some respects becomes part of the individualistic endeavor, through parenthood's capacity to "mature" or "grow" the Self in highly valued ways.

The perceived "naturalness" of having children seems to be so fundamental that it questions the reality of the child choice. Several researchers have commented that the choice to have or not to have children in contemporary Norway hardly is a choice at all. The choice, it seems, is restricted to *when* to have children (see for instance Kvamme 2000). In the next section I pursue the important aspect of timing in making the child choice.

The Perfect Time and the Perfect Man

The possibility to choose *when* to have children emerges as an opportunity to balance the "individualistic" and the "relational" value systems. Contraceptives and abortion on demand brings some degree of control over one's "biology" and the social security system guarantees the economic ability to have children. From this perspective, a couple is free to decide for themselves when the "time is right."

To "be ready for children" refers to ideas about certain conditions that have to be met before one decides to bring children into the world. These conditions obviously can differ from person to person, and from one social grouping to another. The following is perceived by most in my material as an ideal situation: to have lived in an independent household for some years; to have finished one's education; to have been employed for at least a year; to have lived with (or been married to) the partner of choice for some time and to have done some traveling or other self-developing activities. At this point, it is time to settle down and have kids. Let us look more closely at this sequence.

The move away from the parental home is a substantial step for young Norwegians towards "becoming who one wants to be." As opposed to young Spaniards' association of "freedom" with lack of economic and social responsibility (Douglass, Chapter 9 in this volume), young Norwegians seem to associate "freedom" largely with independence (Gullestad 1992: 184), and, specifically, independence from the parental home. All the women that I quote in the text moved away from the parental home between the ages of 19 and 21 years.

Education is, for the women quoted, an important part of the creation of the Self. The Norwegian state presents knowledge as the country's most important resource, and equal access to education is a core value: 83 percent of people aged

25 to 64 have education in addition to compulsory school, 54 percent of people over 16 years of age have upper secondary education, while 26 percent have higher education (information from Ministry of Education, Research and Church Affairs). Not only is education important for preparing for a future occupation, but also student life itself is valued for its freedom and for its sociality. The years as students are portrayed as important for finding an independent platform in life, for getting a clear idea of "what I really stand for" (Vera).

The student years are described as "fun," "free" and "interesting," but they are also characterized by a "constant lack of money." The first "real" job is an important next step in further realizing one's Self. A job is a prerequisite for most people to be able to buy their own home, which is the preferred arrangement for the women in my material. The home is a core symbol in Norwegian culture (Gullestad 1992), and to own one's own home is highly valued. To have a stable income is also important for being entitled to parental leave and parental benefit. As mentioned earlier, parental benefits are calculated on the basis of income. A woman who does not have a job is entitled to a lump sum grant, but this sum is on an average considerably lower than what she would get if she were entitled to income-based benefits.

Many women and men are on the search for the "perfect" partner for a long time. As one matures it is likely that one becomes more self-aware, more knowledgeable of what one considers to be the most important characteristics for a reasonable match. It is my impression that "the right partner" is the most important of the required conditions for choosing a life with children. Siv, a 39-year-old accountant, is quite specific on this point: "Stuart is the only man ever that I could imagine having a child with. And I have met a few! [She laughs]. If it hadn't been for him, I would never have become a mother. No matter how perfect the situation was otherwise. Honestly! And that's because I am one hundred percent sure that he is the perfect father." It is important to untangle Siv's argumentation here. She has not chosen Stuart *because* he would be a perfect father, but she has chosen *to become a mother* because, in her mind, Stuart will be a perfect father. Siv says that she would rather have chosen a childfree life with Stuart, than a life as a mother with another man. Another woman in my material, Greta, who had lived as a single mom for several years, put it the other way around. She told me that she had been searching for the perfect man for a long time, and as she already had one child and wanted more children, she was explicitly looking for "fatherly" qualities in potential men (along with, of course, other "indefinable" qualities that she could fall in love with). Greta is 32 years old, has a university degree, but no job. When she finally finds the "perfect" man, they decide to try to become pregnant almost immediately.

Most of the other women that I have interviewed state that the ideal situation is for the couple to have been together for quite some time prior to getting pregnant.

This is also a reason to postpone having children, to "really experience and enjoy the romance first, to firmly anchor the relationship between us," as one woman explained it to me. At the same time, having children is seen as a "natural" continuance of a functioning romantic relationship, if the time otherwise seems "right." All of the women quoted in this text take it as a matter of course that their partner will share in the day-to-day care of the child. "If I didn't think so, I probably wouldn't have gotten pregnant," Lena told me.

The cultural insistence on "the right order" of events perplexes several of the women I have spoken to. Randi, a 33-year-old with a higher university degree, for instance, comments on the ambiguity that characterizes her social circle's ideas of a "perfect life." On the one hand she says that to have children is emphasized as "the greatest thing in life." On the other hand, there are strict demands on *when* this is to happen. "Young adults" should not get established too early, they should not become too mainstream, they should develop themselves with regards to traveling and education and they should provide themselves with a good "taste of life." In these social circles, Randi explains, there is a negative evaluation of those women who see motherhood as the only source of the good life. If you say that you want children, and that that is the *only* thing you plan for your life, you are regarded as an "old-fashioned" woman, trapped in "old-fashioned" gender-roles. Thus, there is a certain social consensus as to when "time" is considered to be "right." Randi explains:

> So when you are in your early twenties, and *especially* if you are a woman, you should not openly admit that you want children. At least not that to have children is the *only* thing you want. Then you become a certain *sort* of woman, which is not good. But as you grow older, and have done a lot of other things, *then* you can say that you are ready for a family without being regarded as a weirdo. Suddenly an openly admitted wish for a child is regarded more or less as "natural," and to say that you do *not* want children is more questionable at this stage. [Laughs] It definitely is walking a tightrope.

The moral disapproval of women who "only" want children in their early twenties and the moral disapproval of women who do *not* want children when they are in their thirties, together capture, I believe, the normative force of the construction of the "right time" and the "right sequence." I concur with Randi: it is walking a tightrope.[7]

However, it is almost impossible to regulate life to such an extent that the perfect partner and the perfect time concur. The search for the perfect partner and the waiting for the perfect time is therefore a possible contributory factor for some time-contingent demographics: observed mean age for all first births has steadily increased from 24.7 years in 1980 to 27.7 years in 2002. Women born in 1967, with post-secondary educations, had a median age for first childbirth at 30.7 years; 19 percent of the women with higher educations born between 1954 and 1958 were childless at the age of 40 (Lappegård 1999). The relatively high age for first births may have further implications. First, biological fertility may diminish as the woman closes upon her forties. The long wait for the perfect time and the perfect man may therefore imply an increased amount of involuntarily infertile couples. Second, by having the first child relatively late in the reproductive life, the final size of the family may be affected.

I will dwell somewhat upon the latter allegation. It is most usual for Norwegian couples to aim for two children, but one-child and three-children families are also within the "normal" family-size. Lappegård (1999, 2002) states that it is in the group of women with high educations that we find most women with no children or only one child, but that there is a tendency of increased third-child births in this group as well. Two of the women in my material have, at the time of writing, only one child. One because, as she puts it, "my biology is working against me." She is currently undergoing fertility treatment. The other states that she has chosen to have only one child.

The most frequent argument that I have heard from informants against the single-child family is that children are better off with siblings. Many refer to their own childhood when they describe their idea of the ideal family size with arguments like "I myself have found much support in my siblings." In a survey from 1999, the ideal total number of children was reported to be 2.6 on average (Lyngstad and Noack 2000), and as we can see when we compare this number with the fertility rate, there is a gap between the ideal and the real family size. Quite a few women that I have spoken to, who got pregnant for the first time in their late twenties or early thirties, state that they had originally dreamed of three children. For many of them, as they work their way through the first pregnancy and the following years, the dream changes, and they settle for two children, or even one child.

This change of heart has multifaceted reasons. Having children, especially toddlers, is perceived to be time- and energy-consuming. When one starts out rather late with the first pregnancy, any subsequent children will have to come within a limited amount of time. Some women say that they still want three children, but that the third pregnancy is hard to achieve for biological reasons. Others say that they do not have the energy to be pregnant and have two toddlers simultaneously. Some women report that their bodies do not feel ready for another pregnancy as they age towards their forties. Some say that they can cope with career and family life with two children, but that a third child would be too much and would imply that something else had to be sacrificed. Some say that with two children they can continue to travel, but that having three children is more impractical in such a respect. To have two children seems to be perceived as a manageable or practical family size, where one can balance to some extent both self-actualization and family life.

At the beginning of this section, I proposed that the possibility of individually choosing the "right time" to have children is a way to balance between self-realization and relational values. Exemplifying with highly educated women, I have illustrated that this choice is influenced by social expectations, biology and accidental circumstances. The "ideal order of events" – with education, career and the "perfect man" as the most important constituents – could be reformulated as "reasons to postpone childbirth."

Balancing Relational and Individualistic Values

Compared to that of many other European countries, the Norwegian fertility rate is relatively high. Still, it is below replacement level. I contend that the cultural tension between relational and individualistic values is an important context in which to interpret these peculiarities of the Norwegian birthrate. On the one hand, both men and women are expected to be independent and to construct individually meaningful lives: they value their possibilities to realize themselves through travel, education, career and romance. On the other hand the relational values, represented by the home and the family, are also seen as fundamental. The cultural valuation of a family life is inscribed in the individual and manifests itself as a naturally based wish for children. This wish is naturalized to the degree that for some it even affects the interpretation of the body, as in the way Lena reads her body to "want" a pregnancy.

Many Norwegian women seem to want the best of both worlds: they want to become mothers and have a fulfilling family life, and they want to have fulfilling careers as well. To some extent, the Norwegian state tries to make this combination possible. In this chapter I have suggested two ways in which the women themselves attempt to resolve the tension between the two value-systems, both of which potentially influence procreative choices. First, by being able to individually identify the "right time," one can balance the relational and individualistic values in one's own life-course. As I have shown, though, there are social, biological and accidental circumstances that may affect the order of events. Second, these two value systems are somehow collapsed, in which becoming a parent is presented as part of the individualistic endeavor, through parenthood's capacity to "mature" the Self in highly valued ways.

Still, the demands of a family life *do* represent challenges for women (and men) who also want to tend to their careers. In an interview shortly after her second child was born (and the first one was a toddler) Lena smilingly said to me: "We'll probably be full-time parents forever, but maybe not as all-consuming as we are now. Right now I have to admit I feel very much as I am only 'mom', but I believe that soon I'll be more back to normal. Toddlerhood doesn't last forever!" For the women I have talked to having children is not the finishing line. Life is to be savored; goals are to be reached, also as a mother.

Notes

1. Some 76 percent of married or cohabiting women with youngest child under the age of 3 years are employed.
2. My intentions for the fieldwork were to trace and discuss ideas of pregnancy, the pregnant body and the fetal body.
3. Approximately 77 percent of the population live in densely populated areas; 29 percent of the population live in the four largest cities of Norway.
4. The information presented here is gathered from an electronic version of a booklet, which is accessible at ODIN (an electronic information service provided by the Government and the Ministries of Norway): http://odin.dep.no/archive/bfdvedlegg/01/01/Smaab034.pdf
5. On an individual basis one may in such cases reach an agreement with the employer to provide full pay.
6. The women's names have been altered.
7. This judgement, though, is context-sensitive as to, for instance, whether the woman has a partner or not.

References

Arrhenius, S. (1999), *En ekte kvinne: En kritikk av den nye biologismen*, Oslo: Spartacus Forlag.

Björnberg, U. (1999), "Familiers pligter og ansvar: Skandinaviske familier i Europa," in L. Dencik and P.S. Jørgensen (eds), *Børn og Familie i det Postmoderne Samfund*, Copenhagen: Hans Reitzels Forlag.

Franklin, S. (1997), *Embodied Progress: A Cultural Account of Assisted Reproduction*, London and New York: Routledge.

Gullestad, M. (1992), *The Art of Social Relations: Essays on Culture, Social Action and Everyday Life in Modern Norway*, Oslo: Scandinavian University Press.

Howell, S. (2001), "Self-Conscious Kinship: Some Contested Values in Norwegian Transnational Adoption," in S. Franklin and S. McKinnon (eds), *Relative Values: Reconfiguring Kinship Studies*, Durham, NC and London: Duke University Press.

Jensen, A-M. (2003), *Fra nyttebarn til byttebarn*, Oslo: Gyldendal Akademisk.

Kautto, M., Fritzell, J., Hvinden, B., Kvist, J. and Uusitalo, H. (2001), "Introduction: How Distinct are the Nordic Welfare States?," in M. Kautto, J. Fritzell, B. Hvinden, J. Kvist and H. Uusitalo (eds), *Nordic Welfare States in the European Context*, London and New York: Routledge.

Kvamme, S.M. (2000), "Ei død mor er ei god mor," *Syn og Segn*, 2: 4–15.

Kvande, E. and Arntzen, A. (1986), *Fra "peppermø" til Superkvinne'*, working paper from the research programme "Technology and Women's Work,"

Trondheim, Norway: IFIM/SINTEF.

Lappegård, T. (1999), "Akademikere får også barn, bare senere," *Samfunnsspeilet*, no. 5, Oslo: Statistics Norway.

—— (2002), *Education Attainment and Fertility Pattern among Norwegian Women*, Oslo: Statistics Norway.

Leiulfsrud, H. (2004), "Familie og sosial ulikhet i velferdssamfunnet," in A-L. Ellingsæter and A. Leira (eds), *Velferdsstaten og familien: Utfordringer og dilemmaer*, Oslo: Gyldendal Akademisk.

Lyngstad, T. and Noack, T. (2000), "Norske fruktbarhetsidealer 1977–1999: Idealene består," *Samfunnsspeilet*, no. 3, Oslo: Statistic Norway.

Mørkhagen, P. (2002), *The Position of Women in Norway*, UDA147ENG, produced by Nytt for Norge for the Ministry of Foreign Affairs, http://odin.dep.no/odin/engelsk/norway/social/032091-991525/index-dok000-b-f-a.html

Oláh, L. (2001), *Gendering Family Dynamics: The Case of Sweden and Hungary*, dissertation series, Stockholm: Stockholm University Demography Unit 3.

Rostgaard, T. and Lehto, J. (2001), "Health and Social Care Systems: How Different is the Nordic Model?," in M. Kautto, J. Fritzell, B. Hvinden, J. Kvist and H. Uusitalo (eds), *Nordic Welfare States in the European Context*, London: Routledge.

Samuelsberg, R. (2001), *Trygghet, sikkerhet og likestilling*, UDA746NOR, produced by Nytt for Norge for the Ministry of Foreign Affairs, http://odin.dep.no/ud/norsk/generell/p30000701/p30000708/032091-991447/index-dok000-b-n-a.html

Tjørnhøj-Thomsen, T. (1998), *Tilblivelseshistorier. Barnløshed, slægtskab og forplantningsteknologi i Danmark*, Phd dissertation, University of Copenhagen.

"Now It is Completely the Other Way Around": Political Economies of Fertility in Re-unified Germany

Susan L. Erikson

Listen to me, we did not know where we stood after re-unification. Many people lost their jobs, and did not have any money. And if you have a child, how is that supposed to work? After re-unification almost nobody had babies. It was really noticeable. (Renate, 33, saleswoman from eastern Germany; all names are pseudonyms)

Following a baby boom in the 1960s, below-replacement declines in German fertility were first noted in both East and West Germany in the early 1970s. West Germany joined the ranks of countries with the "lowest low fertility" (below 1.3 children per woman) in the mid-1980s, an event forestalled in East Germany until after re-unification with aggressive family-friendly state policy. The current fertility rate in re-unified Germany of 1.29 (Eurostat 2003) places Germany among those European nations with lowest low fertility.

What is interesting about the German case is how its aggregate fertility rate has two narratives to tell. One narrative, the west German version, is about the contemporary opportunities and constraints that shape fertility decisions for people living in a prosperous late-capitalist nation, a story not unlike those of the central and southern European nations with lowest low fertility – Greece, Spain, Italy and Austria. The other narrative, the east German version, is about how the everyday struggles faced by people transitioning from a communist welfare state to a market economy shape fertility decisions, a story similar to other eastern European nations with lowest low fertility – Bulgaria, the Czech Republic, Lithuania, Latvia, Poland, Romania, Slovenia and the Slovak Republic. (Throughout the text, a capitalized East and West refers to the two Germanys before unification, and a lower-case east and west refers to these regions of Germany after unification.) Germany's dual fertility narrative situates west German fertility worries as end-of-the-millennium business-as-usual concerns of an economically privileged European nation, and locates the east German Fall-of-the-Wall fertility shakeup as a product of the social tumult and confusion that accompanied life in many postsocialist nations.

Beginning in 1991, Germany saw a decline in aggregate post-unification fertility because the low fertility rates of former West Germany, which had long stood as "German" fertility rates for Euro-American population demographers, fell even lower when rates in the former East German states – 0.8 in 1992–5 (Statistisches Bundesamt 2001) – were factored in. The Fall-of-the-Wall fertility shakeup in east Germany, reflected on later in the chapter by interviewees almost a decade after it occurred, serves as the primary ethnographic reference point of this chapter. Using ethnographic data to examine the fertility decline after German re-unification in terms of the geopolitical east–west divide, this chapter has three aims: first, to demonstrate the bifurcated nature of fertility in Germany, and second, in so doing, to contest the way in which east German fertility contingencies have been subsumed by west German paradigms of fertility in contemporary population demographics and discourses. A third aim is to provide a counterpoint to the decidedly economically deterministic arguments typically proffered to explain Germany's lowest low fertility rates. I aim to show that fertility rates are instead more complex convergences of state and economic pressures; educational and career trends; and cultures of motherhood.

The chapter's title quotes a phrase used by two former East Germans in separate interviews. They both used the exact same phrase – *"Jetzt ist es total andersherum"* ("Now it is completely the other way around") – to describe the upside-down state of family affairs in east Germany after re-unification. When asked to explain the early 1990s dip in fertility in the east, one of the interviewees responded:

> We were 20 when re-unification happened. Usually you would have married at 18 or 20 and had children then. It was a prerequisite to be married in order to get an apartment. You married and had a child first, and then you built your own life. Now it is completely the other way around. First you live your life, and then you have children when you are about 30. (Crista, 30, bank teller from eastern Germany)

In the context of the interviews, the phrase "Now it is completely the other way around" also connoted a newfound element of choice, a supposed liberty to make different kinds of family planning decisions. Detailing the political and economic correlations and convergences that shape "the-other-way-around"-ness for former East Germans is a primary focus of this chapter.

Methodology

The ethnographic data presented here were collected during interviews conducted with women and their partners whom I met in two university hospitals, one located in former East Germany and one located in former West Germany, in 1998–2000.

Although the primary focus of my research was on how women use prenatal diagnostic technologies rather than on fertility per se, the quantitative and qualitative
data I collected speak to attitudes that I believe inform the patterns of childbearing
in re-unified German society. As to the chapter's temporal perspective, it is both
contemporary and retrospective. Interviewees were asked to reflect on their current
lives as well as on what their lives had been like before and during the years immediately following re-unification.

Almost all of the interviewees –a total of 140 people, 69 at West Hospital and
71 at East Hospital – were interviewed either before or after a prenatal care
appointment in the hospital clinic. A few interviews were conducted in interviewees' homes. Women were the target research population, but when their partners were present, both were interviewed. Partners were present during 32 percent
of the east interviews, and at 21 percent of the west interviews. This chapter is also
informed by an additional data set, one that was collected while observing a total
of 449 obstetrical exams, split almost equally between east and west hospitals.
During these exams attitudes about childbearing and concerns about fertility were
discussed between obstetrician and patient, and I collected data in these settings as
a participant observer.

For the interview data used in this chapter, interviewees were asked semi-struc-
tured questions about first, their perspectives of each other, "Easties" (*Ossis*) of
"Westies" (*Wessis*), and Westies of Easties, second, if and how re-unification had
changed their lives, and third, if they could explain the dramatic dip in fertility in
the east that occurred between 1992 and 1995. For the last question I used as a prop
a graph that appeared in *Der Spiegel*, a popular newsweekly. Figure 3.1, titled (in
translation) "Fewer Births in the East" (Der Spiegel 1999), illustrates the dramatic
decline since re-unification in births in the "new" (east) German states as compared
with the "old" (west) German states. (The graph is used here with permission.)

With notable exceptions (e.g. Gal and Klingman 2000; Kreyenfeld 2000a,
2000b, 2002; Dölling, Hahn and Scholz 2000; Maleck-Lewy and Ferree 2000), fertility studies in Germany have relied on demographic statistics rather than ethnographic data. Demographers typically use case-controlled retrospective methodologies, noting statistical trends after-the-fact and long after opportunities to talk
to the people who "lived" the statistical trend have passed. This chapter attempts
to address a gap in the German fertility literature by giving voice to the people who
are in a position to reflect on childbearing decisions since the early 1990s. Special
attention is paid to what people said about delaying and forgoing childbearing for
specific political, economic and social reasons after re-unification.

There is a decided bias in the ethnographic data and commentary presented here
– it is primarily an east Germany narrative – for two reasons. First, the same question asked of both west and east interviewees, evoked more detailed responses
from the east German interviewees. As a population the East Hospital interviewees

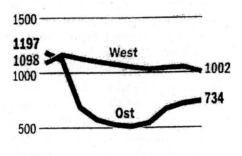

Weniger Geburten im Osten

Nur noch 734 Babys je 100 000 Einwohner kamen 1998 in Ostdeutschland zur Welt

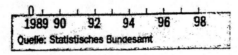

Figure 3.1 Interview Question Prompt, and Total Fertility Rates for East and West Germany since Re-unification, 1989–1998. (Translation: "Fewer Births in the East: Only 734 babies per 100,000 inhabitants were born in 1998 in eastern Germany.")
Source: Der Spiegel Panorama, December 10, 1999.

were much more likely to integrate talk about their pregnancies in a larger social context (rather than the more strictly medicalized context commonly evoked by their West Hospital counterparts), thereby providing much more ethnographic data with which to contextualize the fertility decline in eastern Germany. Second, as a scholar interested in human behavior at the junctures of reproduction and political economy, I am particularly interested in the difference that political economies of place make. Germany's united–divided–re-united history provides an uncommon opportunity to analyze such differences. Re-unification turned east Germans lives "the other way around" while it affected west German lifeways hardly at all. In this sense, the mostly unaltered nature of west German reproductive practice after re-unification can serve as a kind of a control against which the altered east German experience can be compared and contrasted.

A Political Economy of Fertility

This chapter emphasizes the degree to which political economy – in short, normative state and market pressures – shapes reproductive behavior. Despite re-unification in

1989, Germany's divided history means that differences in political economy shape differences in women's reproductive experiences that are residually evident today. The economic, political, and cultural realities of east Germans' lives, lives in which a centralized government subsidized family life, have been, for example, considerably reconfigured since re-unification. Daycare, job security and family-friendly employment and housing policies normalized women's work outside the home and in effect shaped fertility decisions in east Germany.

> We were calmer back then, everything was more secure. We didn't have to think that much, everything just happened automatically. You went to work, you knew exactly that you would go to work again the next day, and that your wages were fixed. The mental pressure was not as big as it is today. And the competition, it wasn't like today because everyone had a job, nobody had to be afraid. (Petra, 29, nurse from eastern Germany)

> Nobody really knew what would happen, and that's why they decided to postpone the wish to have a child because they first of all wanted to see how life would go on. (Gabi, 22, train conductor from eastern Germany)

> We were pulled out of this sleeping society and all of a sudden people had to take care of their own lives. The costs were different, the advertisements were different . . . then there was unemployment . . . All this insecurity caused many people not even to think about children. (Peter, 29, Gabi's husband, also a train conductor from eastern Germany)

Lowest low fertility is not a completely new phenomenon in Germany (Grossmann 1995, 1997). There have been other historical moments during the twentieth century when fertility rates have fallen below replacement level in Germany. After both world wars, Germany saw fertility declines. But, as with the decline following re-unification, each decline had characteristics that distinguished them: the first, documented by the 1925 census that calculated an average of one child per family (Grossman 1995: 3), was a product of Germany's "New Woman" phenomenon and the newfound availability of contraception and abortion promulgated by Weimar Republic reforms in the mid-1920s. The second decline following the Second World War resulted from the mix of economic despair, general demoralization, and the widespread availability of abortion on demand at state expense following the mass rapes committed at war's end by, most pervasively, Russian soldiers (Grossman 1997). The third decline in fertility after re-unification had its own characteristics, many of which are explored below, and provides yet a third example in the twentieth century of the contingent nature of fertility.

How Ideas Shape Policy, How Policy Shapes Fertility

The specific values that shape policy as well as the *proclivity* to use policy to shape values and behavior are enormously variable throughout the world. Specifically with regard to family policy, Germany's tendency to use policy to affect behavior goes back to Bismarck's inception of welfare state policies. Even in Bismarck's late-nineteenth-century employment policy, we see political cultures accommodating workers' homelife (*Heimat*). Motherhood, maternity care, postpartum homecare and household help were some of the domains written into employment policy in the late-nineteenth- and early-twentieth-century public policy, remarkable in and of themselves for the time, but noteworthy too because they were domains deemed *worthy* of regulation by the legislative body.

An historical overview of German family policy is necessary to appreciate the sustained high correlation over time between ideas and policy in Germany. For example, the fertility decline in Germany following the First World War correlates with policy attempting to regulate gendered ideologies of modernity. Family policy constituted during the Weimar Republic tacked back and forth between those that supported women as factory laborers – including policies granting access to contraception and abortion – and those which promoted women as mothers. A reconstitution of motherhood and family life, meaning smaller families and working mothers, was believed to be essential to Germany's modernization process, but postwar concerns about the high number of marriage-age men killed in the war, 2 million "surplus" women and a marked decline in the birthrate made for a incoherent family policy trajectory during the Weimar years.

In the 1930s, the National Socialists' ideologies of "fit" motherhood informed policies designed to redress the low fertility rate. Pronatalist policies for biologically "fit and desirable" women coexisted with racist antenatal and sterilization policies for women deemed unfit to reproduce by the Third Reich. The policies were insidiously discriminatory and sometimes murderous in intent, and turned back many of the reproductive rights acquired during the Weimar Republic. They did, however, achieve their intended goal, albeit temporarily, of reviving the low birthrate.

The fertility decline in Germany immediately after the Second World War was a response to the widespread despair and economic stresses experienced by a defeated nation. The birthrate soon revived, though, to over two children per woman by the 1950s in both Germanys. But what is interesting about fertility in postwar Germany was the inception of two German narratives, each making selective use of ideologies of womanhood, motherhood, and the family from Germany's past to promote agendas that were decidedly economic and gendered.

In East Germany, state policy was geared to enable modern working women, women who were employed outside the home providing essential services for the new nation-state, but who were also mothers of children. Drawing on socialist theories of women's emancipation through paid labor, an echo of late-nineteenth-century feminist and early-twentieth-century Weimar liberation discourses, the state promoted an ideal of the working mother. In West Germany, policy was designed to enable women as wives and mothers, and was informed by romanticized notions of women pleasantly cultivating *Heim und Herd* (house and home). For example, it was not until 1957 that West German women were able to seek employment without their husbands' consent. The nuclear male-breadwinner/female-housewife family not only was assumed to be the cultural norm, but also is the organizational gender arrangement upon which West German family policy has been dependent since the 1950s.

One final point about policy: feminist scholars (esp. Einhorn 1993; Nickel 1993) have pointed out that the gender equity picture promoted by socialist governments was misleading. Gender equity policy, they contend, came at a great cost to women in socialist countries. Women throughout Eastern Europe bore the "triple burden" of housework, childrearing and work in the formal economy with little assistance from their domestic partners or husbands, a factor that no doubt shaped how many children a woman ultimately had. In practice, the measurable effects of this burden on East German women seems somewhat contingent on rural versus urban locales, as well as class. But for women with higher levels of education, the "triple burden" may have been preferable to under- or unemployment. East German women were more likely to be employed in jobs requiring higher levels of education, and the postwar employment trajectory over time was more favorable for well-educated women than in West Germany. In 1950, for example, women made up 15 percent of all gynecologists and obstetricians in both East and West Germany. By 1989, the percentage had increased to 54 percent in the East and declined to only 23 percent in the West (Arabin *et al.* 1999).

At my fieldsites, the absolute number of female physicians who combined having a family with a career in medicine in East Hospital far exceeded that in West Hospital (see Table 3.1).

Table 3.1 Female Physicians: Women and Women with Children, Germany

	East Hospital (n=37)	West Hospital (n=20)
Total number of physicians	37 (100.0%)	20 (100.0%)
Female physicians	18 (48.6%)	8 (40.0%)
Female physicians with children	11 (61.1%)	1 (12.5%)

As many of the female physicians were in their thirties and forties, these data lead me to believe that bearing the "triple burden" in former East Germany had been, if not fair, at least manageable. In the West combining motherhood with a career in medicine was in practice nearly untenable because of, I suggest, an even more restrictive culture of motherhood, a point I explore further later in the chapter. It is not my intent to minimize the real, often limiting effects state policy imposed on East German citizens' freedoms, but rather to join other scholars whose work attempts to redress the erasure of East German lifeways that deserve, at the very least, to be points of discussion in fertility discourses (e.g. Funk 1993; Dölling *et al.* 2000).

The emphasis in this section on how policy shapes but does not dictate fertility decisions is borne of an interest in the way infrastructural opportunities and constraints create opportunities of certain kinds. The East German government cultivated an employment climate that made it common sensical to have children and work outside the home. Having children in East Germany qualified parents for the opportunity to have an apartment of their own. Having children meant parents received a sizable monthly stipend (*Kindergeld*) to subsidize the costs of raising each child. Having children in East Germany, where every adult was guaranteed a job, meant that a pregnancy did not threaten one's job security, even if a woman opted to take a one-year "mother's pause". In the East German case, policies structured opportunities that encouraged and supported reproductive demographics that benefited the state, and provided the opportunity for women to pursue work outside the home and motherhood simultaneously. Conversely, in West Germany, educational opportunities, and political and economic freedoms converged to provide women with virtually limitless career opportunities *until* she had a child, after which most women took the three-year "mother's pause". *Kindergeld* was also available in the West, though it was not as substantial as in the East. If women worked after having a child, they usually took on part-time employment. As articulated by the interviewee below, both scenarios were opportunities and constraints of particular kinds.

> It used to be that women were supposed to go back to work again. You almost didn't have an opportunity *not* to do that. It was hard for a woman to say: "I want to stay home with my children." Now it's hard to say: "I want to go back to work again." (Helga, 36, university lecturer from eastern Germany)

Re-unification yielded experiences encoded differently for women from former East and former West Germany, and those experiential differentials of course shaped fertility decision-making. Life for former West Germans changed imperceptibly at re-unification. For former East Germans, it was "completely the other way around." Re-unification has meant unemployment, expensive housing options, and policies that reflect gender norms of West Germany. Women of childbearing age who grew up in former East Germany expected that the state would provide financial and infrastructural support for combining employment and family. Nostalgia for these incentives, though not always for the entire socialist form of government, arose in over half of my interviews with former East German women and their partners.

> [East Germany] was a country that was friendlier towards children than Germany is now. All women used to work and have a family. They worked full time . . . Some things

are better now and some things shouldn't have been abolished, like the social system . . . If people are happier now . . . well, I don't really see that. (Andrea, 35, medical technician from eastern Germany)

It was normal [then] that we could not buy everything and we could not travel everywhere. Now you can travel everywhere and you can buy everything, but you can lose your job, which really did not exist before. Everyone had a job [and] there were kindergartens and enough daycare. Children were more cared for, the state was friendlier towards children than it is now. Now it is not. (Helene, 23, painter from eastern Germany)

The family was valued more [then], I think. Now, if I did my job the way I am supposed to, I wouldn't have time for family. That's the bad thing. Everything additional to work [now] just does not fit in any more. (Markus, 46, legal advisor from eastern Germany)

For former East Germans, changes in policy, then, meant some opportunities lost, others gained, and, as a result, reproduction redefined.

Characterizing Difference

The cover story for German newsweekly *Der Spiegel* November 22, 1999, bore the headline, "Die neuen Waffen der Frau" ("The New Weapons of Women"). The cover art featured the bottom half of a woman (her upper torso was off camera) in a short skirt and stockings lying on her stomach. Poised precariously on the soles of her black pumps, as if she might attempt to juggle from this impossible position, were a computer, symbolizing work, and a baby carriage, symbolizing family (Figure 3.2). The featured article was a story about German women who work, some of whom had children (Weingarten and Wellershoff 1999).

What irked several of the east German interviewees to whom I showed the cover during interviews was the question of "new" for whom? Combining motherhood and work in the formal economy was the norm in former East Germany. As one interviewee put it, "During DDR-time [East Germany before re-unification] it was completely *normal* to be pregnant" (Magda, age 26, nurse from eastern Germany, original emphasis). Others agreed:

The women who are mothers now grew up in DDR-time. That means they learned to go to work every day. They have to earn their living on their own. I could never sit at home and wait for my husband to earn money. Not ever. For a woman in western Germany, that works. They were raised differently. (Sabine, 34, teacher from eastern Germany)

Many men in the west don't understand when women work. Their wives are at home and raise the children and the men work. So they just don't understand how a woman can work and have children. (Gabi, 22, train conductor from eastern Germany)

Figure 3.2 *Der Spiegel* cover, November 22, 1999.

Of course there are many west German women who work in the formal economy as successful scientists, politicians, lawyers, professors, administrators and in a number of other professions. Many of them have children. But most west German women tend to have careers and children sequentially rather than simultaneously, as was common in East Germany. Magda, Sabine and Gabi's comments are interesting not so much because what they say is wholly verifiable (it is not), but that they, and several other East Hospital interviewees who made like-minded comments, perceived west German women exclusively as housewives, women uninterested in working in the formal economy.

Re-unification turned Ossi lives "the other way around," a harsh reality that went largely unrecognized by their *Wessi* (west German) counterparts. Of those west German interviewees who had an opinion (n=46), 67 percent believed that there was no difference in the reproductive experiences of their east German counterparts, and 33 percent believed that Ossis were backward (*rückständig*). Obviously, these perceptions do not directly affect reproductive decision-making, but they do provide insight into the "divided" nature of contemporary Germany a decade after re-unification.

Converging Domains of Difference

As a means by which to organize the discussion of east–west differences, I present in subsections below maternity policy, original quantitative data from East and West hospitals on common fertility variables, as well as qualitative analysis. Especially because a stated aim of this chapter is to promote an argument that fertility rates in any given place at a particular historical moment are contingent on convergences of domains, special attention has been paid to the aggregate and integrated effect state policy, education, employment, daycare availability, and mothering ideology had convergently, rather than attributing fertility to a single component part.

Mutterschutzgesetz (Mother Protection Law) and Respective Ideologies of Motherhood

In the east motherhood was nothing special. Women worked until six weeks before the birth . . . They didn't carry their bellies around as a proud symbol. It was there, and then there was a child, and that was it. It was nothing special you had to put emphasis on. In the west it is more of an achievement, something special . . . Pregnancy was never anything special in the east and in that environment of course the number of children was higher. (Sabine, 34, English teacher from eastern Germany)

Mutterschutzgesetz, a comprehensive set of state policies regulating employment terms for working and nursing mothers (i.e. hours, breaks, leave, financial support), have been in place in Germany for over a century. I pair these policies with the respective East and West cultures of motherhood because I believe they significantly shaped the differences in women's attitudes toward childbearing at re-unification and, residually, still today. The policies themselves were a reflection of values and ideologies of the respective Germanys, and, dialogically and simultaneously, they shaped values and ideologies of motherhood, a point that is often neglected in more economically determinist analyses of fertility.

Despite somewhat parallel development of *Mutterschutzgesetz* in the former East and West Germanys, one of the most significant differences was in the "mother's pause" (*Mutterpause*), time off before and after the birth of a child. What was a "baby year" (*Babyjahr*) in East Germany was a three-year maternity leave in West Germany. In both cases, in theory, a woman was guaranteed a job at *Mutterpause* end. Before re-unification, East German women were usually able to return to the same or a similar job. West German women, however, were more likely after three years to return to a different job, or to find the job itself terminated. Although some West German women successfully resumed careers after having children, most West German women with children who worked outside the home were employed part-time, and there was a general tendency to have a career and children *sequentially*, rather than simultaneously as was common in East Germany.

The respective *Mutterpause* policies, which are much more extensive than outlined here (see also Erikson 2001), helped shape important differences in women's ability to combine motherhood with work in the formal economy. In the East, mothers working in the formal economy were the norm. Not so in the West. Women had virtually limitless opportunity to pursue careers of their choice *until* they had children at which point the cultural expectation was that she would stay home for at least three years. Daycare options were nearly non-existent, a point I address later in this section, which I believe contributed to an incompatibility of motherhood and work outside the home for most West German women.

On a personal note, the respective cultures of motherhood were palpable for me as a working mother. While conducting fieldwork at both hospitals, my children lived with my parents-in-law in a town about 150 kilometers from my West Hospital site and 250 kilometers from my East Hospital site. Typically I would see my children only on the weekends. When West Hospital staff learned I had children, they commiserated with my children, emphasizing how sad they must be without me, and how even the most wonderful grandmother could not replace my motherly love and attention. While I felt quite comfortable with my children's situation, over the time I spent in former West Germany I became increasingly self-editing about mentioning I even had children. Conversely, conversations about the same situation with East Hospital staff revolved around how lucky I was to have such an ideal childcare situation, and that it was good and very healthy for children to be cared for by adults other than their parents. Koch *et al.* (2001) report similar findings in a 2000 study with 65 percent of the respondents in west German agreeing that a child suffers when the mother is employed versus 33 percent of the respondents agreeing in east Germany.

With re-unification, different kinds of concerns arose for former East Germany women from the resulting clash of motherhood cultures. The *Mutterpause* had been something most East German women had been able to take for granted before re-unification, and its parameters had hegemonically inscribed family and work life.

With my second daughter you could stay at home and still get your full wages for one year . . . Children were never in the way [then]. They were never a reason for an employer to treat the mothers differently or to dismiss them. That was just not the case. (Lana, 44, engineer from eastern Germany)

After re-unification, the economic, social and philosophical transitions required of east Germans were significant. Even though East and West maternity policies were fairly similar, the economic and social milieus within which women negotiated them were different, and affected women's transitional *experiences* of policy. Some interviewees feared pregnancy would disqualify them from *Mutterpause* rights guaranteed on paper, but not in practice.

I was really worried with my second pregnancy because with my first pregnancy I had only been working three months before I got pregnant. They are not allowed to dismiss you but they do it anyway. I had to go to court and that was horrible. They sent me letters saying I had gotten pregnant on purpose. That was really hard. I talked to my boss and finally he said that he would tolerate a second pregnancy, but that is very rare nowadays, maybe one in two hundred. (Ute, 25, factory worker from eastern Germany)

It does depend a lot on the employer whether you have a job. You never know whether you might not be given notice after your maternity leave. Everything is a little uncertain at the moment. That's why many people go back to work earlier than they legally have to, for fear of losing their job. (Christiana, 32, unemployed worker from eastern Germany)

Others considered the extended *Mutterpause* a nice option, one that better served them and their children.

I am taking three years off and I don't know if I will go and look for something new immediately because I was unemployed [when I got pregnant] . . . I am not the kind of person that goes crazy if she has to stay home. There is enough to do. I am happy to be home when my children come home from school. I want them to have someone who is there for them so that they can talk to someone and that I can make them something to eat . . . We could use the money [from me working] but what is the use if I am a mental wreck in the evening? (Michaela, 36, homemaker from eastern Germany)

Still others saw unemployment as a ploy to acculturate east German women into west German gender norms. One woman characterized her opinion this way.

The trend is very much for the woman to stay at home. You can see this from the unemployment statistics. At the moment we have a very regressive political situation, it is very conservative and very much supporting the idea that men go to work and that women stay home with children. There is no one saying we need to get these unemployed women back to work . . . Now it is very hard to say "I want to go back to work." . . .I think that all eastern German women have the impression that their situation is completely changed. (Helga, 36, university professor from eastern Germany)

While divergent in opinion, each woman spoke to the larger point of this article: That political economies cultivate cultures of motherhood that shape a willingness to have, as in Michaela's case, or to delay and forgo having children.

Contemporary German Fertility

At re-unification in 1989, total fertility rates for both Germanys were about the same. But the rates soon diverged, as the east's rate plummeted from 1,197/100,000 inhabitants in 1989 to approximately 500/100,000 in 1994. In 2003 re-unified Germany's TFR leveled out at 1.29 (Eurostat 2003a), though rates in former East German states have stabilized slightly lower, at about 1.1 (Mai 2001), than former West German rates (see Figure 3.3).

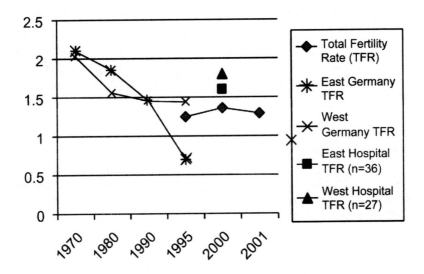

Figure 3.3 Total Fertility Rates for East and West Germany, Re-unified Germany, and East and West Hospitals, 1970–2001.
Sources: Eurostat 2003a; Winkler 1990; Mai 2001; Author's original data.

TFRs at East and West Hospital populations were predictably higher than the national because women without children were not part of the prenatal care setting where I conducted my research.

Age at First Child

Traditionally, population demographers have used the notion of educational and professional opportunity to explain low fertility rates, the assumption being that when women have and exercise educational and professional opportunities they not only limit the number of children they have, but also delay or forgo child-bearing, thereby creating an aggregate "late" age of first child. This opportunity equals fewer children and older mothers' formula depends on women being able to actively control – through contraception, family planning and abortion options – the number of children they have so that they can pursue educational and professional options they believe will enhance their quality of life. Age at first child, then, has been identified as a signifier of the degree to which women control their reproductive capacities as well as the freedom they have in their society to choose particular life trajectories.

Prior to re-unification, however, East German women had both educational and professional opportunities *as well as* opportunities to have children. Having children, in fact, enhanced quality of life (i.e. married couples with children were given priority ranking for apartments). Age at first child (AFC) in the East German case, 22.2 years in 1989 (Bundesinstitut für Bevölkerungswissenschaft 1999), was

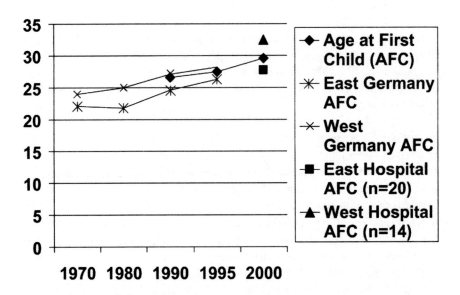

Figure 3.4 Age at First Child for East and West Germany, Re-unified Germany, and East and West Hospitals, 1970–2000.
Sources: Eurostat 2003b; Council of Europe 2002; Bundesinstitut für Bevölkerungswissenschaft 1999; Statistisches Bundesamt 2001; Statistisches Bundesampt Deutschland 2003; author's original data.

not an indicator of educational and professional limits for women, but rather it was indicative of a social structure that made possible the simultaneous pursuit of a career and childrearing.

Michaela Kreyenfeld (2000a, 2000b, 2002) has written about the fertility decline in eastern Germany and contends that it is too early to tell precisely what the post-re-unification later AFC indicator means for eastern German women. Her preliminary statistical analyses suggest that eastern German women have on average postponed the onset of childbearing, though they are still younger at first birth than women in western Germany. It is impossible to tell if they will resume patterns of higher fertility over their reproductive life stage. In the case of my East and West Hospital cohorts, eastern German women were younger at first child (see Figure 3.4), and, still experiencing slightly lower rates of overall fertility a decade after re-unification. Additionally, the average age of the female inter- viewees at first birth was slightly higher than the national average as both hosp- itals, in addition to serving as the site of primary prenatal care delivery for women in the surrounding areas, were also tertiary prenatal care sites, serving pregnant patients with more complicated pregnancies, patients who as a popula- tion are older.

Education and Employment

> Women in West Germany did not work in the same areas we did. We in the east have very many female engineers and other highly educated women. [Now] I see in our company that the colleagues from western Germany are mostly male. There are only very few women, and even fewer women who have children. (Lana, 44, engineer from eastern Germany)

Education and employment are paired here because, although education level and employment are often cited as independent causal factors for delayed or forgone fertility (e.g. Sayn-Wittgenstein 2000; Kreyenfeld 2000a, 2000b), the quantitative data I collected did not distinguish meaningfully between the two. What the data collected do reveal, however, are the small degrees of difference between the pro- fessions that women prepared for (Figure 3.5). Statistically, then, it appears that there is little difference between the education and employment options pursued by German women interested in childbearing.

Despite the relative uniformity of the quantitative data, however, ethnographic data shows that East and West Hospital cohorts have historically and contem- porarily different relationships to employment. Female employment rates in East Germany prior to re-unification had been steady at around 90 percent (Rueschemeyer 1993) compared with 50 percent mostly part-time employment in West Germany (Einhorn 1993). Since their initial post-re-unification fall, employ- ment rates have not risen substantially. By 1993, female unemployment was 21.5

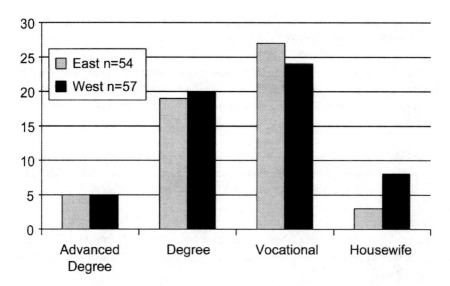

Figure 3.5 Education required by East and West Hospital Cohorts' Professions.
Source: author's original data.

percent in eastern Germany, compared to 8.8 in western Germany (Engelbrech 1994). At time of writing (May 2003), female unemployment in eastern Germany was almost 20 percent, and just over 8 percent in western Germany (Statistisches Bundesamt Deutschland 2003).

Job security was the most often mentioned reason for low fertility by East Hospital interviewees. No West Hospital interviewee identified unemployment as a palpable threat. For East Hospital interviewees, however, the threat of unemployment loomed large as a determinant of fertility. When asked to explain the post-re-unification fertility decline, 41 percent attributed it to unemployment and uncertainty.

> I believe that people want to give children a protected, financially secure future, and there was not that anymore. So many people lost their jobs. The future was so insecure that nobody dared bring a child into this world. (Sabine, 34, English teacher from eastern Germany)

> Unemployment back then wasn't a problem, only now. If you always have to worry about keeping your job, well. . .We had more security for family and children before. You could go back to your job afterwards, which is now not as certain any more. (Kirsten, 33, physical therapist from eastern Germany)

> During DDR-times everybody had their jobs and women had children in their early twenties. That was normal, and today many people are unemployed or only have very

insecure jobs. They think twice about whether they can afford children now. (Claudia, 25, medical resident from eastern Germany)

For East Hospital interviewees, there was a great deal of "interview" overlap between job security and daycare, many women mentioning both in virtually the same breath. Daycare is discussed next, but was linked with employment in the minds of many, as with Crista:

People lived calmer because they did not have to think about things. They knew they would get daycare, they had their jobs somewhere, Even if it was not exactly what they wanted, they had a job. (Crista, 30, bank teller from eastern Germany)

Daycare

After job security, the availability of daycare was cited by 31 percent of the east German interviewees as the reason for the fertility decline. Annette's comment is typical:

[Now] there is always the problem of childcare and preschool openings, they are lacking everywhere, and that was never the case in [East Germany] times. Then you knew you'd get support, but nowadays, you have to fight for everything. (Annette, 39, computer programmer from eastern Germany)

Although several western Germans I spoke with characterized East German daycare as militaristic, of the east German interviewees who addressed the issue of daycare, the vast majority – some with past experience, others anticipating future experience – was satisfied with the quality of daycare available to them and believed children benefited from the experience.

I personally was always satisfied with it. I never had problems with it. The children liked going there, they were never seriously sick at that time . . . We never had the impression that the child was lacking something. I never thought so. (Lana, 44, engineer from eastern Germany)

I want my child to grow up among children and not protected only by me, its mother . . . I think it's very important to give this to children [or] it becomes a huge problem when they get all their love from only their parents. (Sabine, 34, English teacher from eastern Germany)

By 1989, the East German government had achieved its goal of 100 percent *Kindergartenplätze* (preschool placement) "for every child whose parents want it" (Müller-Rieger 1997: 141). This translated to about 95 percent of children between ages 3 and 6 attending preschool (Schmude 1996: 175), and another 80 percent of children under 3 years of age in state-sponsored *Krippenplatz* (literally, crib place).

Because the availability of childcare was considered essential for the predictability of female laborers and their productive outputs, childcare centers were well established throughout East Germany by the early 1980s, up from only 17 percent of full placement in 1949 (Müller-Rieger 1997: 141).

Presently, preschool availability in eastern Germany falls far short of demand for two main reasons: first, following re-unification some preschools were closed for administrative and consolidation reasons during the government's reorganization, and, second, there are fewer children needing daycare. Female unemployment and longer maternity leaves mean that more women are at home able to take care of their own children and relatives' children. This has resulted in less uniform availability, especially in more rural areas that had been fully served prior to re-unification. One interviewee, a preschool teacher from a small town, was relocated because there were fewer children overall.

In west Germany, even as recently as the early 1990s, 64 percent of west German women quit working in the formal economy after having a child because, first, there were few childcare options; second, there was an assumption that women should and want to stay at home to look after small children; and third, public opinion was that a young child needs its mother at all times and that mother–child separation is traumatic for the child (Fagnani 1996). Only 3 percent of children under 3 were (and are) cared for in public daycare centers, and fewer than 40 percent of three year olds attended nursery school (Fagnani 1996: 134). The conditions for stay-at-home motherhood set up by (formerly West German, now pan-German) *Mutterschutz* policy are further reinforced by the scarcity of public and informal daycare options for women who would like to be employed outside the home.

Conclusion

All the encouragement to have children is gone. (Sabine, 34, English teacher from eastern Germany)

In this chapter, I aimed to show that, first, demographic statistics alone tell us little about the *intra*national variability of fertility experiences in Germany. Germany's geopolitical division cultivated notable differences in childbearing practices. As a result, in Germany there are two fertility narratives. Gone-but-not-forgotten nationalisms continue to inform German women's willingness (and lack thereof) to bear children, merging in unexpected ways with larger pan-German post-unification opportunities, constraints and ideologies of motherhood. As shown in this case, demographic statistics are important starting points, but ethnographic data are essential for understanding *experiences* of fertility.

Second, the German case is illustrative with regard to the shaping power of policy because as a society Germany has long regulated women's reproductive activities. Policies – regulating everything from contraception to housing – made certain reproductive choices possible, and, over time, shaped what was likely for the majority. It was a dialogical process: Cultural practices resulted from policy, and those cultural practices then informed subsequent policy reform. Indeed, the policy/cultural trajectories of the two Germanys made a difference, not as much in the rates of fertility as in, again, the *experiences* of fertility.

Third, lowest low fertility rates have too often relied on economic explanations that are unreflexively exclusive and deterministic. I suggest that we are better served by explanatory frames that help us to identify and unpack place-specific societal domains – in the German case, for example, policy, (un)employment, daycare and ideologies of motherhood – that converge and result in practices at particular historical moments. Such analyses would not be in lieu of the demographic generalizations commonly used to assess fertility in nation-states, but rather would be used conjunctively.

All of this points to the place-specific and historical particularness of fertility. The post-re-unification fertility decline was the third marked decline in Germany in the twentieth century, and each instance had its own particular configuration. Contemporarily, while there is no reason to question the fact of the aggregate pan-Europe fertility decline over the course of the twentieth century, apocalyptic analyses predicting the end of civilization as we know it tell us very little about the people making particular decisions at particular historical moments. We are better served by ethnographically informed analyses that help us to unpack the particular economic, political and social convergences that result in particular fertility practices in particular locales at particular historical moments.

Predictably, the *intra*national differences noted in this chapter will disappear over time, though they may be replaced by other *intra*national variations (i.e. ethnicity, class) in Germany. Current fertility differences resulting from Germany's divided history will grow increasingly less remarkable as the number of women who lived and/or remember the culture of motherhood in East Germany decreases. Indeed, among my interviewees, the women aged 30–45 years who had grown up in a socialist system that encouraged childbearing, were the most articulate about why, since re-unification, they and other eastern German women delayed or opted not to bear children. They were also the most ardent defenders of the East German benefits for working mothers. Some of the interviewees, however, were children of 8–10 years of age at re-unification with no strong recollection of socialist politics or what it was to live in a socialist system. "There has to be assimilation . . . The change comes with the generation growing up now," as Lana put it, and, as my interview data indicate, assimilation is already happening.

Still, after re-unification, family life became "the other way around" for many east Germans. Fertility decisions were reshaped by a different political economy, one that problemitized the simultaneous pursuit of work and parenting. The impact of state policy and market forces on fertility cannot be underestimated, and in the German case we find proof positive that political economies of place make a difference in experiences of reproduction.

Acknowledgments

This chapter is based on research supported by the Wenner-Gren Foundation for Anthropological Research, Inc., Grant no. 6591; National Science Foundation, Grant no. 9816337; the Institute of International Education; and the University of Colorado-Boulder. Two other outstanding debts: first, I am forever indebted to the two hospital staffs and patients who remain anonymous here, but on whom my research was dependent; and second, I thank Carrie B. Douglass for her editorial guidance and infinite patience.

References

Arabin, B., Raum, E., Mohnhaupt, A. and Schwartz, F.W. (1999), "Entwicklung der Qualität un subjektiven Einschätzung der Perinatal medizin in Ost- und West-Berlin zwischen 1950 und 1990," *frauenheilkunde plus*, 11: 508–509.

Bundesinstitut für Bevölkerungswissenschaft (1999), "Altersspezifische Geburtenziffern für Ostdeutschland für den Zeitraum 1952–1988," Wiesbaden.

Council of Europe (2002), *Recent Demographic Developments in Europe*, Strasbourg: Council of Europe Publishing.

Der Spiegel (1999), Graph: "Wegniger Geburten im Osten," *Der Spiegel Panorama*, December 10.

Dölling, I., Hahn, D. and Scholz, S. (2000), "Birth Strike in the New Federal States: Is Sterilization an Act of Resistance?," in S. Gal and G. Kligman (eds), *Reproducing Gender: Politics, Publics, and Everyday Life after Socialism*, Princeton, NJ: Princeton University Press.

Einhorn, B. (1993), *Cinderella Goes to Market: Citizenship, Gender and Women's Movements in East Central Europe*, London: Verso.

Engelbrech, G. (1994), "Frauen nur Reservearmee für den Arbeitsmarkt?," *Die Frau in unserer Zeit*, 1: 14–23.

Erikson, S.L. (2001), "Maternity Care Policies and Maternity Care Practices: A Tale of Two Germanys," in R. DeVries, C. Benoit, E.R. Van Teijlingen and S. Wrede (eds), *Birth by Design: Pregnancy, Maternity Care, and Midwifery in North America and Europe*, New York: Routledge.

Eurostat (2003a), "Total Fertility Rate", *Eurostat*, January 29.

—— (2003b), "Mean Age of Women at Birth of First Child", *Eurostat*, January 29.

Fagnani, J. (1996), "Family Policies and Working Mothers: A Comparison of France and West Germany," in M.D. Garcia-Ramon and J. Monk (eds), *Women of the European Union: The Politics of Work and Daily Life*, New York: Routledge.

Funk, N. (1993), "Abortion and German Re-unification," in N. Funk and M. Mueller (eds), *Gender Politics and Post-Communism: Reflections from Eastern Europe and the Former Soviet Union*, New York: Routledge.

Gal, S. and Klingman, G. (2000), *The Politics of Gender after Socialism: A Comparative-Historical Essay*, Princeton, NJ: Princeton University Press.

Grossmann, A. (1995), *Reforming Sex: The German Movement for Birth Control and Abortion Reform, 1920–1950*, Oxford: Oxford University Press.

—— (1997), "The Debate that will Not End," in M. Berg and G. Cocks (eds), *Medicine and Modernity: Public Health and Medical Care in Nineteenth- and Twentieth-Century Germany*, Cambridge: Cambridge University Press.

Koch, A., Wasmer, M., Harkness, J. and Scholz, E. (2001), "Konzeption und Durchführung der Allegemeinen Bevölkerungsumfrage der Sozialwessen-schaften (ALLBUS) 2000," *ZUMA Methodenbericht 2001/05*.

Kreyenfeld, M. (2000a), "Employment Careers and the Time of First Births in East Germany," working paper WP 2000–004 March, Rostock: Max-Planck-Institute für demographische Forschung.

—— (2000b), "Educational Attainment and First Births: East Germany before and after Unification," working paper WP 2000–011 December, Rostock: Max-Planck-Institute für demographische Forschung.

—— (2002), "Crisis or Adaptation Reconsidered: A Comparison of East and West German Fertility Patters in the First Six Years After the 'Wende,' working paper WP 2002–032 July, Rostock: Max-Planck-Institute für demographische Forschung.

Mai, R. (2001), "Fertility Decline in the Regions of East Germany, 1991–1999," poster presented at the EURESCO Conference "The Second Demographic Transition in Europe," June 23–28, Bad Herrenalb.

Maleck-Lewy, E. and Ferree, M.M. (2000) "Talking about Women and Wombs: The Discourse of Abortion and Reproductive Rights in the G.D.R. during and after the *Wende*," in S. Gal and G. Kligman (eds), *Reproducing Gender: Politics, Publics, and Everyday Life after Socialism*, Princeton, NJ: Princeton University Press.

Müller-Rieger, M. (1997), "'*Wenn Mutti früh zur Arbeit geht ...*': Zur Geschichte des Kindergartens in der DDR," Dresden: Argon/Deutschen Hygiene-Museums.

Nickel, H-M. (1993), "Women in the German Democratic Republic and in the New Federal States: Looking Backward and Forward (Five Thesis)," in N. Funk and M. Mueller (eds), *Gender Politics and Post-Communism: Reflections from*

Eastern Europe and the Former Soviet Union, New York: Routledge.

Rueschemeyer, M. (1993), "Women in East Germany: From State Socialism to Capitalist Welfare State," in V.M. Moghadam (ed.), *Democratic Reform and the Position of Women in Transitional Economies*, Oxford: Clarendon Press.

Sayn-Wittgenstein, F. (2000), "Is the Time to First Child Influenced by Women's Professional Interest?," unpublished paper presented at Population Association of America, March 23–25, Los Angeles.

Schmude, J. (1996), "Contrasting Developments in Female Labour Force Participation in East and West Germany since 1945," in M.D. Garcia-Ramon and J. Monk (eds), *Women of the European Union: The Politics of Work and Daily Life*, New York: Routledge.

Statistisches Bundesamt (2001), *Bevölkerung und Erwerbstätigkeit: Gebiet und Bevölkerung 1999*, Stuttgart: Metzler-Poeschel.

Statistisches Bundesamt Deutschland (2003), http://www.destatis.de/, accessed June 9, 2003.

Weingarten, S. and Wellershoff, M. (1999), "Fordert, was ihr kriegen könnt", *Der Spiegel*, November 22: 84–109.

Winkler, G. (1990), *Sozialreport '90: Daten und Fakten zur sozialen Lage in der DDR*, Berlin: Verlag Die Wirtschaft.

–4–

"Our Nation is Dying": Interpreting Patterns of Childbearing in Post-Soviet Russia

Cynthia Gabriel

On my first day in Nizhni Novgorod in 2000, I was greeted by a highway billboard with a picture of a pregnant woman gazing at her swollen belly. The caption read, "My husband is an optimist." I commented to Valentina, a physician, and her son, Danil, a government employee, that this sign must refer to the economic crisis. I guessed that this woman's husband didn't think Russia's economic future looked as bleak as many others. Danil laughingly tossed off a different interpretation. "Perhaps," he suggested, "he thinks his children won't die before they're 50 like the rest of us."

During my fieldwork in 2000 and 2002, concerns about the Russian birthrate and the mortality rate were omnipresent. Often, conversations, newspaper articles, academic research, political speeches or artistic productions begin with a cursory statement about the "catastrophic decline" of the Russian population (Artukhov 2002). Even more often, the reference is left unvoiced, but its echoing reverberation is still felt. If there is one concern that unites Russians across class and space, this seems to be it.

Like women in other low birthrate countries, women in Russia generally have only one and sometimes two children. Less than 3 percent of Russian women born after 1964 have more than two children (Kharkova and Andreev 2000). But there are at least two ways that Russia's demographic picture differs from that of Europe and, indeed, the world. These are, in the first place, the pronounced tendency of Russian women to give birth relatively early in the reproductive cycle. The vast majority of births in Russia occur to women aged between 18 and 24. This is in sharp contrast to all non-Eastern European countries, where fertility tends to peak in the 25–29 age group (Zakharov and Ivanova 2001). Second, in marked contrast to most other countries in the world where birthrates are declining, Russia's birthrate decline is accompanied by a concomitant *increase* in adult mortality, especially adult male mortality. At the same time that fewer babies are being born in Russia, more people are dying at earlier ages. Life expectancies are among the lowest in the world for industrialized countries (Shkolnikov and Mesle 2001).

I offer four possible, interrelated, cultural and political reasons for the low birthrate. First, I will explore the socio-medical practice of defining women over 28 as "older" mothers who are at greater medical risk than younger women. Then I will look at three concerns Russians bring up when we discuss childbearing. They are worries about childcare, male alcoholism and space. I base my arguments on ethnographic fieldwork in urban areas of European Russian (Yaroslavl, St Petersburg, Moscow and Nizhni Novgorod) and on analysis of demographic data. For part of my research, I worked as a midwifery intern in a St Petersburg maternity hospital. More ethnographic research is needed in other parts of Russia to investigate specific demographic trends, particularly in rural areas.

First, the medical approach to childbearing in Russia emphasizes the cultural desirability of early childbearing. Most medical professionals assume that "older mothers" (over 28 years) have significantly higher risks of giving birth to undesirable babies. They believe that these mothers have more complications in pregnancy and labor than younger mothers. Birth professionals, due to these beliefs, patrol and control this socio-medical category of "at-risk" older mothers through medical practices. For instance, they encourage older mothers to have abortions. Women who refuse can face harassment and poor quality care. Many women undergo Cesarean sections (C-sections) due solely to maternal age.

This cultural-medical construction of appropriate childbearing age is hard to understand in light of the extreme concern most Russians, including birth professionals, express about the low birthrate (Bodrova 2002). However, it makes sense when I consider the most common childcare solution in Russia: grandmother-provided care. This is the second phenomenon I will explore. Not only is grandparent care an economic necessity, but also it is highly culturally valued. Many of my informants agree with L.M. Pankova (1998), who writes that children are better off when grandparents are involved in their day-to-day lives. Stack and Burton (1994) point out that such cultural values influence demographic trends. Young women who count on their parents for childcare must have children young enough so that their parents will (or will likely) be alive and physically able to take care of them.

I argue that the demographic effects of this reality, grandparent-provided childcare, is magnified in Russia because of the current mortality crisis. The cultural effects of high mortality is the third issue I will explore. Russians (many of them grandparents) are dying earlier than they have in the past at the same time that available childcare options have decreased in number and quality. But in addition, the well-documented reasons for high male mortality – high rates of alcoholism, binge drinking and alcohol-related accidents – have profound implications for childbearing (Cockerham, Snead and Dewaal 2002; Leon *et al.* 1997). Women like

Yanna, divorced in her early twenties with one child and now 32 years old, tell me, "At my age, there are no good men." In both the literal and the abstract, Yanna is right. Literally, there are significantly fewer men than women in Russia. Of the men available, both ethnographic and statistical evidence points to high levels of alcohol consumption among virtually all of them. As Svetlana, a 19-year-old who wants to be a government specialist, puts it: "No matter how carefully I choose a man, I must be prepared for him to become a drinker." Yanna and Svetlana, both of whom desire two children, must navigate these realities as they make child-bearing decisions in the next decades.

Finally, I will take up the issue of space. Demographers and policy-makers do not often make the connection between the birthrate and the urban housing situation, but my Russian informants certainly do. By far the most common answer to my question, "Why don't you have another child?" is, "There's no space." Russian apartments are invariably tiny ("matchbox" is how one reporter describes them). Surprisingly influential is the strong belief that parents should provide living space for their adult children, either in the same or in a separate apartment. Russian law bolsters this cultural view. According to Russian law, children are born with a birthright ownership share in parental real estate property. A few of my informants forthrightly explain that this parental responsibility has kept them from having more children.

Challenging the View that the Economic Crises have Caused the Decline in Russian Births

Viewing Russia's birthrate in the context of falling European birthrates changes the usual discourse. Instead of an indication of economic pathology, the below replacement birthrate in Russia can be seen as part of demographic trends in industrialized countries.[1] The total fertility rate of the European Union is 1.5 children per woman; replacement rate is considered to be 2.2. The trend toward fewer children per woman has been pronounced in Northern and Central Europe since the middle of the twentieth century; however, countries in Eastern and Southern Europe, including Russia, the Cezch Republic, Italy, Spain and Greece, have caught up since the late 1980s.

This is not how the Russian birthrate is normally treated. Western journalists and policy advisors and Russian politicians and demographers all use the low Russian birthrate to signal economic instability and widespread pessimism. In a month-long special series on the state of Russian health and medicine, Michael Wines of the *New York Times* repeatedly makes the connection between the economic crisis and the low birthrate sound deceivingly simple. Russian women, he suggests, are making a rational choice in view of their economic prospects. As one example, from the ominously titled article, "For All Russia, Biological Clock is

Running Out," Wines (2003c) writes, "after a decade of social upheaval and poverty, creating a child here seems less an act of love, lust or even calculation than it is an act of pure will, and perhaps faith."

Wines is far from alone. Dozens of newspaper and magazine articles, American and Russian alike, incorporate birthrate statistics to help bolster arguments about Russian society. Except in the hands of a few demographers like Vishnevsky (2001) and Kharkova and Andreev (2000), the Russian birthrate almost always indicates something bad, especially something bad about the state of Russian medicine, the Russian economy and about Russia's future.

But this assumption that "correlation is causation" has actually been disproved by recent demographic inquiries. Most notably, Kharkova and Andreev set out in 2000 to answer the question, "Did the Economic Crisis Cause the Fertility Decline in Russia?" They painstakingly sifted through data on birthrates to show that the economic conditions of families did not impact the number of children born. They conclude that

> all of the above considerations cast doubt on the hypothesis that the economic crisis is the main and only cause of the fertility level decrease in Russia . . . From the authors' viewpoint, these facts [of the study] are more conforming to the hypothesis that the socio-economic crisis has merely accelerated the long-term process of the second demographic transition in Russia. (Kharkove and Andreev 2000: 233).

I concur with Kharkova and Andreev (2000) wholeheartedly and seek, in this chapter, to outline a demographic approach to the study of Russia's low birthrate that is ethnographically informed. I propose that a richer understanding of this issue will result by considering the cultural and not just the economic context in which childbearing decisions are being made.

Medically Defining the Culturally Appropriate Age to have Children

I argue that the strong medical and cultural message that women over 28 should not have children is an important factor in the low Russian birthrate. This message is widespread throughout European Russia; it underpins discussions of fertility by Russians from a wide variety of social classes. Russian doctors are among the loudest voices lobbying for more children. Birth professionals are worried because their jobs are threatened by the low birthrate. The number of medical jobs available is tied directly to the size of the population in a given area. In Nizhni Novgorod, four out of nine *roddoms* (maternity hospitals) have closed since 1991, taking with them dozens of good jobs.

Yet even as medical practitioners decry the low birthrate, certain widespread medical practices are, in fact, quite discouraging of childbearing. Of particular note is the medically and socially defined appropriate age range of 18 to 28 for giving birth. Creating this category – and then enforcing it through practices such as suggesting abortions to older women, prescribing C-sections based solely on maternal age, and creating a difficult environment for older mothers at the *roddom* – has the effect of limiting the number of births in Russia.

Russian birth professionals with whom I worked in St Petersburg and Nizhni Novgorod relegate pregnant women into two categories: young mothers or "older" mothers.[2] These categories are not limited to the medical field, but are ubiquitous throughout society, in everyday conversations and magazine articles about birth. In fact, the phrase "young mother" is basically a euphemism for "mother" – as used in popular magazines such as *Moi Ryebyonok* (*My Baby*) or *Malish* (*Little One*) or in books on childrearing such as *Vospitaniye Vnukov* (*Caring for Grandchildren*). In 2000 booksellers across Russia sold a popular book called *Advice for Young Mothers*, by which the authors merely meant "new mothers." This phrase distinguishes, culturally, between older mothers (i.e. grandmothers) and mothers of young children – the young mother. But it also hints that to be a mother, one should belong to the category of "young" mother, not "older" mother.

Since the early 1990s, I myself have felt strong pressure to make my reproductive choices fit culturally approved norms. In 1990–1991 as a 20-year-old exchange student, I felt intense pressure to get married and have children. Russians from all walks of life, including fellow university students, sang the praises of having children in one's early twenties and wondered aloud at my strange ideas about "waiting." I was warned that putting off childbearing could lead to serious problems, such as infertility, an inability to attract a man, or dying in childbirth. In 2000, as a 30-year-old, the pressure to have children had turned down dramatically – replaced by vocal disapproval that I had "missed" the appropriate time and would now be an "older" mother if I chose to have children.

Depending on the medical practitioner, the category of "older" mother is defined as beginning anywhere from 24 to 28. This category of older mother, who is ostensibly more at risk medically from giving birth to a child, is based on an explicit assumption about the appropriate, healthy time to give birth. Going through labor and delivery for the first time after 28 is considered extremely risky. Marina, a birth attendant at Roddom #2 in St Petersburg, told me: "The body is designed to give birth when a woman is around 14 or 15. That is the optimal age, biologically speaking. Why else does a woman's period start then?" Or as Zhanna, a pediatrician in Nizhni Novgorod, says: "There is a time when it is just better, physiologically, to have a baby. After 28, everything is less flexible. Things don't stretch the way they do when you're younger. You're just older and it's much, much harder."

Being categorized as an "older" and at-risk mother has important consequences for medical care. First, many older women are advised to have an abortion. Larissa's doctor, when Larissa first became pregnant in 1997 at 29, strongly pressured her to consider abortion. Several women, who were hospitalized in St Petersburg prior to planned C-sections for maternal age, also confided that their doctors had suggested abortions. When I talked with the head doctor of Roddom #2 shortly after she had performed an abortion, she acknowledged that, "Well, it's the saddest part of my job. But we have to do it. Can we really tell a 40-year-old woman 'Go ahead? Have a baby?' That is professionally irresponsible."

Second, if an older mother decides to go ahead with her pregnancy, her medical treatment and birth options are impacted by her categorization. In urban areas, extensive fetal testing is usually performed. Russians from all walks of life associate advanced maternal age (over 28) with fetal abnormalties, especially Down Syndrome.[3] Fear of Down Syndrome was, by far, the single most common response I heard to my own plans to have children in my thirties.

The categorization of "older" mother, in my ethnographic experience in urban areas, almost always leads to a C-section. Marina was advised to have a C-section at 29 based on her advanced age and her extreme nearsightedness. (Nearsightedness is an oft-cited contraindication for allowing a woman to push during labor in Russia.) Marina decided to have a homebirth with the physician Valentina in order to avoid a C-section. Even after a successful vaginal delivery three years earlier, when she became pregnant again in 2000, her doctors repeated their advice to have a C-section. Marina again planned a homebirth with Valentina. Unfortunately, Valentina was unavailable when Marina went into labor and she had to go to the local *roddom*. When she arrived, she had to argue extensively with her caretakers to give birth vaginally.

In the St Petersburg birth clinic where I worked, at least three C-sections (out of about a hundred births) were scheduled in advance for first-time mothers based on maternal age. Two of these three women appeared to accept their situation calmly and agreeably; the third was saddened by her doctors' recommendation for surgery, but felt helpless to challenge it.

On one afternoon, our group of American midwifery interns spent two hours interviewing and doing physical examinations on two of these women: Elvira, a 37-year-old dentist, and Lydia, a 30-year-old English teacher. We informally discussed with them differences between American and Russian medical reasons for performing C-sections. Some of the American interns in our group questioned Elvira's and Lydia's plans to have a surgical delivery, suggesting that these women could insist on vaginal births. Elvira and Lydia were both visibly upset by this interaction, for opposite reasons. Elvira defiantly answered, "I am going to have a C-section. That is the best thing. I'm 37 and I'm a doctor. I know about these things." Lydia, on the other hand, was near tears. She wanted a vaginal birth, but despaired of having any sway over her Russian doctors.

In Nizhni Novgorod, where I worked with pregnant women at state-sponsored childbirth preparation classes, I encountered several women like Elvira who accept and, indeed, advocate the necessity of C-section deliveries for "older" mothers. I met one such woman, Sveta, during the first trimester of her pregnancy. She was 31 years old and pregnant with her first child. At her first prenatal visit, she was told she would have a C-section because of her age. Sveta heard me say that I planned to have a child when I returned to the United States and that I would be 31. She was shocked to hear that I planned a vaginal birth and for the duration of my time in Russia tried to convince me to listen to reason and sign up for a C-section when I returned home. She feared for the life of my as-yet-unconceived child and also told me: "You will ruin your body!"

Even younger mothers who were at the upper limits of the acceptable age range faced approbation at the *roddom*. In one notable case, a 27-year-old woman, Natasha, gave birth vaginally; however, she labored quite loudly. Her doctor did not hide her disgust at Natasha's approach to labor. After the birth, the doctor attempted to suture Natasha, but she flinched every time the doctor touched her. So while I held her hand and her gaze to keep her quiet, the doctor finished suturing – all the while keeping up a running monologue. When Natasha said, "It hurts!" The doctor replied:

Of course it hurts! What did you expect? That it would be easy? It's supposed to hurt! What does a woman your age expect, anyway? You're supposed to be a grandmother, and instead you get it into your head to give birth! What were you doing when you were 20? Running around? Having fun? That's when it wouldn't hurt so much. But you have to make money, make money and then you complain when it hurts.

These medical practices and medically based beliefs about appropriate ages for childbearing fit the statistical model of Russian births very nicely. Abortion and birthrates by age group in Russia have a distinct pattern, different from that in Western Europe and the United States. In general, Russian women have far more abortions than American women. By conservative estimates, Russian women average four abortions each (Popov 2001). But between 18 and 24 – the age range that is defined by Russian medical practitioners as appropriate childbearing years – Russian women have 50 percent fewer abortions than American women (Center for Disease Control 1999). That means that they are having a substantially higher number of abortions than their American counterparts after age 24.

Put another way, births in Russia are very concentrated in the age bracket of 18–24, whereas in North America and Western Europe the years of active childbearing are extended. In fact, "the contribution by mothers aged fifteen to twenty-four accounted for fifty-six percent of TFR in 1990, the all-time high for western European countries and non-European developed countries in the post-war period" (Zakharov and Ivanova 2001). The Russian birthrate does not plateau anywhere, but rises sharply to age 24 and then falls away abruptly. This dramatic peak – along with the strong cultural and medical pressure against so-called "late" childbearing

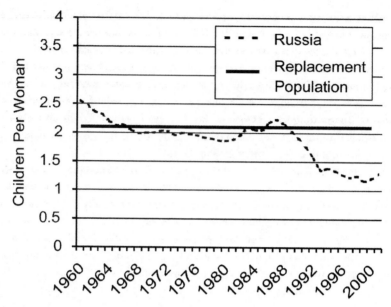

Figure 4.1 Total Fertility Rate, Russia, 1960–2001.
Source: Council of Europe, Social Cohesion, Population, Russian Federation and Population Reference Bureau 2002.

– convinces me that the demographers who compare the current situation in Russia with that of the depression in the United States are somewhat mistaken. Barbara Anderson, a demographer at University of Michigan, claims that in times of economic depression, people everywhere act rationally by delaying childrearing, thereby creating a baby boom after the depression (Wines 2000c). But, at least so far, Russians who "miss" the 18–24 window tend not to have, or to have fewer, children later (Kharkova and Andreev 2000).

Grandparents Taking Care of Children: The Demographic Connection

At first glance, the construction of such a narrow appropriate age range for Russian women to give birth seems paradoxical, given the high level of concern most Russians express about the national birthrate. Surveys conducted by Bodrova during 2000, for instance, confirm what I found to be anecdotally true: the majority of Russians are truly worried about the low birthrate. Bodrova (2002) found that 60.3 percent of 2,407 Russians surveyed thought it was "necessary to take emergency measures to increase the birthrate." Only 18.5 percent responded that such measures were not necessary. This survey, like most of the demographic and statistical data I have reviewed, does not offer much information about what these Russians imagine effective emergency measures to consist of. (Bodrova's survey asks only about implementing abortion restrictions to help increase the birthrate. A majority of respondents did not agree that this was desirable.)[4]

My observations of Russian lives have led me to conclude that grandparent-provided childcare, alcoholism and early mortality among men, and a lack of living space are three interrelated and significant factors in the Russian birthrate. In addition, I posit that grandparent-provided childcare and the early mortality among men underpin the cultural and medical discourse about appropriate childbearing ages. Young women are making childbearing decisions in a particularly difficult cultural context. Childcare options are few and far between; parents, who usually fill this gap, are dying earlier than they used to. This puts pressure on women of childbearing age to have children early.

I should qualify here that while the medical definition of appropriate childbearing ages is widespread throughout Russian society, these three issues (childcare, early mortality and living space) are problems faced mostly by the urban middle class and urban poor. A tiny minority of Russians (often called "New Russians'), whose incomes are more widely divergent from average incomes than in almost any other developed country in the world, are able to buy their way out of childcare dilemmas, government-supplied apartments and even, to a certain degree, early mortality (Rosser 2000; Maximova 1999).

Quality childcare was once considered a right for all Soviet children. Yet even in the best economic years, the "ideal" was never made into a true reality (Geiger 1968; Katkova 1982). Today the situation has deteriorated considerably. Throughout the Soviet period and increasingly in the post-Soviet period, parents are turning to older generations to help with childcare. In one 1998 study in the Tver region of Russia, 44.8 percent of grandmothers were looking after their grandchildren (Parakhonskaya 2002).

The role of grandparents in the lives of many young Russians is considerable; 60 percent of Russians over the legal retirement age (55 years old for women and 60 years old for men) live with family members, usually their children (Parakhonskaya 2002: 104). But this statistic does not begin to tell the whole story. In addition to the many grandparents who live with their children, there are also those who live nearby and interact frequently and those who live in the countryside (who often invite grandchildren to live with them for the entire summer break). In addition, many grandparents help with domestic tasks like cooking, cleaning and making extra money in the informal economy.

I was also struck at the vital role so many older Russians play in the subsistence of their progeny. In the mid-1990s, around 55 million families grew at least some of their own food; subsistence agriculture constituted a majority of Russians' diet (Tho Seeth *et al.* 1998). Most of my Russian acquaintances from cities depend on family members who live at least part of the year in the countryside for substantial portions of their food. For instance, Sasha's mother lives about 100 kilometers from Nizhni Novgorod. During the summer months, Sasha's wife and 13-year-old daughter live with her. After weekend visits to them, Sasha's car is inevitably loaded with produce. During my fieldwork year, he shared this bounty with me. He claims that without his mother's garden, his family would be nutritionally deprived and probably "very sick."

These strong bonds between parents and adult children and between grandparents and grandchildren are even codified in Russian law. According to Statute 55 of Russian Family Law, "A child has the right to interact with both parents, with grandfathers, grandmothers, brothers, sisters and other relatives" regardless of the marital status or wishes of the child's parents (Family Code of the Russian Federation 2000). As for financial support, parents are, of course, obligated to provide for their under-age children. But in addition, Statutes 85, 87, 93, 94 and 95 address the case in which an adult family member is unable to work. These statutes provide that parents, siblings, grandparents and grandchildren (over the age of 18) can all be forced by the courts to provide financial support for one another.

But the contributions of grandparents to their children's families, absolutely crucial to the functioning of so many families, is limited by age and health factors. Russians are keenly aware that their national life expectancies trail those in many other countries: Russian women can expect to live 71.8 years, but Russian men's life expectancy is only 58.9 years (Cockerham *et al.* 2002) In light of these mortality statistics, it makes sense that "the largest proportion of all these [grandparental] contributions [to their children's families] came from the age group 'up until sixty-five years old' (86.1 percent). As age increases, the proportion of giving of all kinds of help decreases" (Parakhonskaya 2002: 107). The stark reality of early mortality is that the number of years grandparents can help their families is limited.

Following Stack and Burton (1994), I believe that just as Russian medical professionals define 18–28 years old as the most appropriate and healthy ages for giving birth to children, Russian grandparents also contribute to the cultural discourse about appropriate childbearing ages. My friend Yanna told me that when she first found out she was pregnant she was unsure whether she wanted to keep the child. But her mother did everything possible to persuade her to keep it, and "finally she [the grandmother] won." I also remember vividly a teenage mother who gave birth at the *roddom* in the summer of 2000. She stood out from the other women as visibly counter-cultural, a self-proclaimed hippie. Her tongue was pierced and she had several tattoos. I anticipated that she would have a complicated relationship with her own parents, based on her counter-cultural views; in reality, she was close to her mother. She agreed to give birth to this child after her mother offered to take care of and raise it. "That's what parents do," said this young woman simply.

Finally, there is my friend Nina. The mother of two children, Nina is definitively done with giving birth. Though the primary reason she gives for not having a third child is lack of space, she also knows that her mother's help cannot go on forever. Every day, her mother, now 61, walks to Nina's apartment and helps feed her two children breakfast. She gets them ready for school, takes care of domestic chores, cooks dinner for the family and picks the children up from school. In the summer, she accompanies Nina's two children to the countryside, where they live together with the children's other grandmother. Nina's mother is active and healthy, but when we discuss her mother's health, Nina gets a worried look. She knows her life would be complicated without her mother's help. "I know I am lucky," she says repeatedly. She is not willing to push her luck with a third child.

Where are All the Good Men? Male Mortality and the Russian Birthrate

Low life expectancies, true for both men and women, dramatically influence the availability of grandparent-provided childcare. The low life expectancy for men, almost thirteen years lower than that for women, has even more implications for the low Russian birthrate. First of all, Russian women who would like to have children (or more children) have trouble finding men of a similar age. Second, numerous studies have shown that the increase in male mortality rates is heavily driven by alcohol-related deaths (Leon *et al.* 1997; Shkolnikov and Mesle 2001; Cockerham *et al.* 2002). This has implications not only because of the loss of men, but also because of the hard-to-quantify effect of excessive alcohol consumption in the lives of many Russian families.

An imbalance between the number of women and the number of men has a long history in Russia. Because of the Civil War, Stalinist repressions, the Second World War, and the war in Afghanistan, many generations of Russian women have grown used to significantly outnumbering their male peers, especially during their reproductive years (Shkolnikov and Mesle 2001). As my friend Yanna plaintively states, "At my age, there are no good men." She is 32. A neighbor in St Petersburg is even more desperate at 43. Most Russian women can quote sex imbalance statistics from memory. The imbalance between men and women in Russia begins at age 15 and increases steadily. Though boys outnumber girls at birth (1.04 boys to 1 girl), by age 65 there are only forty-six men for every 100 women (http://world-facts.globalesl.net).

In other words, as Russians move through their reproductive years, there are fewer and fewer men. The sexes are balanced most equally at the beginning of the reproductive years – exactly when Russian women are having the most babies. The effect is that, for many years (the same years, incidentally, that the birthrate has been falling dramatically) "many women have not had the opportunity to start a family" (Parakhonskaya 2002: 103). The vast majority of adult men – 87.3 percent – have children, but more than one out of five Russian women have never had the opportunity. Of adult women over 55, 21.9 percent have never had a child (Parakhonskaya 2002: 103).[5]

The toll of pandemic male alcohol abuse on Russian family life and the Russian birthrate cannot be underestimated. As indicated, numerous studies have linked the low life expectancy of Russian men directly to alcohol consumption. In the 1990s, "Russia had the highest per capita consumption of pure alcohol in the world – 14.5 liters per annum" (or approximately 4 gallons) (Cockerham *et al.* 2002). "When it is noted that adult males consume ninety percent of the alcohol in Russia, yet comprise twenty-five percent of the population, it is apparent that the drinking practices of this group far exceed per capita consumption and reflect a tremendous concentration of drinking" (Cockerham *et al.* 2002).

Demographers have concluded that alcohol-related deaths (from alcohol poisoning, injury and violence) account for almost all of the increase in Russian male mortality since the early 1980s. They reached this conclusion, in large part, because of the anomalous statistics from the years 1985–1987, when Gorbachev implemented stringent anti-alcohol policies. In those years, male mortality from these alcohol-related causes dropped noticeably (Leon *et al.* 1997; Shkolnikov and Mesle 2001).

I posit that alcohol abuse among men is also a factor in the low Russian birthrate because of the impact it has on the daily lives of not only Russian men, but also their families. This was brought home to me one day in 1991 when I asked a Russian classmate what her father did for a living. "You know, he's at that age," she replied. I knew what she meant. The father in the family where I lived in 1990–1991 was also "at that age." His mother, his wife and his two daughters all seemed determined to avoid naming the problem in front of me, but his heavy drinking was impossible to cover up. Feminists write about the burden placed on many women who must be the primary wage-earner in families where men have become chronically alcoholic. For example, Yarskaya and Yarskaya-Smirnova (2002: 75) quote the director of one office who oversees 250 women workers: "Practically every second or even two out of three [of these women] have problems at home, there is serious drinking, serious pathology at home. So there is my problem, the problem of our work center, a singularly female problem. I feel sorry for my women, but there is nothing I can do to help them."

Let me return to the example of Nina, who maintains that space is the primary deterrent in her life from having more children. She admits, however, that she is also worried about the ability of her own mother to continue to provide childcare for too many more years in the future. But there is another ghost haunting Nina's story: her husband's drinking. Though Nina never complained to me about it, our mutual friends often discussed her husband, Marat's, drinking. Though Marat was only occasionally home when I visited, on a substantial number of occasions when he was home, he was visibly intoxicated. Nina, not surprisingly, is the family's primary breadwinner. I hypothesize that male alcoholism is another factor in the reluctance or inability of many Russian women over 28 to bear children.

"There's No Room for More of Us!"

As regards the lack of space, it is clearly a problem – one that any visitor to Russia notices immediately. Most urban Russians I know live in multigenerational set-tings of two, three and even four generations together. Young couples who have struck out on their own invariably live in one-room dormitories or tiny studio apartments. Most of the urban housing built since the Second World War in Russia has been one- to four-room apartments, the vast majority having two or three rooms. As Patrick Flood (2002) notes, such architectural decisions were made in the context of building socialism. The Soviet state, which for many years focused on building industry, in part by encouraging women to participate in the work-force, "discouraged childbirth through its housing policies, under-producing undersized apartments in urban areas, with a typical ten-year wait for a young couple to get a flat barely large enough for two" (Flood 2002). Only recently, since 1998, have construction projects to build larger-scale apartments in the major cities begun.[6] Still, the number of available apartments (aside from being out of reach financially for most Russians) is miniscule compared to the number of fam-ilies that need expanded housing.

Nina's situation is quite common. She and her husband live with their two chil-dren in a cramped two-room apartment. The children sleep in one room. Nina and her husband use the living room; the couch doubles as their bed. This arrangement (using the living room as a bedroom) is the norm, not the exception, in urban Russia. The kitchen is so small that the family cannot sit all together around the kitchen table. Her mother made a "lucky swap" for a studio apartment in the city nearby, so they do not have to live together. Nina's life is consumed with trying to trade up to a three-room apartment. Nina's decision to switch careers, from accountant to real estate broker, is based on this dream of owning a larger apart-ment. Even though Nina's mother lives nearby and provides free childcare, Nina relates that after their first child, a son, was born, it took her five years to convince her husband to have a second child. She says, "He was worried that we couldn't afford a second child. I was worried that we had no room."

Concern about space is not limited to this transparent concern about not having extra space in one's apartment. It also involves a longer-term concern that seems to be particular to urban Russians: the desire of parents to provide living space for their adult children. An acquaintance in St Petersburg, Olga, who has one teenage son (she had him when she was 16) desperately wants to have a second child. Yet she doesn't feel right about having a second child until she can afford to buy either a second apartment or a larger apartment because she believes it is the parents' duty to provide adult children with living space. She doesn't want to deprive her older son of what she considers his birthright: an apartment.

Petra Rethmann (2000) found this sentiment to be influential in the Russian Far East as well. She tells the story of a Koriak woman, Lidiia, from Ossora, whose life situation has deteriorated dramatically since the end of state socialism. Lidiia feels a parental responsibility to provide her children their own living space. Rethmann writes that "when Zina [Lidiia's daughter] was approximately 15 years old she decided to leave home and move in with her boyfriend." Though Lidiia was angry, she also blamed herself for not being able to provide living space for the couple: "How would she have been able to provide some space for the couple? She did not have the money to buy a new place. And, of course, she could understand that Zina wanted to leave home because she had no room of her own" (Rethmann 2000: 32).

Russian law corresponds with this sentiment and may, in surprising ways, play a role in some families' decisions about having children. Russian law provides that when children are born, they automatically own a certain percentage of their parents' real estate. If a couple lives together in an apartment that they own jointly and they have one child, each person now owns one-third of the apartment. If the couple has a second child, each person now owns one-quarter of the apartment. If a family receives an apartment from the government and children are registered as owners (which increases the size of the apartment to which the family is entitled), the children retain ownership over their portion of the apartment into adulthood.

In September, 2000, I watched an episode of a Russian television program called *The Suit is On* – the Russian equivalent of *People's Court*. In this half-hour program, a mother and adopted daughter are fighting over an apartment. The 20-year-old daughter cannot get along with her mother and wants to live on her own. She claims that she owns half of her mother's apartment and wants to force her mother to sell the apartment so that they can buy separate apartments. Complicating the case is the fact that the mother never officially and legally adopted the daughter, even though they have lived together for twelve years. The judge must rule whether the adopted daughter has rights to her mother's apartment even though she was never officially adopted. The judge returns the verdict that the daughter does indeed have rights to the mother's apartment, but that the daughter cannot force her mother to sell the apartment. Instead, the judge requires that the mother allow the daughter to continue living in the apartment. If the daughter chooses not to live with her mother, she will continue to own half of the apartment but will have to find accommodation elsewhere.

In real life, I watched these complications play out in another way. My friend Igor opened his own business during the boom years before the 1998 crisis. During the boom, he bought an expensive $25,000 two-room modern apartment. In 2000, he got married and had a child. According to Russian law, his son now owns one-third of his apartment. According to another Russian law, Igor cannot move into any apartment in which his son will have *less* square footage than he now owns. This child protection law, defended vehemently by many Russians I know as a sensible measure to protect children from selfish parents, now severely limits Igor's options. Igor would very much like to sell his expensive apartment now, move into a smaller apartment and use the cash to expand his business, but finds that he is not allowed to do so. Igor advises his entrepreneur friends not to have children if they own their own business. "It just doesn't make sense," he says. "It limits your ability to grow your business."

Not surprisingly, then, a study by Andrei Artukhov (2002) found that "living conditions" were, in fact, the number one factor listed by couples in their consideration of how many children to have. Artukhov suggests a novel way for the Russian government to encourage childbearing. Since the Russian government is still, technically, the owner of many apartment complexes in Russia, Artukhov thinks that a new form of privatization, aimed at helping families with more than two children, would be effective. In his model "young families" (this is his phrase – he thinks it especially important to help young families in which the mother is younger than 30 years old) would be given access to credit to buy apartments. If the couple has one or two children, they would only have to pay back only part of the debt, "but if they have a third, then they would not have to return the money" (Artukhov 2002: 110). These policies are already being tested in some Russian regions.

Conclusion: Toward an Ethnographic Demography

In conclusion, then, I offer four interrelated points as ways to understand the cultural context of the low Russian birthrate. I am arguing against the facile economic crisis causation theory which remains in vogue among many western journalists, policy advisors and policy-makers. In particular, I take exception to the opinion of such influential writers as Michael Wines (2000a, 2002b, 2002c) of the *New York Times* and Stephen Massey (2002) of the East West Institute, that the economic problems faced by the Russian medical system are mostly to blame for the low life expectancies and "dramatic demographic decline" (Tedstrom 2002). Certainly, the economic crises have influenced the lives of Russians, including their reproductive lives. But such representations miss two important points. First, blaming the low Russian birthrate on the economic situation since 1991 ignores the long-term fertility trends toward smaller families and a below replacement birthrate. These trends are well documented in Russia. Second, as an ethnographer and cultural anthropologist, I advocate a policy and research approach that takes into account the complex interplay of international economic dynamics with local, Russian cultural systems.

In addition to looking for a scholarly approach that incorporates economic and social theory together, I also hope to bring together what is often two separate lines of demographic inquiry: studies about the Russian birthrate and studies about Russian mortality. Though some publications, such as *Dire Demographics* (DaVanzo and Grammich 2001), do attempt to provide analysis of these two issues simultaneously, they generally do so in separate chapters or sections. An integrated approach, in which the cultural realities of living with a low birthrate and a high mortality rate are explored, is rare indeed.

But this dual reality is, in fact, the situation facing Russians. They are simultaneously aware of both truths. Their reproductive decisions are being made not only in the context of deep-seated concerns about "not enough children being born" (the words of one Russian informant), but also in the context of fathers and potential fathers dying young and grandparents (who provide nearly half of Russia's childcare) also dying earlier than they used to. I argue that a strong cultural belief in the desirability and necessity of women giving birth in the narrow age range of 18 to 28, bolstered by medical rationales and medical practice, is a very important contributor to the Russian birthrate. However, I do not see this belief as an isolated factor that can be easily changed. Instead, I argue here that it is deeply imbedded in other cultural practices and discourses, such as the widespread preference for and reliance on grandparent-provided childcare and the absence of men at later ages in the reproductive cycle. Likewise, though the economic crisis certainly impacts the ability of Russians to buy or rent larger apartments, cultural beliefs and practices – such as the belief that parents are responsible for providing living space for adult children – are also important in shaping fertility decisions.

Notes

1. Michele Rivkin-Fish in an article in *American Anthropologist* challenges the use of "demographic transition theory." She points out many of the problematic assumptions that are built into this theory, for instance "its presumption that shifts in . . . practices surrounding reproduction occur in patterns shared across cultures" (Riukin-Fish 2003: 289). She notes that demographers within Russia who have embraced the view that the shift toward low fertility in Russia is "inevitable" have done so against the background of an extreme pronatalist state. Arguing that modernization always results in lower fertility rates helped these demographers contest interventionism. "Vishnevskii and his supporters," she writes, were among the first and most visible to endorse demographic transition theory in Russia, and they "believed that leaving decisions about fertility to individual families would benefit society" (Riukin-Fish 2003: 295). In other

words, despite its flaws, this theory has allowed for progressive social advocacy.

Rivkin-Fish analyzes the use of transition theory within Russian demography; however, a similar argument can be made for western experts on Russia. That is, despite its significant drawbacks, demographic transition theory helps destabilize certain western assumptions. When Russia's demographic "crisis" is refigured as a "natural" decline, different questions can be explored ethnographically *and* statistically. In other words, the use of demographic transition theory, in this case, *allows* for a more nuanced and ethnographically informed demography, which is exactly what Rivkin-Fish and many challengers of transition theory favor.

2. Valentina, a homebirth physician in Nizhni Novgorod, is a notable exception. Just like many homebirth midwives in the United States, she and her views about birth are considered odd by many of her medical colleagues.

3. It is true that the risk of bearing a baby with Down Syndrome increases steadily with maternal age. In the age bracket 20–24, the frequency of babies born with Down Syndrome is 1 in 1250. At 32, an age when tests specifically to rule out Down Syndrome associated with maternal age are not recommended in the United States, the chances are 1 in 750. By 35, the chances have increased to 1 in 350, and by 40 to 1 in 100 (Hook, Cross and Schreinemachers 1983). I include these statistics to show that what is at stake here is not whether Russians or Americans are "right," but rather that we have defined, culturally, our acceptable levels of risk differently (see also Rapp 1999).

4. The *American Anthropologist* article by Rivkin-Fish points out many of the problems with interventionist measures to increase the Russian birthrate. Rivkin-Fish (2003) rightly questions the desirability of attempting to influence (especially to increase) the Russian birthrate; however, I was struck by the resounding unanimity with which my informants from urban areas of European Russia (some of whom were unemployed, most of whom were university-educated professionals and some of whom were among the newly rich) bemoaned the birthrate decline as entirely negative. Many of them suggested interventionist state measures. Most often, I heard calls to raise state subsidies for children (especially in larger families). One young woman (mother of two) had recently accepted a job with 500 rubles per month salary (an exceedingly low salary; transportation costs to and from work for this woman totaled 125 rubles per month). She felt betrayed by a government that promotes higher birthrates but that cannot protect women with children from facing discrimination in hiring.

5. Although there are certainly many women who choose not to have children, there are also many who are disappointed. Bodrova (2002: 100) found that women who did not have any children desired the same number (or even more)

children as their counterparts who had already given birth to at least one child.
6. Some wealthy "New Russians" are building houses on the outskirts of cities.
But these expensive houses do not answer the needs of most Russians. See
Caroline Humphrey's chapter "The Villas of the 'New Russians'" for an in-
depth analysis of this phenomenon (2002: 175–201).

References

Artukhov, A.V. (2002), "Gosudarstvennaya Semeinaya Politika I Yeyo Osobennosti
V Rossii," *Sotsiologicheskiye Issledovaniye*, 7: 108–110.

Bodrova, V.V. (2002), "Reproduktivnoye Povedeniye Kak Faktor Depopulatsii V
Rossii," *Sotsiologicheskiye Issledovaniye*, 6: 96–102.

Center for Disease Control (1999), *Maternal and Child Health Statistics: Russian
Federation and United States, Selected Years 1985–95*, series 5, no. 10,
http://www.cdc.gov/nchs/data/series/sr_05/sr05_010e.pdf.

Cockerham, W.C., Snead, M.C. and Dewaal, D.F. (2002) "Health Lifestyles in
Russia and the Socialist Heritage," *Journal of Health and Social Behavior*,
43(1): 42–55.

DaVanzo, J. and Grammich, C. (eds) (2001), *Dire Demographics: Population
Trends in the Russian Federation*, Santa Monica, CA: RAND.

Flood, P.J. (2002), "Abortion and the Right to Life in Post-Communist Eastern
Europe and Russia," *East European Quarterly*, 36(2): 191–226.

Geiger, H.K. (1968), *The Family in Soviet Russia*, Cambridge, MA: Harvard
University Press.

Hook, E.B., Cross, P.K. and Schreinemachers, D.M. (1983), "Chromosomal
Abnormality Rates at Amniocentesis and in Live-born Infants," *Journal of the
American Medical Association*, 249: 2034–2038.

Humphrey, C. (2002), *The Unmaking of Soviet Life*, Ithaca, NY: Cornell University
Press.

Katkova, I. (1982), "Maternal Care of Infants," in G. Lapidus (ed.), *Women, Work,
and Family in the Soviet Union*, New York: M.E. Sharpe.

Kharkova, T. and Andreev, E. (2000), "Did the Economic Crisis Cause the Fertility
Decline in Russia? Evidence from the 1994 Microcensus," *European Journal of
Population*, 16: 211–233.

Leon, D.A., Chenet, L., Shkolnikov, V. and Zakharov, S. (1997), "Huge Variation
in Russian Mortality Rates 1984–94: Artefact, Alcohol, or What?," *The Lancet*,
350(9075): 383–388.

Massey, S.M. (2002), *Russia's Maternal and Child Health Crisis: Socio-Economic
Implications and the Path Forward*, accessed January 8, 2003 at
http://psp.iews.org/highlights.cfm?view=detailandid=33.

Maximova, Tamara T.M. (1999), *Socio-economic Conditions and Health in*

Russia, departmental publication, Department of Complex Studies of Population Health and Social-Hygienic Monitoring, Semashko Research Institute, Russian Academy of Medical Sciences, Moscow, Russia, http://members.tripod.com/~Tokourov/socio1

Pankova, L.M. (1998), *Vospitaniye Vnukov*, St Petersburg: Peter Press.

Parakhonskaya, G. (2002), "Pozhiloi Chelovyek V Semye," *Sotsiologicheskiye Issledovaniye*, 6: 103–110.

Popov, A.A. (2001), "Family Planning and Induced Abortion in Post-Soviet Russia of the Early 1990s: Unmet Needs in Information Supply," in J. DaVanzo and C. Grammich (eds), *Dire Demographics: Population Trends in the Russian Federation*, Santa Monica, CA: RAND.

Rapp, R. (1999), *Testing Women, Testing the Fetus: The Social Impact of Amniocentesis in America*, New York: Routledge.

Rethmann, P. (2000), "A Hopeless Life? The Story of a Koriak Woman in the Russian Far East," *Anthropologica*, 42(1): 29–42.

Rivkin-Fish, M. (2003), "Anthropology, Demography, and the Search for a Critical Analysis of Fertility: Insights from Russia," *American Anthropologist*, 105(2): 289–301.

Rosser, Jr, J.B. (2000), "Income Inequality and the Informal Economy in Transition Economies," *Journal of Comparative Economics*, 28(1): 156–171.

Shkolnikov, V.M. and Mesle, F. (2001), "The Russian Epidemiological Crisis as Mirrored by Mortality," in J. DaVanzo and C. Grammich (eds), *Dire Demographics: Population Trends in the Russian Federation*, Santa Monica, CA: RAND.

Stack, C.B. and Burton, L.M. (1994), "Kinscripts: Reflections on Family, Generation and Culture," in E.N. Glenn, G. Chang and L.R. Forcey (eds), *Mothering: Ideology, Experience, and Agency*, New York: Routledge.

Tedstrom, J.E. (2002), Email to newsgroup titled *Russia's Maternal and Child Health Crisis: Socio-Economic Implications and the Path Forward – EWI Policy Brief by Stephen M. Massey*, December 10.

Tho Seeth, H., Chachnov, S., Surinov, A. and von Braun, J. (1998), "Russian Poverty: Muddling through Economic Transition with Garden Plots," *World Development*, 26: 1611–1623.

Vishnevsky, A.G. (2001), "Family, Fertility, and Demographic Dynamics in Russia: Analysis and Forecast," in J. DaVanzo and C. Grammich (eds), *Dire Demographics: Population Trends in the Russian Federation*, Santa Monica, CA: RAND.

Wines, M. (2000a), "In Russia, the Ill and Infirm Include Health Care Itself," *The New York Times*, December 4: A1, A8.

—— (2000b), "Capitalism Comes to Russian Health Care," *New York Times*, December 4: A1, A14.

—— (2000c), "For All Russia, Biological Clock is Running Out," *New York Times*, December 4: A1, A10.

"World Facts": at http://worldfacts.globalesl.net.

Yarskaya, V.N. and Yarskaya-Smirnova, E.R. (2002), "'Ne Muzhskoye eto delo . . .' Gendernii Analiz Zanyatosti V Sotsialnoi Sferye," *Sotsiologicheskiye Issledovaniye*, 6: 74–81.

Zakharov, S.V. and Ivanova, E.I. (2001), "Fertility Decline and Recent Changes in Russia: On the Threshold of the Second Demographic Transition," in J. DaVanzo and C. Grammich (eds), *Dire Demographics: Population Trends in the Russian Federation*, Santa Monica, CA: RAND.

–5–

The Economy of Birthrates
in the Czech Republic

Rebecca Nash

Distress over birthrates in the Czech Republic has remained consistent from the socialist (1948–1989) to the postsocialist (1989 to the present) eras.[1] Although rates are lower in the current period, the present-day alarm resembles concern that emerged from socialist documents and narratives. Indeed, within academic and governmental communities since the mid-1950s, there has always been a birthrate crisis (save a reprieve during the 1970s) – always a sense that Czech families were not producing enough offspring. Because of the continuity of crisis, I argue that demographic discourses reveal more about social anxiety and the way that reproduction makes politics than they do about what economists and demographers identify as the objective consequences of reproductive behavior.

Nonetheless, within a shared framework of unease, socialist and postsocialist demographic discourses differ in significant ways. The language of birthrates is shaped by economic and political symbols, which shift with changing state forms. For example, during the socialist period low birthrates prophesied the loss of collective manpower, the failure of redistributive policies and the futility of pronatalist social engineering. Quantifiable national prowess depended on working hands, which often served as a metaphor for concern with low birthrates in socialist-era state texts. More recently, the Czech Republic's position within Europe, westernization, the growth of individualism and reduced emphasis on state support for families supply the idioms of stunted growth and deficit through which experts and non-experts document a dwindling population.

I observed during my fieldwork in Prague that journalists and quantitative social scientists always reported and wrote of lowered birthrates as indicative of future social and economic problems. Yet parents and policy-makers alike often respected the decision of Czechs of childbearing age who put off or never had children for financial reasons, or to work, travel and study. Those Czechs not having children were contributing to the transition out of socialism and into postsocialism: They were establishing responsibility for the self (rather than "taking," *brát*, social provisions) despite not reproducing citizens.

In her research on the mystery of high mortality rates in Brazil, Nancy Scheper-Hughes encourages the study of what she calls "demography without numbers," a qualitative approach that asks anthropologists to "point to demography's gaps, to suggest what may be missing, and to indicate what still needs to be construed" (Scheper-Hughes 1997: 203). In other words, cultural anthropologists should ask the questions that demographers do not ask. For me this led to an inquiry into class-coded differences emerging from discussions of reproductive behavior in the Czech Republic. Low-income Czechs actually having children are not considered to be solutions to social reproduction. The paradoxes of demographic science are ways in which to witness class and ethnic distinctions and the moral coding of reproductive behavior among low-income Czechs, particularly women. To those for whom following Western European patterns (from NATO membership in 1999 to falling birthrates) was interpreted as understandable and even desirable, Czech households with above average numbers of children stood for deferred membership in Europe and the market – and the prolonged role of the state in family life. Low birthrates offer the key to social and economic transformation.

I carried out the field research on which this chapter is based in 1999–2000. My doctoral dissertation explores the relationship between the state and families in the postsocialist era from a variety of angles. I conducted ethnographic work in a welfare office, a family court and a state facility for women with children. I also collected family histories with Prague families and interviewed social policy makers, family activists, and men and women who worked in family policy during the socialist era. When I asked questions about the family in the late 1990s and about the state's role in family life, birthrates appeared as an index of both the state–family dynamic and of anxiousness about a "family crisis" (*krize rodiny*) circulating in public discourse as well as in family settings.

This chapter begins with a survey of the continuity of coverage of birthrates across the socialist and postsocialist periods. I also compare metaphors used in the socialist versus the postsocialist eras by state planners and demographers. I then focus on positive receptions of low birthrates by parents, young people and other family members during the current era. I conclude with a visit to the birthrate makers, as I call them. These Czechs with children, here single mothers, were much more concerned with their own entitlement to new needs-based financial awards for families than they were with the state's barrenness.

The Continuity of Demographic Crisis

In a November 2001 interview with *Radio Praha*, Czech sociologist Ivo Možný remarked that, since the end of communist rule in 1989, many Czech women have chosen to take advantage of new freedoms rather than establish families. To him this explained the rise in average ages at first childbirth, which climbed during the

1990s from the low twenties to the late twenties and into the mid-to-late thirties. Možný elaborated, "in the early 1990s women who previously would have started having children postponed them. We are now experiencing a dramatic moment in Czech demographic history because those same women are in their early thirties. We will soon see how many of those postponed children will really be born." He added, "we are generally shifting towards the western type of the family again" (*Radio Praha* 2001).

Reproductive statistics from other parts of Europe are ubiquitous in discussions of Czech birthrates, serving as a standard by which sociologists like Možný, but also demographers, policy-makers and mothers and fathers evaluate reproductive behavior at home. This comparative framework is not new to those working in historical demography, who have long sought to characterize family typologies according to "European patterns" or "Eastern European patterns" of childbearing age, family size and marriage rates (see Hajnal 1965; Rychtaříková 1994). According to these categorizations, European (i.e. Western European) families are thought to consist of two parents and one or two children, while Eastern European families have a greater number of children and, often, three-generation households. In the Czech Republic, the dramatic political changes that took place when the socialist era ended in 1989 serve as a threshold event and the moment at which the state and its people made a "return to [Western] Europe" (see Kumar 2001: 61–62, 82–83). Families participate in a return to Europe within demographic discussions: as in Western Europe, specialists like Možný tell us, marriage rates in the Czech Republic are lower and children are fewer (Čermáková *et al.* 2000: 59–77).

Here we see that political and economic models are tied to models of the family and family size. To remark that Czech families resemble smaller, western families is to indicate that Czech economic and political systems are western as well, especially as Czechs face state membership in political-economic institutions such as the European Union. Thus, debates about birthrates in the Czech Republic are not just about birthrates (see Zielińska 2000). In this case, reproductive politics is about geopolitical belonging.

As in many other parts of postsocialist Europe (see Gabriel and Stoilková, Chapters 4 and 6 in this volume), reports of low birthrates circulate in the media on a regular basis. Just a few newspaper headlines offer a sampling of the urgent tone with which birthrates are reported in the Czech Republic: "The number of children born last year was the lowest" (*Mladá fronta dnes* 2000a); "Children continually decrease, city hall therefore closes nursery schools" (*Mladá fronta dnes* 2000b); "Czechs have one of the lowest birthrates in the world" (*Lidové noviny* 2000a); and "The Least Number of Children Born since the Austro-Hungarian Empire" (*Dnešní Jablonecko* 2002). Moreover, the *World Population Data Sheet* reports that, out of the forty countries with below replacement level fertility rates, the Czech Republic ranks very low with 1.1 children born per woman in the year

2000 (cited in McDonald 2001; see also Table 1). All over East Central Europe decreasing birthrates are credited to the events of 1989 and understood as a symptom of social upheaval.

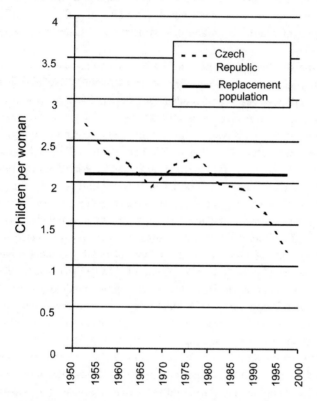

Figure 5.1 Total Fertility Rate, Czech Republic, 1950–2000.
Source: Population Division of the Department of Economic and Social Affairs of the United Nations Secretariat, *World Population Prospects: The 2002 Revision and World Urbanization Prospects: The 2001 Revision*, http://esa.un.org/unpp

Yet low birthrates are not new to the region. And in the Czech Republic, many of the demographers who compiled the statistics and interpreted them in the post-socialist era were doing similar work during the socialist era, when they recorded a steady rise in birthrates between 1970 and 1975 (what is referred to with Czech pronunciation as the "*baby boom*" and its literal translation "*populační třesk*"), but otherwise witnessed downturns throughout the 1950s, 1960s and 1980s (Čermáková *et al.* 2000; Rychtaříková 1994; Wolchik 2000). Many headlines from the socialist period mirror those from the post-1989 period: "The current population situation in the ČSSR: worsening population development evident since 1967 continues to deepen" (*Rudé právo* 1968); "We are smaller and smaller" (*Rudé právo* 1969); "Unfavorable population development in the ČSSR" (*Radio Prague Domestic* RFE/EE 1973); and "Does Czechoslovakia also have a population problem?" (*Tvorba* 1975). These appeared later, in the 1980s: "The number of children in families falls" (*Svobodné slovo* 1987) and "To have, or not have children?" (Novák and Capponiová 1988).

During the socialist era low birthrate trends were linked to "demographic transitions," sometimes called the "demographic revolution," which took place throughout Europe in the late nineteenth and early twentieth centuries. At that time, families started having fewer children and transitioned from a so-called "traditional" to a "modern" family structure, which in Czechoslovakia meant two or three children per family rather than four or more (Rychtaříková 1994: 144; Kuchařová and Tuček 1999: 10; *Tvorba* 1975; Možný and Rabušic 1999: 105; see Kligman 1998: 42–70). Czechoslovak modernity rested on family size. Yet demographers argued that families were becoming too small and ultimately limiting the modernization/industrial potential of the republic.[2]

Although current birthrate statistics are thought to be underpinned by a combination of opportunity, newfound freedoms, and dramatic economic insecurities that arose in the early 1990s, this cursory comparison of media coverage of birthrates demonstrates that concern over low birthrates has endured regardless of ideological and historical moment. Yet, although the tone of birthrate coverage is consistent over time, its content and policy responses differ between the two periods. The varied substance of demographic distress calls into question the neutrality of population sciences and what is often taken by economists, politicians and demographers as the self-evident causes and consequences of "lowest-ever fertility levels" (Day 1992: xvi; see Greenhalgh 1995: 875). Moreover, the symbols representing trends during the socialist era were bound to the redistributive, collectivist character of the state; while the language of postsocialist trends recalls increasing orientation toward an emerging market economy and individualism.

Contrasting Metaphors of Social Reproduction and Production Socialism

During the initial phase of socialist rule (1948 to the mid-1950s), the government of the Czechoslovak Socialist Republic (*ČSSR*) placed an emphasis on women's equality in the home and workplace, congratulating itself on the dramatic rise in women's employment and the liberation of women (Bartošová 1978; Kozera 1997: 7–10; Šolcová 1984). The state pressured families to lean on collectivist institutions and to share the upbringing of children with new state organizations. A "slow decline" of birthrates in the 1950s, however, startled social policy makers and economists into paying greater attention to family units, marking the launch of thirty years of pronatalist family policy (Bartošová 1978; Heitlinger 1979; Wolchik 2000). Although state planners continued expanding compulsory activities and services outside of the home, policy documents and party platforms increasingly valued the socialization of children that took place within families.

According to articles and studies from the late 1960s and 1970s, a variety of factors were thought to contribute to the low birthrates. These included a series of developments related to women's roles, such as the increase in women enrolled in institutions of higher education, an unwillingness to have children because the mother would not be able to work, an insufficient length of maternity leave, the high abortion rate and relatively high ages of women at first childbirth. Economists and demographers understood other causes of low birthrates in Czechoslovakia to be the unavailability of apartments and the inability of most to buy an apartment, the expense of establishing a household and, finally, the high cost of children in general.

The tone of population reports was scientific and grim. As told by media sources and state publications alike, low birthrates threatened loss of manpower, specifically when aging members of the population retire. Because the socialist states were labor-intensive regimes as opposed to capital intensive, low numbers of working bodies were especially worrisome. Population loss undermined what Gail Kligman calls, in the Romanian case, "the productionist orientation of communist regimes" (1998: 44). In addition, younger generations were not filling emptied places in the workforce (Heitlinger 1979: 177). An aging population breeding no youth and no future generations, it follows, cannot fulfill material production objectives. In an article in 1968, demographer Milan Kučera explained that if population trends were to persist downward as steadily as they had since 1964, Czechoslovakia would eventually grow too old for itself. He suggested that when fewer babies are born the population ages more quickly than it would otherwise: "without [necessary] precautions ... the population could worsen and the future effect would be older residents, then the breakdown of further economic and social development would take place" (*Rudé právo* 1968: 5). In the demographic reports from this era, images of chronic, unproductive elderliness, with no emerging economic producers and caretakers, predominated.

Elsewhere, Emilián Hamerník, the Minister of Labor and Social Affairs in the early 1970s, insisted, "The population of Czechoslovakia today is among the oldest in Europe" (Hamerník 1971: 1). These public spokesmen frequently used the verb *stárnout*, meaning "to be getting on in years" and "to age." For example, two Slovak pediatricians explained, "*že národ biologicky stárne*" or, "the nation is biologically aging" as a result of unfavorable population development (Cilingová and Kratochivíl 1971: 435). The frail – the least productive and least useful segments of society – were soon to outweigh the fit within Czechoslovak society.

Spokespersons often warned of the need for enough hands (*ruce*) to carry on work for society at large. Youthful hands work not only toward economic ends, but in the service of social reproduction. Here, Hamerník explains the repercussions of continued low birthrates:

> The importance of this [population] problem is critical to our future development and the future outlook of our socialist society . . . the continual worsening of the population's age structure and decreasing birthrates suggest that, in the next era, population development will not be in harmony with our stated objectives and needs. Said most simply, if population growth does not improve, it will have very serious effects on the future of our nation. (Hamerník 1971: 1)

Hamerník also addressed the potential outcome of age disparities, including wage imbalances, a decreased workforce, the weakening of certain fields and specializations and an inability to predict and rely upon future development and growth so critical to a planned economy.

The state cared deeply about increasing the population and established a Population Commission in 1962 which responded to the low birthrates with a broad range of pronatalist measures. Women were the targeted recipients of state support, which included lengthier maternity leaves over time (one year in 1962, two in 1970, and three years by 1976), increased maternity benefits and a one-time-only birthing award per child for basic expenses. The Secretary of the Government Population Commission explained the relationship between family policies and population policy: "Our socialist society gives families with children considerable help most of all to facilitate their social and economic situation . . . Also in order to have enough working hands in the future to contribute to society and in order to have energetic, young generations" (Havelka 1972).

Rising birthrates in the early to mid-1970s suggested to some that child benefits, low-interest loans for newlyweds, housing development and increased public nurseries had an effect on reproductive behavior. Between 1970 and 1975 (the era of the so-called "boom"), fertility rates rose from roughly 1.9 children per woman to 2.5 (Rychtaříková 1994: 140). Yet following a return to low rates in the mid-to-late 1970s, Czechoslovak policy-makers and demographers concluded that pronatalist awards did not have real effects on population growth (Wolchik 2000: 66; *Czechoslovak Situation Report* 1988).

By the late 1970s, population rates had returned to pre-boom norms and the cycle of concern and efforts to solve the problem continued. If ages at which Czech mothers bear their first child had remained at standards characteristic of the late socialist era (the late teens and low twenties), the baby-boomers would now be raising their own children. But, just as they came of average childbearing age, the world changed. Many of these men and women are not having children. And the rates continue to fall.

Postsocialism

Judge Brabcová is a professor of family law at Charles University's Law Faculty in Prague.[3] "Look", Judge Brabcová said to me in late 2000,

> how many children are born? Look at how the rates are falling – the people, the children. It's because no one says to people that the state is interested in families prospering, in families having at least two children. It's just the opposite. Most of the current ideologues say it's up to each individual, the state cannot worry about it. And people must solve their own problems. Those [leaders] don't say, "We are interested, we will help you."

During my research Czechs sometimes interpreted previous state interest in birthrates as a dedication to families and households that has vanished since 1989. The state's relationship with families, then, was judged according to the attention paid to birthrates and continued redistribution of state funds to families with children. Moreover, as Judge Brabcová suggested, the size of the population was no longer as elaborately bound to the survival of the state and socialism. She interpreted shifts in population discourse as an indication that politicians, and by extension the state, did not care as much about Czech families.

Despite what its Czech critics said, the state after 1989 remained concerned with the relationship between family life and reproductive patterns. I observed during interviews at the Ministry of Labor and Social Affairs, in press coverage of government-sponsored research, and in conversation with state employees within a range of family services offices that the postsocialist government was focused on trying to develop new ways of increasing population size and halting the drops in birth and fertility rates.

Research institutes based out of the Ministry of Labor and Social Affairs worked to understand post-1989 reproductive behavior. Citing the Director of Demographic Studies at the Faculty of Natural Sciences, sociologists Věra Kuchařová and Milan Tuček describe socio-economic variables understood to be discouraging young Czechs from having children in the postsocialist era as "inflation, unemployment, drops in real wages and drops in the value of family benefits, problems on the housing market, and feelings of uncertainty caused by pessimism about future development" (Kuchařová and Tuček 1999: 6). Analysts had often blamed housing shortages and uncertainty about the future for low birthrates during the socialist era (Freiová 1999), but unemployment and inflation are altogether new (official) phenomena because prior to 1989 unemployment was illegal and the state regulated the cost of food, goods and rent.

Despite new causal explanations for the low birthrate trends, such as unemployment, present-day analysts continue to be concerned that the population will vanish because of steady declines over time. The imbalance of the population (many old, few young) remains characteristic of demographic forecasts as well. The baby-boomers born in the 1970s are one of the largest Czech generations, but they are not reproducing enough, it is claimed, and some economists expect population "waves" (*vlny*) to cause future instability.

One article from the newspaper *Lidové noviny* draws on metaphors of the tree of life (*strom života*) to translate the economic repercussions of irregular population growth into a popular awareness (*Lidové noviny* 2000a, 2000b). Currently the tree is a healthy one: its green leafy top represents the retired population of pensioners, who are supported by the labor of their young, working trunk, i.e. the baby-boomer generation. Now the tree has a "relatively strong foundation and many young people of productive age" to bear older generations. Yet by about 2030, some demographers argue, the trunk will age and transform into a more elderly and abundant crown but have little support from its dwindling younger stalk, resulting in one of the narrowest support bases (the population of working age) in all of Europe.

It is important to recognize that, like the socialist era, recent demographic analysis points toward the future. Population statistics for the year 1999 were released in February 2000: the population totaled approximately 10,278,000, or 11,000 fewer than in 1998 (also a year of record lows in Czech demographic history; *Lidové noviny* 2000a). The real effects of this "negative" growth, demographers explain, will be apparent between 2030 and 2050. The release of figures from 1999 triggered concerned coverage anticipating what the Czech Republic will look like around the year 2030. Reports also explained that births were at "their lowest ever" and that the number of dying exceeded those born. For example, 20,000 more people died in the Czech Republic than were born in 1999. Dead bodies outpaced the creation of new ones and the tree of life was pruned from both ends. The dead would ideally be replaced by newborns, but both demographic categories (the deceased and the unborn) contributed equally to future economic strain.

In a public hearing in the Czech Senate in June 2001, seasoned demographer Milan Kučera spoke in a language of accumulated debt (rather than environmental/naturalist references to the tree of life), as if those Czechs who do not reproduce today are taking out loans that can never be paid off. Given rising costs of living, Czechs may lighten personal economic burdens today by not having children, he warned, but society will "pay" in the future:

> Deformation of the age structure is such that within twenty to thirty years the Czech population will not be able to regenerate itself. The number of potential [future] parents will be so low that it will be impossible to raise birthrates, to raise the number of children born. The demographic debt (*zadlužení*) of long-term losses of children will be insurmountable. (*Veřejné slyšení* 2001: 23)

The reference to bad demographic credit and irresponsible social "spending" reappeared in Kučera's public testimony when he argued that young people today feel more pressure to consume than become selfless, parental persons: "Look at leasing terms, at loan offers, at the choice of goods in catalogues – young people can have all of this immediately. Can we protect ourselves from this?" (ibid. 24).

As a corrective, he concluded, the state should compensate for both economic strain and the pressure to spend accompanying capitalism by rewarding families who have children. State awards would, he insisted, counteract negative effects of new, unfamiliar and threatening consumerism. Kučera saw positive value in the state's paternalistic role; as during the socialist era, financial redistribution can preserve family life and foster social reproduction in the face of western influences. Birthing might work like the economy, the economy might influence birthrates, but legislators should make state resources available when families are affected and thus remedy influences of the market economy.

Many Czechs drew on an economistic language when explaining that the economy both suffers from recent low birthrates and contributes to, and causes, further low population growth. Often the links they drew between the economy and family life, however, were more literal than embellished. When I inquired during family history interviews why young Czechs were not having babies, I received pat answers like "there are no apartments" or "it's too expensive." Czechs framed low birthrates in terms of the consequence of general economic insecurity, uncertainty and deprivation. Lower birthrates were perceived as a tax on the transition to capitalism despite the fact that the Czechoslovak statistical office had also recorded birthrates as progressively lower during most of the socialist era.

Many family spokespersons now blame the falling birthrate on the absence of an affirmative family policy, such as the one which state representatives refined throughout the socialist period. Yet, despite widespread criticism of the state by those who come from a range of family organizations, many in the Czech government do not take below replacement level birthrates lightly and often contribute to the circulation of alarmist language used by demographers and the Czech and European press. Unlike the period during the early 1990s, when many family subsidies and bonuses were trimmed and cut, the current government frequently proposes redistributive policies familiar to the pre-1989 era. The government of Social Democrats, for example, has attempted to pass birth-incentive legislation and spoke of reintroducing across-the-board benefits for families with children (*Právo* 2001; *Lidové noviny* 2000c).[4] Defending his proposals for the reintroduction of such benefits (against his critics who insist benefits should not go to the wealthy) the leader of the Social Democrats asked poignantly, "what family with children is wealthy?" (cited in *Právo* 2001).

In postsocialist times the tree of life symbolizes the forces necessary for healthy population development: deeply grounded roots and the billowing strength of generation following generation. Those who refer to the tree as potentially destabilized use the anxious, concerned tones of socialist demographers of the 1970s, 1980s and 1990s in the Czech Republic. Another more economistic metaphor, that of debt and repayment, interrogates the demographic costs of membership in the market economy. Socialist-era demographers, however, more frequently used a labor-oriented symbol in their calls for higher birthrates: then, hands were needed to multiply and fortify society. Perhaps a time-bound logic codes the use of these metaphors – demographic debt recalls market forces. In contrast, hands call to mind the combined effort necessary to build a self-sustaining, egalitarian and redistributive economy. Czechs used all three symbols, however, to evoke and make tangible the dangers and fears of low population growth.

Given the complexity of demographic discussions in the Czech Republic it is useful to investigate their full range of meanings. I now turn toward interpretations of low birthrates which suggest that there is something to them of value, rather than prominent images of quantitative loss and social impotence heard in demographic and political circles. Indeed, the following material suggests that the state, society and individuals have much to gain from low birthrates.

Reasoning Low Birthrates

Unlike the socialist era, some Czechs in the postsocialist era tied "all-time" birthrate lows to geopolitical benefits. Population patterns put the Czech Republic, to borrow a phrase from Ann Anagnost (1997: 133) "in its place in the global community." Whether they interpreted low birthrates as a curse or a blessing, demographers and economists in the recent period consistently associated low birthrates with similar trends in western Europe, where birthrates and marriage rates were also falling. For example, influential sociologists of the family, Ivo Možný and Ladislav Rabušic, wrote in 1999, "It is certain that Czech society, as far as the formation of families, births, and deaths are concerned is becoming more similar to European standards," and "The opening of the borders to Western Europe has brought with it also the acceptance of their cultural models . . . this means a return to the West European family model, from which Czech society had been separated for half a century" (Možný and Rabušic 1999: 94, 101). The Czech population "problem" in the postsocialist period was eased by increasingly looking and behaving like families and individuals in the West – of which many Czechs such as Možný and Rabušic (1999: 133) considered themselves to have always been a part.

During his November 2001 radio interview, Ivo Možný suggested that putting off having children in the postsocialist Czech Republic is a perfectly reasonable (*rozumná*) thing to do given opportunities to work, travel, study and simply be free and single. Czechs in a variety of settings hinted that, amidst widespread concern, it made good sense not to have children. Even those informants who one moment fretted over the economic strain that low birthrates are thought to contribute to, would the next moment perk up and say, "Of course, young people are taking advantage of the opportunity to work, travel and study."

Yet opportunities to "work, travel and study" come only to particular Czechs (many of whom live in larger cities, especially Prague). These workers, travelers and students are those who supposedly contribute toward building a vibrant economy. Thanks to their upward mobility, work ethic and self-interest, they are the most desired reproducers. Yet paradoxically, because of the time spent working, traveling and studying, these potential parents are not yet choosing to have children.

It is important to stress that no one involved in demographic discussions with whom I came into contact considered the possibility of demanding or requiring Czechs to reproduce in greater numbers. For example, demographers and writers of state policy argued that social engineering characteristic of the socialist era was undemocratic. At a public hearing in June 2001 family sociologist Rabušic cautioned that aggressive pronatalist policies were out of the question:

> Theoretically we could raise fertility if we forced Czechs to give birth to a greater number of children, even if they don't want to. Yes, it is crude, but European culture knows of examples, such as the case of Romania, when several societies stopped at nothing. Nevertheless, that method is unthinkable in a democratic society, unacceptable, and we will not raise it as a possibility. (*Veřejné slyšení* 2001: 13)

In addition to rejecting crude pronatalism, many demographers, consultants and policy-makers working for the state were reluctant to replicate or mirror socialist-era policy formulations by encouraging Czechs to have children through elaborate benefits. They insisted that calls by Social Democrats to increase birth allowances and re-universalize benefits were motivated solely by an interest in winning votes from those nostalgic for communism.

Still, while not coercive, expert voices shape understandings of when and in which cases Czechs should bear children as well as the impression that those working, traveling and studying are behaving "reasonably" (in contrast to *egoista* in Spain, see Douglass, Chapter 9 in this volume). Reasonable behavior, it seemed, went hand in hand with, and facilitated, a successful transformation from a state-run economy to privatization – despite falling birthrates. Rather than pressure Czechs to have children, state reformers drew on a language of individual opportunity and self-interest, suggesting that the decision to have children is and should be self-regulated. In these formulations, the state's responsibility was to create the economic conditions within which Czechs may have families if they so choose.

Take, for example, remarks by a policy advisor at the Ministry of Labor and Social Affairs, in November 2000. Like Rabušic, he touches on the inconceivability of interventionist population policy in the post-1989 era:

We don't have a family policy . . . nor do we have a population policy. It would probably be useful to open the discussion, but the experts are overwhelmingly against
engaging in the idea . . . We don't want to give people money to have children, nor do
we want to give people money for having children. *Basically, people should be left to
make money so that they can have as many children as they like* [pause] *so that nothing
prevents this.* (emphasis added)

This policy advisor underscored the growth of, and increasing value in, individual
profit and initiative. The state's key task, then, was to foster positive economic conditions, which were the solution to low birthrates. As he further explained, "A prosperous economy would raise salaries and influence the birthrates; we don't want to
say, 'If you have a child we will give you 10,000 crowns or 20,000.' No, dear God,
no." Desirable reproductive behavior, then, would be made possible through the
development of a market economy.

Many of my informants in older generations were the most understanding (and
even encouraging) of decisions by younger family members to put children off
until later in life. Thus young Czechs with a certain amount of mobility and education, who are rethinking traditional family patterns, often receive sympathy
given how dramatically the world they face differs from their parents' world of the
socialist 1970s and 1980s. Then, as one informant like many told me, "there was
nothing to do but have the classic family: two kids, a weekend cottage and a dog."
Young Czechs and their parents today believe that the cost of having this "classic"
family interferes with individual achievement. Many of the family members I
interviewed agreed that younger generations should not be having children until
they have achieved their personal goals. Financial independence was the primary
aim of these young Czechs, and "working, traveling and studying" served as a
method of increasing standards of living as well as a slogan for the achievements
that Czechs past childbearing age, who raised their children during the socialist
era, often felt they were denied.

Often, as Krause (2001) reminds us, women are the first to be implicated in
reproductive decision-making. For women, having children in both eras presented
a dramatic change in lifestyle because men and women alike often assumed that
women stay at home with children on lengthy parental work leaves (three to four
years). One middle-aged informant, Mrs Boudová, told me while reflecting on her
own unhappy marriage that a woman's decision to conceive, marry and leave work
(usually in that order) should be made carefully. In hindsight, she felt that she
should have waited until she was older to have her first child and that her daughters, both in their mid-to-late twenties, should now wait. Here she refers to her
second daughter, Marcela:

If I had been reasonable, I would have postponed my first child and not had her at 26
. . . I hope that Marcela doesn't intend to have children for the time being, and I am

bringing her up to feel that she can wait until after she turns 30. People should first realize their needs and secure their own contentment.

For Mrs Boudová, personal goals included independence and self-reliance, as well as independence from the state. Self-actualization and careful timing of child-bearing contributed to her belief that Czechs should not lean on official support: "too many people don't think independently, they don't try to solve their own problems," she told me. She dismissed demographers' fears that Czechs are not having enough children:

> the demographers yell that low numbers of children are born, but Marcela's generation realizes that life is more than children, more than sitting at home and staying with the kids. And increasing numbers of people realize that they must earn what they have. They can't expect free goods and a flat and those kinds of things . . . it's more complicated today [than during the socialist era] and to rely on the means of the state is irresponsible.

As the state privatizes so too must Czechs in their everyday lives, although this has proven difficult for women in the workplace.

The socialist state required that women's jobs be held for them during maternity leave. Employers today are also required by law to hold a primary caretaker's job for up to three years of, what is now, "parental leave."[5] Yet currently – when opportunities to advance are both highly desired and competitive – many Czechs women worry about blatant sexist discrimination in hiring practices, and told me that they were asked during job interviews whether or not they planned to have children (see also Čermáková *et al.* 2000: 21–30). Young women realized that anti-discriminatory laws were not being enforced. Thus a need to support oneself in the face of shrinking state contributions to families, concerns over discriminatory hiring practices, and growing discourses of self-fulfillment and individual achievement combined to make prolonged childlessness seem the most logical and sensible choice.

In addition to the practicalities of job stability and employment, there was a pervasive sentiment among family members I spoke with that their young offspring should see the world. Although her two sons are still in their teens, Mrs Procházková, a mother in her late forties, made planning for their travel and study abroad a top priority. Opportunities for present-day youth were again informed by what the socialist era denied older generations. During our interview, Mrs Procházková returned again and again to the theme of travel abroad and her inability to meet foreigners, master a foreign language and perhaps even work in a foreign country. She was not able to take advantage of the freedoms her kids have and she regrets it: "My entire life it bothered me terribly that I didn't have the possibility of going to some foreign workplace, where I could have learned to speak [another language] fluently and grown accustomed to life and the people there."

The inability to travel abroad, particularly during the 1970s and 1980s, was spoken of similarly by many Czechs.

Another way in which the decision not to have children appeared beneficial was through comparisons of the reproductive behavior of young Czechs to other young Europeans. For example, an extreme form of newfound European-ness is the "singles" phenomenon. Singles are hyper-individualist, free and consumers. The singles phenomenon refers to men and women of marriageable age who choose, in uncommon Czech fashion, not to marry but work and, even more damning in the eyes of some, play. Some singles live together, but without any intention of marrying soon or ever having children. Although media interviews and my discussions with real-life singles reveal that these Czechs continue to value family and marriage, they are far from ready to commit themselves to either.

The weekly intellectual magazine *Respekt* explains that a "single" has it all. A single is at the top of his or her field, such as business, the arts, journalism, or academia. The singles spend the majority of their time working, are rarely at home, and are uncommitted romantically, though they do date. They value their profession most of all and do not stay attached for long. Life is wonderful and the singles are successful (*skvělý a úspěšný*). Their lifestyle is high profile and attractive:

> Singles influence society, not only on personal levels, but also the media climate and commercials, which often draw on their fast, dynamic, efficient lives – the contrast of hard work and fun, which society is fascinated by. On the one hand there is responsibility, work meetings, a career and creative work, and on the other a night life in a wondrous, glamorous night club and parties. (Eckhardtová and Čápová 2000: 13)

In these kinds of depictions, singles are portrayed as part of a global youth culture; their lifestyles have more in common with those of young professionals in New York and Paris than with their parents' communist youths: "Czech singles bring new feelings and values, which the communist regime threw away, especially self-assurance. Singles can say to themselves, 'Everything that I earn, I earn myself. I don't owe anyone anything'" (Eckhardtová and Čápová 2000: 12).

Admittedly, the singles phenomenon is largely a media construction of fantastic, bizarre Euro-yuppies. I never met a young twenty- or thirty-something Czech willing and able to jet off to Argentina at a moment's notice, as the *Respekt* authors suggest one might (ibid: 12). Certainly, though, within discourses of low birthrates, images of "singles" stood for many things. "Singles" meant not only a radical new lifestyle for both men and women, but also the Czech Republic's new place in Europe and the world, the reconfiguration of values for the family, work and demographic distress.

Positive interpretations of low birthrates counterbalance the negative interpretations. Despite the pessimistic coverage in the press, pronatalist proposals by some leading government officials, and worry by some Czech family members themselves, "not having babies" translates into sound decision-making in the face of economic uncertainty. Moreover, the postponement of reproduction by a whole generation of young people is interpreted to mean that they are the beneficiaries and creators of postsocialist promise.

Furthermore, the non-reproductive behavior of young, mobile, and educated Czechs appears "reasonable" when compared to those women who *are* now having babies in the Czech Republic. Ironically, despite decades of concern over "all-time" birthrate lows, poor women having children are regarded as unreasonable, unmodern and un-European.

The Birthrate Makers

Scheper-Hughes's (1997) call to "point to demography's gaps" prompted me to think about the women who are not part of the problem of the barren state. After examining discourses of the costs and benefits of low birthrates, it appears that poor women who have children and receive state support are the "gap" in Czech demography. These women are winners on paper, if you take an increase in birthrates as an absolute goal, because they maintain and even surpass birthrate goals. But they are losers in their daily lives because their reproductive behavior is not seen as *reasonable*.

The exemption of these women from resolutions to the postsocialist population predicament was made clear during my fieldwork. I would visit sites where the birthrate alarm was paramount and then move to others, such as a facility for mothers with children on the outskirts of Prague, where low birthrates were not the problem. There, I was always surrounded by children. The seeming surplus of children at the home countered popular images of a baby-less Czech society. By way of conclusion, I point out contradictions within policies toward families, as well as how concerns about the number of children born per woman vary according to class and ethnic categories.

While demographers and social policy-makers nervously await the arrival of more baby citizens, the mothers I worked with in the home lost patience with the state during daily, weekly and monthly trips to a variety of local offices. Rather than foster a sense that their children were valued by the state, their stories present state employees as complicating and unfairly obstructing the nurturance of young Czechs. In this way, the mothers would have concurred with family spokespersons who bemoan the decreasing value of the family to the postsocialist government. Unlike the socialist era, when all families received the same amount of money from their local office, today's applicants must wait in line to claim entitlement based on low income, figure out both how and how often to file paperwork and shuttle from office to office – usually with children in tow. I was struck by a seeming opposition between the state's insistence that it needed more children and the needs of poorer families.

To take only two of many examples: Mrs Blažková is a Romani woman, or gypsy, and lived with her five children in the home. When I asked Mrs Blažková to tell me about her experiences filing her paperwork for living minimum benefits for families, she explained:

> [I go to get money for the children] for camp, or sometimes [if] it [happens that I need] food and help . . . [T]hey give me problems in the benefits office . . . in February I gave birth – yeah, and on the sixth of February I was supposed to take my papers for money to the family benefits office. I was in the hospital, so I couldn't you know. So they stopped; the entire month I was with the children without money.

Mrs Blažková expressed a common confusion with state procedures. The mothers in the home often appealed to administrators for clarification – worried and concerned by what they had been told by the accountants in the benefits offices. Romani mothers, in particular, felt they were treated unfairly.

Mrs Wagnerová (an ethnic Czech) had four children and, at the time of our interview, was on maternity leave. She had been living in the home for three years. She told me about what it was like to go to the family benefits office in her district,

> when I was expecting Tereza I [went to the benefits office and] said, "I no longer live with my husband, we live separately, we are getting a divorce." But I was pregnant you see. And they asked, "You don't live with your husband? But you are pregnant?" I said again to them . . . [that] though we no longer share a household we are nevertheless having a baby. And they immediately stopped the benefits. They said, "You are pregnant with your husband, let him take care of you."

This mother was bewildered by state demands for various documents, authorizations and confirmation certificates, such as required proof that the father of her children was not contributing to the children's support. She felt she was entitled to state resources for her children, regardless of her marital status. Many of the mothers living in the facility told stories of having been deprived of state support because of some minor paperwork mishap on their part – such as Mrs Blažková's – or because of what they considered an arbitrary legal rule or, more often, because of the ignorance (they claimed) on the part of the benefits accountants.

As we have seen, some government officials proposed benefits in the service of fostering financial security for potential parents. Still others resisted the resocialization of population politics. Regardless of measures taken, clients who *already* qualify for family benefits feel distant from a state hungry for population growth. Thus the administration of social policy for the disadvantaged works outside of demographic agendas and suggests competing familial ideologies within the state.

Poorer families with children are caught in the wake of shifting state–family relations as the economy changes from a redistributive to a needs- and means-based system. And while struggling families with children work to maneuver new and unfamiliar support mechanisms, demographic appeals are targeted solely toward up-and-coming European Czechs.

Finally, one would think that those in the alarmed camp would have been comforted by high fertility rates among some women, such as residents of the facility for poor mothers. Yet within discussions of why Czechs are not having babies, and why they should or should not, emerge unflattering images of those who actually are. One retired policy-maker remarked to me that too few people are having children. "Well," she paused, "everyone but Roma and Catholics." The Romani population in particular symbolize state parasites extraordinaire. And, a seasoned social worker suggested to me that family benefits for poor families be limited to those who have no more than two children. Furthermore, a number of commentators noted that there is an inverse relationship between an individual's salary and the number of children he or she has: The lower the income, the more children born (these kinds of statistics characterize the literature on birthrates in developing countries). The association between family income and family size serves as a boundary around a demographic "crisis" that is also circumscribed by and framed in terms of one's (in)dependence from public systems of support. This conundrum fueled some policy-makers' desires to focus foremost on improving the economy, rather than on ways to provide incentives or "reward" those who are having children, such as the women in the home.

Conclusion

Small families were both cause for concern and reassurance in recent Czech demographic discussions. Spokespersons often claimed that Czech society is potentially destabilized by low birthrates, which will restrict the ability to build a strong workforce, support older generations and benefit from participation in the "modern" world. But to be modern, democratic and European requires the decreasing size of families and, even for the time being, few to zero children per family. Poorer, disadvantaged women who are having children in the Czech Republic represent the limits on calls to raise birthrates; they represent the end of a problem that has been unnerving more than a few Czech demographers, economists and families since the 1950s.

Notes

1. On January 1, 1993 Czechoslovakia became the two separate states of the Czech Republic and Slovakia.

2. Keeping in mind the labor-intensive orientation of socialism, it is important to point out that these states imported labor from each other, such as from Vietnam, Poland and Yugoslavia in the Czechoslovak case (see Kligman 1998: 267 n.19).
3. I have changed the names of all of my interviewees to protect their privacy.
4. The Czech Parliament voted against re-universalizing benefits for families with children in March 2002.
5. Although a parent is entitled to up to four years' paid leave with young children, employers are not required to hold jobs after the third year of leave.

References

Anagnost, A. (1997), *National Past-Times*, Durham, NC: Duke University Press.

Bartošová, M. (1978), *Populační Politika v ČSSR 1945–1975*, Prague: Československý výzkumný ústav práce a sociálních věda, výzkumný práce řada B, č. 76.

Čermáková, M., Hašková, H., Křížková, A., Linková, M., Maříková, H. and Musilová, M. (2000), *Relations and Changes of Gender Differences in the Czech Society in the 90s*, Prague: Czech Academy of Sciences, Sociology Institute.

Cilingová, E. and Kratochvíl, S. (1971), "Motivační faktory ve vztahu k narození třetího dítěte," *Československá psychologie*, 5(říjen): 435–442.

Czechoslovak Situation Report RFE/EE (1988), Demographic Policy, 15 February.

Day, L. (1992), *The Future of Low-Birthrate Populations*, New York: Routledge.

Dnešní Jablonecko (2002), "Od dob Rakouska-Uherska se nyní rodí nejméně dětí," 13 dubna.

Eckhardtová, D. and Čápová, H. (2000), "Štěstí přeje osamělým: Proč by všichni chtěli žít jako singles," *Respekt*, 4–10 (září): 11–13.

Freiová, M. (1999), *Reflections on Family Policy*, Prague: Civic Institute.

Greenhalgh, S. (1995), "The Power in/of Population," *Current Anthropology*, 36(5): 875–878.

Hajnal, J. (1965), "European Marriage Patterns in Perspective," in D.V. Glass and D.E.C. Eversley (eds), *Population in History*, Chicago: Aldine.

Hamerník, E. (1971), "Co znamená populace ve vývoji a výhledu naší společnosti," *Národní výbory*, 42(21 října): 1–3.

Havelka, J. (1972), "Abychom měli více dětí!," *Politická actualita*, Radio Hvezda [frequency 1230], 25 prosince.

Heitlinger, A. (1979), *Women and State Socialism*, Montreal: McGill-Queen's University Press.

Kligman, G. (1998), *The Politics of Duplicity*, Berkeley, CA: University of California Press.

Kozera, N. (1997), *Czech Women in the Labor Market: Work and Family in a Transition Economy*, working paper 97: (6), Prague: Czech Academy of Sciences, Sociology Institute.

Krause, E. (2001), "'Empty Cradles' and the Quiet Revolution: Demographic Discourse and Cultural Struggles of Gender, Race and Class in Italy," *Cultural Anthropology*, 16(4): 576–612.

Kuchařová, V. and Tuček, M. (1999), *Sociálně ekonomické souvislosti rodinného chování mladé generace v České republice*, Prague: Studie národohospodářského ústavu Josefa Hlávky.

Kumar, K. (2001), *1989: Revolutionary Ideas and Ideals*, Minneapolis, MN: University of Minnesota Press.

Lidové noviny (2000a), "Česko má jedno z nejnižších porodností na světě", 12 července.

—— (2000b), "Svět se přelidňuje, Evropa však vymírá," 12 července.

—— (2000c), "Špidla chce vrátit přídavky všem dětem," 28 července.

McDonald, P. (2001), "Low Fertility not Politically Sustainable," *Population Today*, 29(6): 3, 8.

Mladá fronta dnes (2000a), "Počet narozených dětí byl loni nejnižší", 29 března.

—— (2000b), "Dětí neustále ubývá, radnice proto ruší mateřské školy", 15 června.

Možný I. and Rabušic, L. (1999), "The Czech Family, the Marriage Market, and the Reproductive Climate," in J. Večerník and P. Matějů (eds), *Ten Years of Rebuilding Capitalism*, Prague: Academia.

Novák, T. and Capponiová, V. (1988), "Mít, či nemít děti?" *Učitelské Noviny*, 5–19: 11.

Právo (2001), "Plošné přídavky na děti by měly zvýšit porodnost, je přesvědčen Špidla," 25 října.

Radio Prague Domestic RFE/EE (1973), "Unfavorable Population Development in the ČSSR," 6 April.

Radio Praha [http://www.radio.cz/] (2001), "A Conversation with Ivo Možný," interviewed by Daniela Lazarová, 2 November.

Rudé právo (1968), "Současná populační situace ČSSR: Zhoršování populačního vývoje projevujícího se již několik let, se v roce 1967 dále prohloubilo," 5 března.

—— (1969), "Je nás stále míň," 16 května.

Rychtaříková, J. (1994), "Czech and Slovak Families in the European Context," *Journal of Family History*, 19(2): 131–147.

Scheper-Hughes, N. (1997), "Demography without Numbers," in D. Kertzer and T. Fricke (eds), *Anthropological Demography*, Chicago: University of Chicago Press.

Šolcová, M. a kolektiv (1984), *Sociální politika KSČ*, Prague: Nakladatelství Svoboda.

Svobodné slovo (1987), "V rodinách ubývá děti," 13 října.

Tvorba (1975), "Má také Československo svůj populační problém?," 9 dubna.

Veřejné slyšení (2001), "Stenografický Záznam Veřejného Slýšení VZSP: 'Demografický Vývoj České Republiky'," Český Senát, 13 června.

Wolchik, S. (2000), "Reproductive Policies in the Czech and Slovak Republics," in S. Gal and G. Kligman (eds), *Reproducing Gender*, Princeton, NJ: Princeton University Press.

Zielińska, E. (2000), "Between Ideology, Politics, and Common Sense: The Discourse of Reproductive Rights in Poland," in S. Gal and G. Kligman (eds), *Reproducing Gender*, Princeton, NJ: Princeton University Press.

–6–

A Quest for Belonging: The Bulgarian Demographic Crisis, Emigration and the Postsocialist Generations

Maria Stoilkova

Bulgaria has recently been described as having experienced a demographic crisis unparalleled among other Eastern European countries. It has one of the lowest birthrates in the world, a high mortality rate among infants and elderly people, and an unprecedented degree of emigration of young people between the ages of 20 to 40. Since 1989, which marked the end of the forty-year period of socialism in Bulgaria, over 10 percent of its population, nearly 0.8 million people, have emigrated to the "West". Compact communities of Bulgarians are now spread out in different parts of Canada, the United States and Western Europe. These surprising demographic developments met a variety of responses in Bulgaria. Some journalists, drawing on the opinions of established experts in the field of demographics, described the population collapse as an event of apocalyptic dimensions conjuring up images of the Bulgarian nation as a sinking ship being deserted by its passengers – the young émigrés.[1] A more nuanced response that took shape in political speeches and community debates attempted to ease the high societal stress promoting an explanation of the demographic crisis as part of the "necessary evil" of the Bulgarian transition on the road to achieving the high standards of living of the wealthy democratic societies.

Such depictions inevitably identify the hopes of the nation as embodied in the young people of the country. Yet, they tend to gloss over how issues of reproduction – at once, biological, social and economic – have become understood by a generation of young Bulgarians as full of irreconcilable contradictions. The expectations of social prosperity, which Bulgaria's opening to the global economy promised to deliver, have not been fulfilled by the postsocialist realities of a shrinking labor market, cuts to social programs, and lack of professional and social mobility.

In this chapter, I offer an interpretation of the current "demographic crisis" in Bulgaria that is neither a statistical table of bodies and numbers, nor a cynical portrait of national betrayal enacted by the youth fleeing the country and refusing to reproduce. Rather, looking at several social arenas – the labor market, the welfare system, the media and the family – I elucidate how shifts in demographic patterns are precipitated by a set of cultural struggles. I argue that in its statistical sense the decline of birthrates in Bulgaria that occurred after the fall of socialism is related to the mass emigration of members of a generation of fertile age. Yet, what a statistical eye underplays are also the particular conditions and experiences that the postsocialist generations had to confront as they went on to redefine their social and gender roles. The birthrate decline in Bulgaria, albeit aggravated only after the fall of socialism, had already been evident during the preceding decade. In postsocialist public discourse, however, heightened interest in demographic issues came to express critical societal concerns about the deteriorating conditions of life after socialism. I show how demographic shifts in birthrates and family-making represent a cultural adjustment to economic and social upheavals in Bulgaria both before and after 1989, involving new definitions of both social and gender identities and new understandings of what it is to be "modern". Finally, I suggest that we may need a new lens for our demographic statistics in order to account for national bodies that are no longer bounded by territory in the same way they have been imagined in the past.

This chapter emerged from a larger anthropological study, which I pursued between 1999 and 2002, tracing the migration of young Bulgarians to the United States. It is also based on survey data, opinion polls and demographic studies published in Bulgaria. My arguments build upon observations from two main domains of experience: the production and reception of discourses and lived experiences (Marody and Giza-Poleszczuk 2000: 163). Discourses about reproductive practices are the explanations people provide about their decisions to have or not have children, to marry or not marry, to prolong living with their parents or not. They provide insight into how people understand life situations and the roles individuals play in them. Through these discussions people reason possible strategies for action. Lived experiences, on the other hand, are produced by a set of constraints that define available choices for action. These constraints include the size and the shape of the labor market, the structure and quality of education, the level of salaries and services, the health system, social welfare and childcare facilities, among other things. Imagining new possibilities for self-actualization after socialism draws powerfully on one additional source: the media and the imagery encoded in popular culture and in advertising (Marody and Giza-Poleszczuk 2000).

Statistics Talk

The interest of popular media in demographic statistics in the late 1990s was sudden but not accidental. Before explaining this phenomenon, first we should mention that despite the media's recent interest in the reproductive culture, Bulgaria's birthrates have been in decline since the mid-1980s. Table 6.1 contextualizes the birthrates in Bulgaria in a set of other demographic and economic indexes (see also Figure 6.1).

Table 6.1 Demographic and Economic Indices, Bulgaria, 1960–2000

Year	2000	1999	1998	1997	1996	1993	1990	1980	1960
Fertility (TFR)	1.3	1.23	1.11	1.09	1.24	1.46	1.81	2.01	2.31
Infant mortality (per 1000 live births)	13.3 3	14.6	14.4	17.5	15.6	15.5	14.8	20.2	45.1
Unemployment (percent of total labor force)	16.3	14.1	12.2	13.9	14.2	21.4	1.7	—	—
GDP (constant 1995 US\$ × 10^{10}	1.23	1.16	1.13	1.09	1.18	1.25	1.5	1.18	—

Source: The 2002 World Development Indicators, CD-Rom, © copyright International Bank for Reconstruction and developoment, Washington DC.

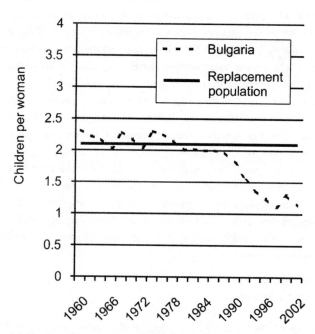

Figure 6.1 Total Fertility Rate, Bulgaria, 1960–2002.
Source: Eurostat, Population and Social Conditions, Demography, Fertility Indicators, 29 January, 2003.

According to Boyan Znepolski, a Bulgarian media critic, the alarming demographic data at the beginning of the 1990s became a crucial point of reference in a number of over-politicized public and media conversations. It was used to frame public criticism against the mounting hardships of Bulgaria's transition to capitalism (Znepolski 2002). For instance, one context in which the media has used demographic data has been to censure the state's withdrawal from responsibility to support families. While in the past state control of the reproductive domain was rationalized as necessary to assure the healthy life of the nation, in the post-1989 era new-found liberal ideologies ruled out direct state intervention. At the same time, the media's insistent fixation on the diminishing birthrates as a way of criticizing the state has also drawn attention to the ethnic Bulgarians, who appear to have been most affected by this demographic trend, and by implication has also unleashed popular "fears" about the supposed rise in reproductive activity among the ethnic minorities of Roma and Turkish populations, in particular.[2] Disturbing instances of harassment of Roma woman by medical personnel in delivery rooms have been frequently reported in the media.

The decline in birthrates, which began in Bulgaria in the mid-1980s, can be read in a couple of ways. First, marriage is traditionally viewed by Bulgarians as most suitable to the social task of raising children. Yet, it has been the model of the single-child family that established itself as a norm in the early 1970s. The declining pattern in birthrates is also associated with a decrease in the number of marriages and a rise in the number of divorces throughout the 1970s and the 1980s.[3] Since the late 1970s demographers have also observed an escalation in the number of couples who choose to cohabitate rather than marry, and of those who, upon marriage, do not pursue reproduction at all (Stoilova 2001: 108).

A radical drop in birthrates in Bulgaria, however, occurred at the beginning of the postsocialist era in the 1990s. This drop illuminates the state's diminished spending on social services, which made the prospects for starting families discouraging. At the same time in comparison to the rest of Europe, quite interestingly, Bulgarian women give birth to a first child earlier and at an average age of 23 years.[4] Reasons for early motherhood could include the prevalence of certain cultural norms which valorize young motherhood, the recent elimination of sex education in high-schools, as well as the new cultural "trend" among the *nouveaux riches* of marrying much younger women. I will return to this interesting new phenomenon later in this chapter.

The Postsocialist Landscape

It was the early fall of 2001. The US government was still negotiating conditions under which to launch a military attack against Afghanistan. On a calm evening in Sofia I was sitting with Desi,[4] a recent mother and a journalist from Bulgaria's prominent financial weekly *Capital*. The Mohito café, which she chose for our meeting, entertained a large crowd of fashionably dressed young people. An unsuspecting visitor might have been surprised to find such a scene in a country where the average monthly salary does not exceed $120, and with rates of unemployment, especially among the young, that in some parts of the country reach nearly 30 percent (Bell 1998). To a Bulgarian, on the other hand, this is a familiar scene. The burgeoning Sofia night life caters to a wide spectrum of clientele responding to the restructuring Bulgarian society with its emerging wealthy middle class.[6] Night life culture has emerged as the single most accessible consumer benefit resulting from the broad scope of changes unleashed in the 1990s. As most Bulgarians enjoy vibrant social life, many young people spend all their limited income on savoring their relationships with friends in such a manner, especially since "no amount of savings from a regular salary ever allows [them] to invest in a house, or even a car," as one young man revealed to me.

It is a bit loud in the café but I still can follow Desi's engaging tale about her experience from earlier that day when she visited what she described as a "disturbing" peace rally against the bombings in Afghanistan. Before I could probe further into why she felt the rally was disturbing, she quickly adds with a hint of irony that "rallies in Bulgaria as a rule draw in a bunch of outcasts and elderly citizens waiving placards of their favorite socialist leaders." "Young people have better things to do," she offers by a way of conclusion. She continues: "But most of the time they know that rallying is not the way that 'democratic politics' really works; not in this country, any way. And besides they [the young people] hardly care any more: we no longer see the point in any of this empty political talk about our possible better futures."

Her spirited tongue veers now in another direction and she speaks tenderly about her 1-year-old daughter. With no effort to conceal her resentment she exclaims:

> Can you believe it? I just read today in the paper that the birthrates have slightly increased this year. I really dread the fact that my daughter, too, has become part of *their* statistics, most probably as an evidence of another of their cheap populist pronouncements of how life is improving. It is ridiculous to think that we are giving more births because, imagine, they have most "generously" increased the monthly child allowances from 4 to 8 dollars per child.

Her lamentation ends on a note to which I had already become accustomed during my various conversations with different people in Sofia that summer: "Why would one want to live in such a country?"

This discursive script is revealing of the way younger Bulgarians today address their disillusionment with social and economic developments in their country. Talk about leaving the country absorbs a variety of concerns. It speaks to the sense of alienation that these Bulgarians felt severed them from both the older cohorts, who grew up during socialism, and the younger ones for whom socialism is barely a form of family memory. It raises concerns of being betrayed by the self-serving new political elites and the older generations who, "nostalgically vote 'left' and for political causes that bring only disasters." Finally, it embraces an anxiety over a growing sense of apathy that this cohort feels cripples their society and has prompted many to look abroad for a more energized social environment in which to work and live.

By the signifier "young people" I refer here to the generations that came of age in postsocialist Bulgaria. I am particularly interested in one cohort of Bulgarians born between 1965 and 1975, and now in reproductive age. My research suggests that this generation has emerged as a group with its own identity, which situates them as a cultural bridge between socialism and capitalism. Members of this cohort are characterized by a combination of shared attributes. Most are well educated. They were raised with specific expectations about their social status and professional careers which were crafted within the socialist culture, yet they began their adult life at the dissolution of that culture and during the "transition." Because of these shared experiences, social position and existential orientations, I will refer to this group as the first postsocialist generation.

Members of the first postsocialist generation played a central role in the street demonstrations following the overthrow of the communist government in 1989. Subsequently, they came to represent the political and social Renaissance of the country, which promised limitless opportunities for individual prosperity and freedom. Their "uncontaminated consciousness," free from socialist dogmas and experience, made them the most promising political agent of change.[7] And in fact, this cohort seemed enthusiastic about playing the role of the social vanguard of the country. The unfolding political-economic reforms, however, turned out to be far less advantageous for young Bulgarians than was initially imagined and have begun to alter the very context in which men and women in Bulgaria understood their social roles and identities.

In the early 1990s Bulgaria prepared for a leap into capitalism. This involved restructuring the legal system, the welfare system, national and local political organizations and vital economic activities, which led to dramatic contraction of the industrial sector and the labor market, to high inflation and a drastic reduction of Bulgarians' consumer power. Most of the large state companies, before subjected to a protracted process of privatization, developed enormous debts to the state. Consequently, the state's diminished capacities to manage security, education and health put into question the very social order of the country and encouraged the emergence of organized crime and unrestrained corruption.

Most demoralizing to the socialization of the first postsocialist generation, however, were the conditions of the labor market. During radical economic restructuring, Pierre Bourdieu has argued, shifts in the labor market affect most dramatically precisely the generation that is about to enter the labor force at the time of the shift (Bourdieu 1998: 157). Rapid reorganizations in the economic sector risk a process of deskilling of one whole generation. As a result, young people get less out of their qualifications in comparison to what the previous generation would have obtained. Hence, Bourdieu argues, a combination of resentment and revolt generated in the hearts of these professionally deprived young people bring about a sort of general collective disillusionment, which soon extends to all social institutions and to the state as a whole. Young people's betrayed ambitions make them refuse to accept such fundamental tenets of the new social order, as "career," "status," "marriage" and, in general, what it means to "get on" in society. Bourdieu's insight illuminates the meaning of statements such as the following one collected from another informant: "It is insulting to live in a society where success is measured through speculations, and deception is married with physical abuse, where there are very few who live well, and where those that achieve their prosperity though legal operations and professionalism are even fewer. How do you raise children like that?"

To the majority of young people, it seemed, life in postsocialist Bulgaria was not providing clear definitions of how to succeed and prosper at home. Few of the new opportunities for achieving wealth and social mobility were considered morally acceptable by most Bulgarians. This is not to suggest that Bulgaria failed to project any home-grown examples of accomplishment. A limited elite has managed to prosper immensely from the changes contributing to a social structure with a wealthy few at the top and a vast impoverished majority at the bottom of the social pyramid. To Bulgarians, however, the role models that these *nouveaux riches* offered seem deceitful. They conveyed a complicated mix of skills, which went beyond education, hard work, or personal qualities, characteristics that most Bulgarians value as the routes to ethically acceptable personal accomplishment. I propose that the desire to obtain professional growth and personal prosperity in ethically acceptable ways is what has enticed many young Bulgarians of fertile age to postpone reproduction and instead try their chances for prosperity abroad. This social trend has had a direct impact on the country's reproductive patterns.

Shifting demographic patterns cannot be understood without attending more closely to the social struggles for mobility that have become so central to postsocialist experiences. The social transformation in Bulgaria not only changed the economic conditions under which men and women understood their social roles and identities but, perhaps more importantly, also marked a shift in the system of social distinction towards economic power and money. While in the recent past status and prestige had been judged on the basis of membership in the *intelligentsia* or the *nomenklatura*,[8] and was most often achieved by relevant educational credentials, postsocialism has dismantled these norms and previous loyalties and left a void, emptied of rules for governing social mobility. New opportunities for accumulation of wealth – opportunities whose logic remained for long unclear to the majority of Bulgarians – allowed a limited number of the former economic elite, occupying privileged managerial positions, to preserve their posts in the postsocialist landscape. These men began shaping the new postsocialist affluent class in Bulgaria.

Postsocialist Generations Crafting New Social Identities

The adult social and professional life of the first postsocialist generation began in a context in which societal forms of authority and the social structure were largely tainted. Confronted with the task of charting new trajectories of social and professional mobility, the postsocialist generations had limited choice of models and social groups to emulate. Their inherited social capital – resources, knowledge, and the social networks of their parents, especially if these were entrenched in the party system – was largely discredited. While for a few, the murkiness of the emerging social forms allowed for unrestrained experimentation and advancement through risk-taking, for others it brought growing anxiety and alienation. A passage from an interview with a young Bulgarian may illuminate some of these existential dilemmas. Coming from a family of former state bureaucrats in the early 1990s, Peter had just finished his required military service and was eager to try his luck in the new capitalist market.

> At that time all of my friends were in a hurry to make money. It seemed to us that anyone who dared could succeed. We knew, however, that only the fastest and those who began early enough could make it big. So I tried a couple of different things – I started by opening a small kiosk and selling alcohol. That worked for a while, then I switched to selling clothes which I would buy in Poland or Turkey –this actually only made enough money for basic living expenses. I was getting agitated. Some of my friends dropped the idea of going into businesses and went back to school. Looking at the guys making the big bucks – no one had any education, so I thought going back to school is nonsense. I was convinced that you could make it only through perseverance and I didn't want to waste time in school. Besides, we knew that the educational system was really going down the drain, too.

A new group of young entrepreneurial subjects, whom Peter alludes to, has been unanimously recognized as the most unexpected "winners" of the Bulgarian "wild capitalism." Profiting from the institutional chaos in the country and the weak enforcement of law, these new "businessmen" organized in mafia-esque networks, launched a variety of shady firms, typically in the sphere of insurance and security, but also in export and even banking (Nikolov 1997). They came to be known in Bulgaria derogatively as the "mugs" (*mutri*), the "wrestlers" (*bortcite*) or the "thick necks" (*debelite vratove*). Much despised and feared by ordinary citizens, *bortcite* quickly joined the ranks of the *nouveaux riches* and came to symbolize a new model of economic mobility, yet one considered radically immoral. Interestingly many of these people were also former professional wrestlers.[9] With little education and much arrogance, earning their respect through physical abuse and racketeering, these new postsocialist protagonists had little appeal to their peers from within the former middle stratum of Bulgarian society like Peter.

In 2003 I spoke to Peter again – he was now 30, still single, still living with his parents, and working in a restaurant. He likes his trade, yet it is far from prestigious. "It is a decent job though," he says, "given that there are so many people on the streets looking for one." Peter regrets that he didn't follow the advice of his friends and go back to the university. In the meantime, a few of his friends earned scholarships from foreign universities and have been living abroad ever since. Potentially, they could come back to Bulgaria and join the new professional force in multinational and Bulgarian companies that are experiencing some demand, albeit limited, for well-trained professionals. Peter, on the other hand, feels "trapped." If he leaves his work as a waiter, he will be unable to find anything better at the moment. Moreover, he does not have the financial resources to support himself without a job, if he should decide to take a break and look for more lucrative opportunities. He also feels pressured by his parents, who expected him to complete a university degree, as they both did, and eventually marry.

Not all of those young Bulgarians who made "the right decision" in resuming their education have been economically successful, however. In particular, many educated members of the first postsocialist generation have recognized that they were trained for professions inadequate to the new market conditions. They felt compelled to accept jobs in the newly emergent private sector, yet ones that were still underpaid and ill-defined.[10] Accustomed to a certain standard of living during socialism, which provided for a secure transition to a chosen profession,[11] the first postsocialist generation found their ambitions betrayed in the new context of ever-growing economic uncertainty.

Many companies in the new market economy took advantage of the general regulative havoc at the beginning of the transition to employ young people in dead-end jobs, lacking a promise of professional advancement, contract security or grievance procedures. During the first transitional years, the country had reached levels of social inequality unseen in Bulgaria since the period preceding the Second World War. Low wages and high levels of unemployment had created a reality in which the younger Bulgarians were forced to change jobs frequently and look for employment of any kind, regardless of their specific training (Aleksandrov 2001: 15). Moreover, many of them were now becoming the main breadwinners of their families.

Postsocialism therefore also presented serious challenges to family survival.[12] Throughout the mid-1990s due to continuous high levels of inflation the savings of Bulgarian families were literally wiped out. Moreover, in the past, socialism had discouraged individual forms of savings and hence many families in the postsocialist era had limited resources to meet, for instance, the financial needs of a person between jobs or facing retirement. With older parents at retirement age whose earnings in pensions now hardly suffice for their basic subsistence needs, younger generations in the households are also responsible to provide for their aging parents. This shift in the responsibility of family members has led to the erosion of parenthood models established during socialism when the senior parents, for instance, were often expected to assist their children financially long after they had started independent families of their own, and to provide the newly married couples with housing (Todorova 2000: 167). Such new arrangements in the family obligations and the shortage of cash have also imposed restrictions on the ability of young people to move out of the households of their parents. These conditions seem to nourish negative feelings of being "locked" in a predicament of perpetual adolescence.

For all kinds of young Bulgarians, starting their own families seems discouragingly distant. Both educated young men and women who are trying to respond boldly to the challenges of capitalism and younger working-class people, who are more limited when looking for jobs, feel constrained. Both groups tend to compensate for these imposed restrictions by postponing procreation and exploring more immediate rewards in consumption and entertainment instead. If we examine the thoughts of younger Bulgarians, time and again we find them expressing a sense of finding themselves at an impasse: public expectations view them as those who will bring forth a new form of society, but at the same time, when they attempt to be innovative in their pursuit of new social roles, they are perceived as infantile and lacking in responsible civic attitudes (i.e. they tend to stay with their parents, do not marry and begin families). They are also paralyzed by the lack of economic possibilities that restrict their social activities. The result of this impasse is that many young Bulgarians, who believe their place is in Bulgaria, paradoxically, remain in a state of indefinitely deferred adulthood. To others emigration has emerged as a possible way to execute the passage away from adolescence in a way that is also considered honorable.

Gendered Struggles and Social Mobility

The relationship between the new paths of social mobility that became available in the postsocialist era and the shift in the reproductive behavior of younger generations becomes more evident when addressed though the lens of gender. Moreover, demographics is a powerful script for imagining society in particular gendered ways. When Bulgarian population specialists code the nation "in crisis," in actuality they imply a systemic view of Bulgarian women's fertility as a "problem." The rhetoric of the "demographic crisis" obscures women's economic contributions both during socialism and in the postsocialist period, as they have struggled to combine their productive and reproductive duties. I turn here to several stories of young women who are embracing new career opportunities in postsocialist Bulgaria. These opportunities reflect changing ideas of femininity and reproduction, which are linked to new strategies of social upward mobility. Decisions about marriage, family and children figure prominently in women's chances for social advancement.

At the beginning of the 1990s women began exploring new ways to combine work and motherhood. Some embraced career opportunities tailored to the capitalist markets,[13] conversely, others chose to withdraw completely from the labor market and to devote full attention to their families – a choice that was often unavailable and morally sanctioned during socialism (Daskalova 2000: 340). One Bulgarian sociologist points out that an emphasis on a sense of aesthetics, education and self-development has been important in the socialization of young Bulgarian women during socialism (Stoilova 2001: 109). However, for the older generation of women who grew up in the early years of socialism, the icon of femininity promoted by the socialist ideology was the self-sacrificing mother. This icon celebrated women who sacrificed their careers in devotion to their children. On the other hand, younger women who came of age during the last decade of socialism emphasize, above all, the construction of the Self as a measure of success and satisfaction. They depend more on their own talents for this self-definition.

New strategies of the autonomous Self found articulation in the pages of several trendy lifestyle magazines of the postsocialist era catering to younger and more-educated audiences. Among these *Egoist* and *1(one)* have emerged as provocative public venues for voicing the experiences of postsocialist generations. Dedicated initially to promoting interest in western-style habits of life, leisure and consumption, these magazines have also allowed space for articulating less conventional life experiences and attitudes such as sexual experimentation, traveling and living a life of pleasures and self-indulgence. These topics are discussed as techniques for exploring a new autonomous and self-sufficient existence. The venues of lifestyle magazines were also the first to celebrate gender roles alternative to the dogmatic socialist prescriptions of women as "self-sacrificing mothers" and men as "workers," and to welcome the appearance of vibrant gay and lesbian communities in the mid-1990s. The male gay scene, for instance, has now become an inseparable part of the postsocialist urbanscape. Gays and transvestites, the majority of whom are young and well traveled, are the trend setters of new styles of night life in Sofia. The Bulgarian lesbian movement is also making prominent steps towards organizing on its own.[14] And while young people rely on models from the "West" to guide them in this search for new gendered selves, these selves are creatively embedded in the Bulgarian context.

It was also in the pages of these magazines that young audiences began seriously discussing decisions to marry late or emigrate not as forms of national deception, but as a possible exercise of individual choice. Such choices are being gradually normalized as standard strategies for autonomous self-development in the eyes of the young, and not simply as reactions of immaturity. However, such cultural experimentation takes time to evolve and this "time" requires that one postpone facing the abrupt demands of the more "traditional" dilemmas of family and reproduction.

Alexandra is a member of the first postsocialist generation and a young woman whom I befriended in the early 1990s while she was still an undergraduate at the University of Sofia.

> Those years were incredible, filled with so much hope and enthusiasm. From the perspective of the years passed, I can admit now that it is difficult to explain how we could be so blind to the potential consequences of such radical changes. In any case, personally, I was quite happy about what happened then, because it meant that after graduation I could chose for myself where I wanted to work, or so I believed. You see, when I was accepted at the university I had to sign a contract that upon graduation I would leave Sofia and work in a small town. Instead, because of the changes, I went on to work as a sociologist in one of the most prosperous new polling agencies where we were preparing a variety of surveys for television newscasts.

Alexandra also had a boyfriend at the time who had earned a degree in public engineering, yet who was not as lucky as she was in landing a prestigious job. Later Alexandra decided to go for a doctoral degree, a new form of education in Bulgaria. She had also been taking evening classes in French and English for years. She was living with her mother, a divorcee, and the idea of getting married was not necessarily on her mind at all.

> The most important thing for me is really to evolve intellectually and spiritually. There was no way I could drop my plan in exchange for a kind of cozy domesticity that my mother felt was important to pursue when she was 25. She actually divorced quickly after getting married: it is an unspoken rule that Bulgarian men look for lovers outside marriage. I was never too enthusiastic to be a second-rate wife in somebody else's life. And who was getting married anyway? All of my friends were single and it was great, we could travel and look into all that we thought was exciting. There was a lot of catch up to do and to compensate for the times we missed living in a closed state during socialism. Many people decided to continue their education abroad. Our parents in fact were very encouraging of all this. I guess, though, if you live in a small town there's

really not much to do but to go for marriage. What bothers me most about the culture of marriage here in Bulgaria is that people get married and they simply stop growing. It is another issue altogether that with a child in your hands, obviously, you no longer can experiment with choices. In the meantime me and my friends, we were interested in everything else.

Years passed by and Alexandra realized that she wasn't going to develop further professionally even with her subsequent job and what initially seemed like quite an opportunity to work for Arthur Andersen Investments in Sofia. The barriers to her ambitions in this foreign company, she said, seemed even more evident since all the workers on the managerial level were westerners. Finally, after a series of disappointments, she applied for an immigrant visa to Canada.

> I got married and, surprise! Suddenly I found myself in a small apartment where there were three generations of my husband's family living together, poking constantly into our personal matters. I thought I was looking for a partner in life. Instead I was dealing with a mother's son. It was impossible to think about having a baby on the top of all of us. Now I am waiting for my Canadian immigration papers to go through. But it is not the housing inconveniences that made me apply for immigration papers. Within a year that issue would have been resolved. It is that I don't understand the morals of this place any longer. It seems everyone is in a battle with everyone else and it is all about money. It is disgusting, really.

Alexandra's narrative is revealing of how the events of 1989 and their reformatory rhetoric allowed the first postsocialist generation of women to put their own welfare before that of established family norms. It also meant looking for new definitions of, and possibilities for, womanhood. The shift in family-making – getting married later, postponing or rejecting procreation – represents a cultural adjustment to the changing economic and social landscape in the country. The lure of market capitalism for Alexandra and her friends lay in the possibility for self-reliance, not self-sacrifice. To be "modern" and open to the new possibilities that emerged with the changes in the political regime meant to look at professional women from the cosmopolitan cultures of the "West" for models on how to be independent and successful. These themes permeate many of the discussions of young women in Bulgaria today.

Alexandra's comments on marriage respond to models of family life that were cultivated during socialism and that were changing in the postsocialist era. Communist ideology claimed to resolve the problem of gender inequality by allowing women to participate equally on the labor market. However, state socialism similarly constructed the space of the family as irrelevant to issues of gender inequality (Gal and Kligman 2000: 52). At the same time, in everyday life, the domain of the family was often imagined as a space of "authenticity", where people could experience free speech and political truth. Embedded in this "free" space was also an unequal relationship between men and women. Yet this inequality was obscured because the role of the family in providing refuge from the empty state ideology was considered more important than the presence of gender inequality (Gal and Kligman 2000). Moreover, as Alexandra's story testifies, a hegemonic masculine culture also allowed spouses to have intimate relationships outside marriage, which she perceives as self-degrading.

The inequalities in gender relations inherent in the socialist family model, inequalities which in some respect became even more salient in the postsocialist era (Ghodsee 2001), have now been rendered more visible, especially to ambitious and educated young women. This realization is sharpened by a new self-reflective culture, which incessantly compares the predicaments of life before and after 1989. In particular for younger women from educated backgrounds, an early marriage appears antithetical to the goals of self-fulfillment. As a single woman in her late twenties confided in me: "I don't want to end up like my mom, who keeps saying she has sacrificed everything in the name of her children, and for some supposed responsibility she felt she carried towards the state and society."

Alexandra's romance with the new capitalist opportunities is similar to the stories of thousands of young people who sought to avoid loss of status or economic impoverishment through migration. Although the overall demand for labor in postsocialist Bulgaria diminished significantly, a modest need for highly-skilled workers has been evident. One outcome of this moderate demand has been the emergence of a small group of professional women. Among these are also graduates of western universities who want to pursue careers back in Bulgaria. Because the increasing levels of unemployment have affected women disproportionately, postsocialist professional trajectories demand significant personal compromises from women (Ghodsee 2000: 6). For instance, to new and precarious private businesses women are now considered more expensive laborers than men. One reason for this is that, as the main caretakers of their children, women put additional demands on companies' tight budgets for maternity leaves and social security funds (Ghodsee 2000). On the other hand, women are also perceived as a more flexible and manipulable labor force than men. These professional obstacles have also been prominent in women's decisions to have fewer children.

Another stratum of young women, often with working-class background, from small towns and with less education, has sought to respond differently to pressures created by capitalism. They choose to embark on their own journey of independent modern life, in which marriage to a wealthier man becomes a tool for social mobility and financial security. Viewing oneself comfortably ensconced as a housewife in the deluxe atmosphere of a spacious house is one of the dreams which Svetlana Boym has hailed as "the fusions and confusions of the Western capitalism's special effects" (Boym 1994: 277). Such calculated and materialistic attitudes toward marriage observed in the behavior of these ambitious young women "from the provinces," as these girls are often derogatively called, startled Bulgarians in the early 1990s. They came to represent a model of what has been referred to as postsocialism's "commodified femininity" (Marody and Giza-Poleszczuk 2000: 169). The new form of romance between small-town girls and rich men from the capital found its most complete expression in a widely popular genre of pop-folk music known in Bulgaria as the *chalga*.

The world of *chalga* is driven by money, love, seduction and shiny new cars that dash across the Bulgarian cities with furious speed. It glorifies the owners of these cars – a menagerie of postsocialist "businessmen" and politicians, accompanied by beautiful women – and their ferocious and adventurous lives. *Chalga* is about excessive consumption, as the refrain of one of these songs goes, "one hundred Mercedeses I wish to have, one hundred years to drive them". The appeal of these popular songs, which flourished in the 1990s, lies precisely in the sharp contrast between their portrayal of unbridled materialism and dramatized excess, on the one hand, and socialism's and postsocialism's grim everyday struggles for economic survival, on the other. This new aesthetic, popularized by mass media, advertising and popular culture, offers "idealizations of appearance, personality and behavior," which then become associated with gender concepts and gender relations (Marody and Giza-Poleszczuk 2000: 152).

Kristen Ghodsee (2000: 7) has linked the gendered messages promoted by Bulgarian pop-music to the rampant culture of criminality and the lifestyle of the "mugs" (*mutri*). Expensive clothes, golden necklaces, luxurious cars, mobile phones and attractive beauties have become the signature symbols of this new class of capitalist men. Furthermore, the criminal world advanced its own mafia aesthetic which glorified the short-skirted, gold-digging *mutressa* (the feminine from *mutra*) as the ultimate expression of successful femininity.

The personal stories of many of the young women who have joined the world of the adventurous and risky capitalism are very instructive as to how these young girls have embraced such messages. Their success stories unfold in two arenas: in the entertainment industry or on the fashion catwalks. Many, in fact, are escaping from factory work and the limited opportunities for employment available in smaller towns. Bulgaria's low wages and geographic proximity to cosmopolitan European cities has made the countryside a Mecca for sweat shops. The work conditions in these places, however, are often quite dire and the wages are as low as those in Bangladesh, India or China (Ghodsee 2000).

In search of better prospects for financial stability and personal freedom young women from small towns often relocate in the capital, or in the cities around the touristy Black Sea coast. While less well positioned to pursue professional careers than their more educated and cosmopolitan counterparts from larger cities, these small-town girls exploit their charms and physical appeal to create new personal connections and secure jobs in Sofia. In the context of society's renewed interest in physical attractiveness, young women with working-class backgrounds choose to capitalize on their physical appearance and search for employment in the various modeling agencies, new fashion salons and boutiques or in the numerous night-clubs and discos that are ubiquitous on the new city landscape. Their biggest fans, and possibly future husbands, come from among the *nouveaux riches* who frequent these entertainment sites and who can afford the trophy of a beautiful wife. For these women, entering the world of fashion or the entertainment industry is the starting point of their own battle of involvement with the "brave new world" of capitalism.

In postsocialist Bulgaria, attractiveness (the care of the physical self as opposed to socialism's valorizing of motherhood) is recognized as the key factor behind women's success both with men and in the labor market. Bulgarian newspapers are full of classified ads offering jobs to "young and attractive women." Hence it comes as no surprise that fashion has emerged as a compelling visual commodity and an arena of romance in postsocialist Bulgaria. The popular media regularly features multiple-page spreads on fashion shows or photo shoots (Gray 2002: 2). In addition to the coverage fashion receives in the local newspapers, and regular programs on television, international fashion channels are beamed on big television screens in bars, shops, beauty parlors and even at dental clinics. From an interview with the director of one of the many modeling houses in Sofia we learn that every month the agency receives dozens of pictures of girls as young as 10, "all dead set on becoming a model" (cited in Gray 2002: 2). While parents are often less enthusiastic about their daughters' modeling pursuits, which are seen as "obstacles to other more meaningful professions," the director assures us the girls are taught how to walk and dance, and they are helped to improve their confidence, "which is better than ending up on the streets, doing drugs" (Gray 2002: 2).

Bulgaria averages half a dozen fashion-related events per month and the world of fashion is used by the upper echelons of Bulgarian society – diplomats, politicians and other prominent public figures, some also linked to the organized crime – to show off their new elite statuses. Successful models, on the other hand, utilize these occasions to make connections, establish romantic relationships, and "join the life of glamour." In a newspaper report covering one of these glamour events, a gossip columnist likens fashion and politics as the two most entrenched topics in the public culture of postsocialist Bulgaria.[15] "Fashion equals money equals power," he acknowledges. "People are interested in politics too, of course. But fashion is a better liar. In politics everyone is saying, 'we can't improve the world'. Yet, fashion says, 'life can be beautiful, you can be beautiful too'."

It is social mobility, wealth, and an imagined future of luxurious recreational travel, rather than love or class solidarity, that account for the lure of the new commercialized romances of young women aspiring to material comfort and capitalist men. My research also suggests that even in the most successful of cases, when these mercenary *mutressa* women marry, it is rare that the new couples have more than one child. Hence, new challenges encountered by both educated and working-class women are shaping the country's birthrates.

Reproduction beyond the National Borders

Within the first five years after the collapse of socialism (1990–96) more than 800,000 young people fled the country rushing to reply to what they saw as "a promise for a more decent and respectable life" in the "West." This exodus produced a real emigration craze in Bulgaria. The bulk of people who migrated westward (and specifically to the United States) belonged to the once relatively prosperous socialist middle strata of society. This is a generation whose most productive years, both in terms of work and childbearing, are currently being lived or are ahead of them (Stoilkova 2001: 154). Therefore, the current demographic "crisis" in Bulgaria is the result of generation-specific disadvantages brought about by the new cultural and economic realities of the country, following the dissolution of the socialist system. The persistent drop in birthrates in Bulgaria during the postsocialist era should be attributed to the shifting social behavior of one particular generation that chooses to postpone marriage and procreation and even migrate in response to its disadvantageous position.

Fear of "the death of the nation," due to a demographic collapse, gains public significance when the nation-state is imagined as a bounded territory locked in a specific geographical location and represented by one single (dominant) ethnic group. Reproduction rates are usually measured within the territory of the official boundaries of the nation-state. Yet, my ethnographic experience among those that are seen at home as "fleeing the sinking ship," the members of the Bulgarian diaspora, reveals a group of people who identify in emigration as even "more Bulgarian." Nearly 300,000 young Bulgarians now live and work in the United States. They maintain continuous contact with Bulgaria and support relatives at home. Many are married with children and sharing plans for a possible return to Bulgaria.

At regular meetings of the Bulgarian community in the San Francisco Bay Area, one could hardly guess that young Bulgarians experience any particular quandary in their reproductive experiences. These meetings are relaxed and lively. Young children are running around while their grandmothers, summoned especially from Bulgaria to help with the upbringing of the next generation, proudly attend to their grandchildren. "I am very concerned about the education of my child here in America," confides Eli, a mother of a 3 year old. "I am hoping that as a university professor, my husband could potentially look for a job in some quieter university town with more promising schools, so that we do not end up paying an enormous amount of money for private schooling. We are also not ruling out the option of enrolling our child in a Bulgarian school back home under the caring eyes of the grandparents."

It is difficult to predict whether the majority of these people will one day return, and furthermore whether their children will want to live in their parents' land of origin. However, there is mounting evidence from various parts of the world to testify that diasporic groups are now much more engaged with the life of their home communities than ever before. This puts into question some of the most basic understandings about the boundedness of the national body and its demographic characteristics. "My kid is 1 year old," shared another Bulgarian parent from New York, "and we are flying back to Bulgaria to apply for a Bulgarian passport for the baby. It is a matter of principle for me that my child accepts Bulgarian citizenship, regardless whether she will choose one day to live in the country or not." To claim that the physical reproduction of Bulgaria is endangered is to obscure the engagement of members of the Bulgarian diaspora with projects at home, and their attempts to remain connected to the social life of their country. Obviously the absence of members of the generations in reproductive age, who give birth elsewhere abroad, does affect the number of bodies born in Bulgaria. However, to suggest that this reflects a "decline of the nation," as the Bulgarian press does, is overly alarmist. It ignores the fact that Bulgarian young people in different economic and moral contexts (i.e. abroad) are having children.

Meanwhile, a growing number of Chinese and Middle Eastern families have begun to settle in Bulgaria.[16] Some members of these communities claim that they initially chose Bulgaria as a camping ground on their way to locations in Western Europe, which offer more lucrative employment opportunities. Yet they often stay in the country for longer periods of time, some intermarry and have children. The burgeoning number of small ethnic restaurants and businesses is a testament to the latter. After all, according to the most recent prognostics, Bulgaria is expected to join the European Union by 2007. Like those Bulgarians living abroad, these immigrant groups are not included in demographic calculations of the country; yet their presence will be a decisive influence on future demographic developments.

Conclusion

In this chapter I looked at record low fertility rates in Bulgaria during the 1990s to argue that shifts in demographic patterns should not be regarded independent of cultural struggles accompanying rapid socio-economic changes. I offered a qualitative interpretation of the country's "demographic crisis" by exploring several social arenas – the labor market, the welfare system, the media, and the family. In a statistical sense, the decline of birthrates in Bulgaria after the collapse of state socialism is related and often attributed to the mass emigration of members of one generation in fertile age. Yet, it is also linked to the changing conditions and experiences that an entire postsocialist generation confronts as its members redefine their social and gender statuses. The demographic "crisis" in Bulgaria represents a cultural adjustment to unstable social and economic environment, involving new definitions of gender and social identities and new understandings of what it is to be "modern."

Acknowledgments

I am indebted to Diana Blank, Carrie B. Douglass, Zeynep Gursel, Arthur Mason and Rebecca Nash for their critical engagement, help and trust in completing this chapter.

Notes

1. Since the mid-1990s reports on declining demographic statistics were coined in such titles as *The Demographic Picture of Bulgaria is Worrisome, Bulgaria Struck by a Severe Demographic Crisis* and *The Nation is Vanishing*, which appeared respectively in *Capital* (May 1997, no. 25, and September 2002, no. 39) and *24 Chasa* (March 27, 1998).
2. Currently ethnic Bulgarians comprise 83 percent of the total population. There are altogether more than thirty other ethnic communities residing in the country; among these the Turkish (8.5 percent) and the Roma (2.6 percent) groups are the largest (*2001 World Factbook*, http://www.outfo.org/almanac/world-factbook_01/).
3. The number of teenage pregnacies is also higher than in other European countries. For more details, see Todorova (2000: 153).
4. Poverty is especially severe among single-parent families, single mothers and women divorcees with children, who in 90 percent of the cases are granted parental rights (UNDP 2000).
5. All names of individuals interviewed for this study have been changed.
6. See Daniel Simpson (2002) "An Ex-King Slips Fast as Bulgaria Languishes," *New York Times*, December 13.
7. On the symbolism of youth and the revolutionary protests of 1989 and 1997, see E. Dainov (ed.) (1998). *The Awakening: A Chronicle of the Bulgarian Civic Uprising of January–February 1997*, Sofia: Center for Social Practices, NBU.
8. These two strata during socialism represented the most explicit social divisions within what was conceived on the whole as an egalitarian Bulgaria society. The *nomenklatura* comprised of members of the political elite and upper- and middle-level state bureaucrats. The *intelligentsia,* on the other

hand, was the core substrate of the so-called "socialist middle class" and loosely encompassed anyone who had a university degree. Membership or entry into these two stratas of society provided access to various degrees of privilege and, in general, to higher standards of living.

9. The majority of these young men are of working-class background and came out of the famous vocational sports schools which trained the Bulgarian Olympic wrestling teams during socialism; hence their popular nickname the "thick necks" (*debelite vratove*). These heavily built men were hired as private armies by the new economic oligarchs during postsocialism (Nikolov 1997).

10. As inherited from socialism, the large public sector in Bulgaria offered more secure employment to young people but with significantly less pay than the newly emergent private sector. Furthermore, in the public sector, young people's efforts were blocked by the older employees, who saw in them a threat to their own livelihood and for whom employment in the private sector, catering to younger labor force, were ruled out.

11. During socialism universities managed with governmental programs for allocating graduates directly to available positions on the labor market.

12. Several successive governments in the post-1989 period have postponed the adoption of a new legislation to halt the many negative trends in the life of families, such as the impoverishment of children, the drop in birthrates, the rise in deathrates among children, and the restriction of access to education. The state often justifies this disengaged position by declaring that this would make the country more attractive to infusions of foreign capital. It is widely believed that heightened demands for labor protection and maternity benefits are discouraging foreign investors to move to Bulgaria (see Todorova 2000: 170).

13. The preferred professions for women which respond to the shifting concepts of femininity are those of the freelance journalist, the actress, the artist, the "businesswoman" (often engaged in petty-trading), the photo-model and the designer. This observation is based on a brief scanning of various women magazines.

14. I thank my colleague Robin Brooks for this information.

15. The interview appeared in one of the most popular tabloid magazines *Blyasak* (May, 2002).

16. One example is discussed in an article by Iva Rudnikova (2001), "The Bulgarian Chinatown," *Capital*, no. 48.

References

Alexsandrov, H. (2001), "The Patriarchy, the Generation 'We' and the Users," *Capital*, September: 35 (in Bulgarian).

Bell, J. (ed.) (1998), *Bulgaria in Transition: Politics, Economics, Society and Culture after Communism*, Boulder. CO: Westview Press.

Bourdieu, P. (1998), *Distinction: A Social Critique of the Judgment of Taste*, Cambridge, MA: Harvard University Press.

Boym, S. (1994), *Common Places: Mythologies of Everyday Life in Russia*, Cambridge, MA: Harvard University Press.

Daskalova, K. (2001), "Women's Problems, Women's Discourses in Bulgaria," in S. Gal and G. Kligman (eds) *Reproducing Gender*, Princeton, NJ: Princeton University Press.

Gal, S. and Kligman, G. (2000), *The Politics of Gender after Socialism*, Princeton, NJ: Princeton University Press.

Ghodsee, K. (2000), "Women and Economic Transition: Mobster and Mail-Order Brides in Bulgaria," *CSEES Newsletter* (University of California, Berkeley): 17.

Gray, J. (2002), "Bulgarians Look to the World of Fashion for a Ticket Out of Reality," *Transitions On Line*, electronic version.

Marody, M, and Giza-Poleszczuk, A. (2000), "Changing Images of Identity in Poland: From the Self-Sacrificing to the Self-Investing Woman?" in S Gal and G Kligman (eds) *Reproducing Gender*, Princeton, NJ: Princeton University Press.

Nikolov, J. (1997), "Crime and Corruption and Communism, Organized Crime in Bulgaria," *East European Constitutional Review*, 6. See also, www.law.nyu.edu/eecr/vol6num4/feature/organizedcrime.html.

Stoilkova, M. (2001), "A New Generation of the Bulgarian Transition: in Search of a 'Brighter Future'," in R. Stryker and J. Patico (eds) *The Paradoxes of Progress: Globalization and Postsocialist Cultures*, Berkeley, CA: Kroeber Anthropological Society Papers.

Stoilova, R. (2001), *Inequality and Social Integration*, Sofia: LIK.

Todorova, V. (2000), "Family Law in Bulgaria: Legal Norms and Social Norms," *International Journal of Law, Policy and the Family*, 14: 148–181.

UNDP (2000), *United Nations Development Programme in Bulgaria: Review*, Sofia: Office of UNDP in Bulgaria.

Znepolski, B. (2002), "The Screenplay of Arbitrariness: An Analysis of the Language of the Postcommunist Press," Presented at One Ring to Rule them All: Power and Power Relations in East European Politics and Societies, University of California, Berkeley.

–7–

Underfertility's Challenge to Family and Gender Relations in Urban Greece

Heather Paxson

In Greece, the notion that motherhood "completes" a woman is professed by demographers and policy-makers, and by middle-class woman alike. Yet despite the persistent idealization of motherhood, Greece's total fertility rate (average number of children per woman of reproductive age) fell below replacement level in the early 1980s, plummeting to 1.28 in 1999 (Council of Europe 2001; see also Figure 7.1). During ethnographic research into fertility control and motherhood, I encountered the recurring theme of Greece's "underfertility" (*ipoyenitikótita*). The "demographic problem," as Greeks speak of, is perhaps especially palpable in Athens, where I conducted fieldwork between 1993 and 1995 (Paxson 2004). In 1951, 18 percent of the national population lived in the nation's capital, but following mass urban migration in the wake of the Second World War and Greece's subsequent Civil War, by 1991 well over 30 percent of the population resided in Athens (National Statistical Service of Greece (NSSG) 1992). Urban migration produced an aging rural population, such that fertility rates in urban and rural areas have fallen at much the same pace (Parliament of Greece 1993). Nationwide, deaths outnumbered births beginning in 1998 (NSSG 2002). Athenians share widespread perception not only that "Greece is getting smaller," but also that this constitutes a legitimate cause for concern when compared with neighboring Turkey, Greece's political rival, whose fertility runs at three times Greece's.

For many Athenians, the future strength of their nation would seem to depend on the continued production of Greek bodies, on the reproduction of larger families. This pronatal imperative has been given a gendered charge, not only through a belief that motherhood completes a woman, but by the fact that Greece's declining birthrate was first brought to public attention following a 1960s study into women's birth control practices (Valaoras and Trichopoulos 1970). This state-sponsored study also disclosed a common incidence of repeat abortion (Paxson 1997, 2004; Halkias 1998). A decade of war, famine, poverty and urban relocation pressured Greeks to have smaller families; by the 1950s middle-aged mothers "discovered" medical abortion as a means of family limitation. By the 1980s the

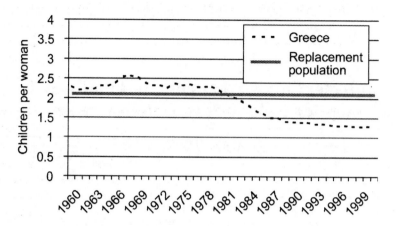

Figure 7.1 Total Fertility Rate, Greece, 1960–1999.
Source: Eurostat 2003.

abortion rate had climbed to three times the live birthrate. Ever since the 1960s study explicitly blamed women's repeat abortions for much of the country's demographic weakening, discussion of Greece's underfertility has made continued reference to the attitudes and behaviors of the nation's women.

Parliamentary transcripts and letters to newspapers have voiced by now familiar recriminations that "modern" – that is, urban middle-class – women are to blame for selfishly "refusing" to have traditionally large families (Halkias 1998). I heard similar complaints at medical conferences and public symposia addressing family planning and demographic issues in Athens. But in my research I found that this officialized recrimination by no means reflects consensus among the urban, middle-class populace – the very group targeted by family planners. Middle-class Athenian women do not describe themselves or their peers as being *selfish* for delaying starting families or for limiting family size. Rather, they depict this as *responsible* behavior, regardless of unfortunate national consequences. A dichotomous model of gender roles as either traditional or modern, often presumed by Greek politicians, obfuscates the economic and cultural factors that impede couples from realizing desires for larger families. It also obscures women's own nuanced, often critical understandings of how, in daily life, people – and "a" people – navigate and embody conflicts between the so-called traditional and modern at the margins of Europe.

To learn where professional and lay theories converge and diverge on questions of reproductive politics, I conducted open-ended interviews with health care and social science professionals as well as with thirty-eight women about their own lives, many but not all of whom are mothers, aged 20 to over 70, living and/or working in the middle-class neighborhood of Pangrati. Some interviews were conducted in English but most were in Greek; translations are mine. Thanks to a fortuitous introduction, I attended several meetings of an Athenian feminist group whose members were concerned about the xenophobia and sexism implied in the reproductive-based demographic model of national well-being that characterized a widely circulated parliamentary report on the country's "Demographic Problem" issued in 1993.

I approach the politics and problems of Greece's supposed "barren state" from three angles. After summarizing state rhetoric and policy, I consider what low birthrates mean to the segment of the population often held accountable for them, middle-class working and professional families, and I do so by attending to class inflections of Athenians' sense that they cannot afford to raise as many children as they might like. Second, I discuss repercussions of personal and national under-fertility for how urban Greeks perceive gender difference, especially what it takes to enact proper femininity in this modern era. Finally, taking my cue from a leftist feminist group in Athens, I offer a critique of how framing of the demographic problem as such is founded on xenophobic, often racialized understandings of how national populations are, or should be, constituted. Looking at demographic issues through a triple filter of class, gender and ethnicity (see also Krause 2001), I argue that to think of Greece as a "barren state" – as do many Greek demographers – obscures how this perception depends on unacknowledged apparati of economic, sexual and nationalist ideologies that constitute the modern Greek nation-state. It also belittles the practical concerns of Greek citizens who aspire to larger families.

Politics and Policy

Since 1990, Greece's most substantial pronatal policy has been to award large families with cash incentives. As of 2001, monthly allowances of about US$150 were given to married couples having a third child, until this child reaches 6 years of age; to families with four or more children, small allowances are offered per unmarried child under the age of 23. While awarding families for meeting the pronatalist goal of a third or fourth child, state policy fails to aid couples in having a first or second child (Paxson 2004).

Following a significant 5.33 percent fall in the national birthrate (number of births per 1,000 of the population) during the decade of the 1980s, in November 1991, a non-partisan parliamentary commission was convened to study the country's demographic situation and recommend relevant policy measures. Issued in 1993, while I was in Athens, their report notes that a range of factors contribute to demographic measurements – migration, population distribution between rural and urban areas, the age spread of the population, deathrate, birthrate. But instead of viewing social and economic factors as having direct impact on the sorts of things demographic statistics purport to measure, and therefore as fair game for policy intervention, authors focus on reproductive attitudes when outlining policy recommendations, which aim at encouraging women to have larger families. No significant changes in policy have been implemented following this report, which nonetheless remains instructive of nationalist and reproductive ideology.

Beyond raising monthly allowances and tax breaks for large families, the report calls for reform of state-operated family planning clinics. Presumably unaware that these clinics, few in number, are used primarily by working-class women for routine gynaecological examinations (Margaritidou and Mesteneos 1992), politicians advocate revamping family planning not to be "identified solely with contraception, abortion and sterility," but so it would aim to "protect the family" and embrace the "support of motherhood, which," the report states, "must be forwarded as a supreme social value" (Parliament of Greece 1993: 19). Policy recommendations are also directed at state education, asking it to "stress at every appropriate moment Greek tradition [of family] and religious sentiment" (Parliament of Greece 1993: 36).

In the 1993 report, parliamentarians depict "motherhood protection" as a national need occasioned by urban modernity: "The new notion of family and society that urbanization occasions (a notion that the countryside is also adopting), housing problems, the cost of education, the lack of appropriate childcare centers, etc. lead to smaller families and the postponement of marriage" (Parliament of Greece 1993: 15). But if socio-economic conditions contribute to demographic outcomes, it is the modernization of women's attitudes that are held accountable for them. Specifically, women having abortions are figured at the heart of Greece's demographic weakness. The report claims that by correctly informing women that abortion can damage their future fertility, and by "forwarding the national and religious traditions of our people, it is possible that forty percent of women will decide not to resort to abortion" and – the implicit corollary – the country will gain more planned children (Parliament of Greece 1993: 19).

Not surprisingly, this government projection has not been realized. Despite an absence of new policy measures, the abortion rate *has* fallen since the early 1990s (although it remains above the live birthrate). Health care professionals interpret this as a result of men's increased condom use to prevent HIV transmission. But contrary to government predictions, the birthrate continues to decline. Fewer abortions have not translated into more births. In forwarding as pronatal policy a family planning agenda aimed at encouraging women to "choose" not to have abortions, Greek policy-makers mistook the *means* of birth limitation – abortion – to be the *causes* of birth limitation. Birthrates in Greece will not rise without comprehensive economic and family policy directed at what urban Greeks perceive as the primary reasons for their own reproductive decisions.

Class and the Making of Modern Families

Depicting the nation's declining birthrate as a matter of economic and historic circumstance, rather than the outcome of individuals' desires, middle-class Athenians are themselves attuned to socio-economic causes of small families. They agree it is "more difficult today" to decide to have children. Niki, a 35-year-old married woman who says she cannot afford children, contextualized her dilemma: "The middle-class Greek, I believe, thinks much more about raising a child. Do they have the economic capability? How will they manage? How to raise it, how to school it? They think about all this a lot, whereas past generations didn't think about it so much." I heard many women voice desires for larger families they felt thwarted by contemporary circumstance.

Women as well as social scientists I interviewed cited the fact that children "cost too much" as the primary cause of the nation's low fertility. In an interview, a midwife told me that Greek women "spend a lot on their children," more than

> in other European countries [where] they don't have to pay for their children's education, [where] they don't think to bequeath a home and money for their children. In Greece people want to educate their children very well, to give them the best clothes, to give them everything. And also to leave them something [as an inheritance], a home. And so they don't have more than two or three [children].

Anna, a 31-year-old administrative assistant and mother of an 8-month-old baby who during the day is looked after by Anna's mother, told me, "I would *like* to have another child. I would like at least one more. But it's difficult because I'm working, and because now we want to have everything for our children. You don't decide easily to have more children because you want to provide them with everything." Middle-class Athenian women tend to discuss their own reproductive agency – a self-reflexivity concerning whether and how to raise children – by claiming hard-won achievement or by stressing external parameters beyond their control.

Demographer Haris Symeonidou's (1990) research has shown that Greek women's employment does not directly affect fertility level. Indeed, that dual incomes are considered necessary for having children helps account for simultaneous low rates of fertility and female employment (Symeonidou 1990). Symeonidiou's research reveals that wage-earning Greek women pursue one of two strategies when they have a first child. Many leave the workforce after marriage or childbirth; for these women, waged work appears as a functional precursor to motherhood (Vaiou 1992: 255). Alternatively, they return to work very shortly after birth, finding caretakers for their infants. Beyond state guaranteed six months' unpaid parental leave to supplement four months' paid leave for childbirth in the public (not private) sector, there is little informal job security for women (Papadopoulos 1998), meaning that once women leave the job market for a year or more it is very difficult to return. The labor activity rate of Greek married women between 25 and 49 years of age has been the lowest in the EU, at 40 percent compared to the EU average of nearly 60 percent (Eurostat 1994, cited in Papadapoulos 1998: 55). Women complained to me that part-time work that would bring extra income but without creating insurmountable childcare demands is difficult to come by. In 1995, 8.4 percent of Greek female employment was part-time, compared with a European Union average of 31.3 percent (Papadopoulos 1998). Women noted, too, that since the overcrowded public school system is organized on a split-day schedule, so that their children can attend school in the mornings one month and afternoons the next, part-time work would be tricky to negotiate.

Lack of quality, affordable daycare is of great concern to working mothers and aspiring parents. Private daycare centers in the mid-1990s charged as much as 600,000 drachmes (US$2,575.00) a year per child, about 50,000 drachmes (US $215.00), a month. This is more than the state provides families to help support three or more children. If a couple has two young children, the fee approximates the monthly salary of a secretary or clerk. And only some of the expensive private centers will accept children under the age of two and a half. Within the few state-run daycare centers in operation it is not uncommon for a sole childcare worker to have as many as fifty small children in her charge. For many families, such conditions are unacceptable. The working mother of a 7-year-old, Litsa, told me, "This is very difficult, where to take your child. I had him at daycare until he went to school. I paid such money! Now he goes to [public] school. But he gets out at twelve-thirty, and someone has to stay with him until three o'clock when I come home. I have anxiety." In Athens, female employment does not reduce women's desire to have children so much as it is the case that the infrastructure cannot accommodate the needs of mothers who work outside the home.

While middle-class urban Greeks are beginning to join other Southern Europeans in employing African, Filipina, and Albanian immigrant women as domestic workers and nannies (Anderson 2000; Lazaridis 2000), most continue to rely for childcare on the unpaid labor of family members. This arrangement suits people not only economically, but because they prefer not to have "strangers" (*kséni*, meaning non-family and/or non-Greek persons) looking after their children. Even professional women rely on the informal social institution by which grandmothers (*yiayiádhes*) in particular are available and willing to help with the social reproduction of their own children's families and thus contribute to their upward socioeconomic mobility. But with women delaying childbirth often into their thirties (the mean age of Greek women at the birth of a first child in the late 1990s was 27) the generation gap is widening, compromising couples' preferred childcare arrangements; even if grandparents are at home during the day, they may be quite elderly. The *yiayiá* institution may be waning (Symeonidou 1990: 149).

Athenians depict additional constraints impinging on parental desire as symptomatic of Greek modernity. I heard of couples, wary of bringing up children in the overpopulated, polluted city of Athens, who decided not to have kids until they can afford to move to tree-lined suburbs. Indeed, a popular explanation for national underfertility blames the pollution-filled haze that hangs over the nation's capital, which, as a symbol of the toxic side of modernity, is held responsible for a (probably exaggerated) drop in sperm counts. Nadia, who tours the city streets as a door-to-door salesperson, believes people are especially vulnerable to modern pollutants of television radiation and car exhaust because the stress (*ánchos*) of "modern life" is making people "soft". Critiquing modern technology and a pace of life for damaging humans' "nature," she sees Athenians drained of virility and fertility: "People aren't as tough as they were when they ate wild foods. And television has radiation – did you know? – which taints the potency of the person. The person has lost sex because of this culture, they don't have sex with the frequency they used to. You hear of couples who have sex every five days, every two months!" The less frequently couples make love, she concluded, the fewer children they make. Two women in their twenties also complained to me that, with people working two jobs to make ends meet, they are too tired at the end of the day to even think about having sex. No wonder, they concluded, "we have underfertility"!

Other women emphasized that maternal obligations – what it takes to be a good mother – are compounded as children are regarded as consumer projects. Galena, a grandmother in her sixties, said, "Before, the family had children to work with them, to help as hands. Now this has changed. The baby is a mouth to feed, a body to clothe. It is not hands. We change as a society, we are not as we were before. Greece now has the same problem as Europe, other developed countries." Indeed, Athenians encounter the sorts of class-inflected attitudes favoring reduced family size and more "conscious" fertility control strategies that anthropologists have identified in a variety of developing economies as important means and measures of individual and national modernity (Schneider and Schneider 1996; Kanaaneh 2002; Krause 2001; Gal and Kligman 2000; Krengel and Greifeld 2000). Social and cultural values concerning how people think about having families and raising children frame these as fiscally expensive undertakings.

Currently a mother's success is dependent not merely on bringing forth children who will inherit the family's name and assets, but on raising *successful* children – children with advanced degrees, who speak two or three languages and can succeed in a competitive job market. Education in Greece, as throughout Southern and postsocialist Eastern Europe, is superseding accumulated inheritance and business connections as the prime mover of social ascent, the securer of high status occupations (Collier 1997; Kligman 1998). Athenian parents routinely send their teenage children to *frontistíria*, private institutes offering foreign language and other classes after public school hours. Parents feel they must push their children in high school since entry into the ten fully subsidized state universities is based on competitive examinations. Many young Greeks study in Britain, Germany, the United States; foreign-trained professionals may never return, creating the "brain-drain" that contributes to Greece's demographic profile. In either case, "quality" children are produced through the acquisition of cultural capital attained through considered parental consumption.

When personal achievement comes to signal social status, reputation is largely based on how one chooses to spend money. Litsa astutely applied this to mothering, explaining that if parental obligations have always been directed at enabling children to get ahead, today Greek consumerist self-fashioning translates being a "good" mother into providing "the best" material goods for one's children, rather than, say, spending quality time with them. When others recognize that a woman chooses to spend her hard earned money on her children – to keep them in the latest fashions, to provide them with extracurriculars – this demonstrates her moral worth as a mother:

> It is very difficult to have a child – these days we are a consumer society. Earlier, when we went to school we used to wear [uniform] pinafores, one would last the year with its tears mended and patched. But now, there's this consumerism. Tomorrow my child will see someone wearing such-and-such shoes and he'll tell me, "Me too!" You'll tell me I should fix it so my kid is not interested in name brands. You'll say I don't *have* to send him to extra classes to do a foreign language – in the past we grew up in another way. I was the last child of five. What my sister would wear one year I would take the next, it didn't matter to us: we weren't bombarded by television. Of course we have done this to our lives. They put this idea into our heads but we are the ones who go and implement it. We are the consumers. Tomorrow at the supermarket we see something new, we try it, we like it – and there's the good discount – so, it's difficult.

Since the 1980s, Athenian parents have felt pressure to provide the best for their children and to produce "the best" children (see Emke-Poulopoulou 1994: 89).

Child psychologist Aliki Andoniou, the mother of a 3 year old, is critical of the consumerist drive of today's mothers: "The mistaken *noötropía* [collective mentality] of the parents predominates, that for a child to be raised properly it must wear Kickers shoes and have a lot of expensive toys. They don't understand these aren't what satisfy a child. And because of this people aren't having kids." Some professionals argue that Greek *familism* – the notion that family relations are pre-eminent social relations, that the family should be a cohesive unit, that family loyalty supersedes all others – when combined with capitalist consumption creates unrealistic expectations for proper parenting. In research among Athenian women conducted in 1989 as part of a comparative EU study into women and poverty, another psychologist I interviewed found that children's private schooling, clothing, shoes, activities are paid for by *women's* contributions to household economies. This financial provisioning represents a modern extension of the maternal responsibility women have long assumed, by which they earn credit for their children's success and character.

What Maila Stivens (1998: 63) writes of middle-class urban Malaysia speaks equally to Athens: "To be a modern mother is to be an active consumer under great pressure to acquire all the commodities necessary for the satisfactory performance of motherhood." In this context, women – and many men – agree it is better to have "one and raise it well," than to have many children and help alleviate the nation's demographic problem. Modern motherhood is foremost about the *quality* of childhood one can offer as a parent; concern for the *quantity* of children produced follows. Were policy-makers to realize this, they might be led to do more to help couples have a first or second child.

Gender and Modern Motherhood

For middle-class Athenians, the ability to provide children with optimal opportunities and material comfort requires first a responsible approach to birth control. Nadia, who has never married at age 40, said to me:

> I tell you, only the foolish ones are having children; the intelligent ones are holding off. Because *proper* persons know what a child demands. Perhaps because the Greek has undergone indigence, before and after the War – [but] back then they had children – those who have grown up now tell you, "I don't want my child to go through what I went through then, I'll have one and it will live well, not many and live in poverty."

Phoebe agrees with her age-mate Nadia that people these days have fewer children out of an appropriate sense of responsibility, which she qualifies as "maturity":

> In Greece we have a low birthrate. Why? I believe it's because things are a little difficult from the economic side. A couple thinks about when they will have a child, and wants to offer their child a good, comfortable life, meaning to have the money to be able to afford the good schools. They begin to think we can have one child only – or no children . . . This, I think up to a point, is an issue of maturity.

To explore how middle-class women go about being what Nadia calls "proper" (*sostós*) persons and demonstrating what Phoebe means by "maturity" (*orimótita*), I considered how Athenians square ideals of modern *adulthood* with notions of proper *femininity*. If women today "are less concerned with reputation in a bounded social group and more concerned with demonstrating 'modernity' in an urban setting and with establishing their own senses of personhood" (Dubisch 1993: 282, references omitted), how is this Greek modernity envisioned? And how do women reconcile this with idealized images of motherhood? In a pro-child, pronatal climate, as one woman, an unmarried physician, said to me, motherhood is something about which every woman must decide: "Deciding against motherhood is just as hard as deciding for motherhood. But it's a decision you have to make. You cannot pass through your life and forget about it. Motherhood you have to consider." What is at stake are urban Greek understandings of what it means to be a mother and a woman, and how these complement and/or complicate one another amidst a looming sense that underfertility writ large is a problem for the nation.

Lela, whose 15-month-old son is largely being brought up by her own mother and father, who live downstairs, said, "I do not think that motherhood has changed from the past. That is, the relationship between mother and child hasn't changed. What *has* changed is the position of the woman in society. Motherhood stays the same, but the woman who works doesn't sit at home and raise the kid, as happened before." In many families the burden of accumulated demands from today's fast-paced world is landing in the lap of those who remain at home: grandparents. Maro, a 38-year-old unmarried dentist who spent much of her adult life trying to move away from her parents, sees this as a problem:

> Because the economic situation is difficult, kids have returned to the family . . . They have a child and leave it with their parents, then take it home for the weekend. The mothers are hanging over them and for I don't know how many it's becoming the same family bond. That is, the mothers are mothering again for their daughters' children. "Since [her] Mother will cook anyway it's better, we are spared from fatigue, hardship, and a few minutes." That's the mentality [*noötropía*]. [A woman's mother, the grand-mother] puts in two casseroles instead of putting in one casserole and she's willing!

Maro is suspicious of younger women's willingness to rely on their mothers' domestic labor, just as she judges the complicity of older women willing to mother again for the next generation. The "modern," wage-earning mother, Maro points out, requires quite "traditional" forms of support, even dependence. "The child of my child is two times my child," an old saying goes, or, as another woman said, "The grandmother is like twice mother." But this is one tradition Maro would like to see left in the past:

> I see that we are turning back with this. I believe one takes a step forward as one arranges one's life on one's own and faces it on one's own. You want to have a child, you assume the responsibilities of having a child; you work, you assume the responsi-bilities of working. I consider it to be a step ahead to stand up in one's life . . . to have it in one's own hands. I think anymore there's a step backwards in this.

For Maro, the modern woman should conduct her life without heavily relying on her natal family, and she should be accountable for her own actions. This sounds similar to the logic of politicians wanting to rely on women's reproductive responsibility and personal choice to solve the demographic problem. The differences are that Maro wants the state to offer more comprehensive social services to enable individuals to realize their goals, and for her, increasing the nation's demographic numbers is insufficient reason to have a child. Indeed, Maro is one of only two women I encountered who described themselves as having consciously decided *not* to become mothers. Bowing to others' expectations that women *should*, by all means, for whatever reasons, become mothers would be to "take another step back" from the kind of modern society that might, potentially, offer women more of a say in their lives.

Maro is the exception. Most Athenian women aspire to motherhood. For them, what relationship, if any, obtains between personal and national underfertility? My friend Phoebe divorced a few years before I met her. She never gave birth during eight years of marriage because she and her former husband "couldn't communicate. I thought about what a problem it would be if we tried to raise a child together and so I decided not to have a child, consciously." Prior to her present administrative position, Phoebe held a variety of office jobs and owned a clothing boutique in the neighborhood. I knew Phoebe as an energetic woman who dressed fashionably, spoke French and English, and enjoyed her work. Aside from the fact that her 30-something brother had moved into her one-bedroom flat after a girlfriend broke up with him, to me Phoebe seemed, like Maro, to be a "modern" woman with independent sensibilities. It was somewhat of a surprise to me when – early in my research – Phoebe described feeling something missing from her life: "I believe that with having a child comes as well the fulfillment of the woman . . . The woman is completed having a child." "Of course" she would like to have children.

I continued to meet middle-class women – single, married, divorced, with and without children – who echoed Phoebe's assurance that motherhood "completes a woman." Weeks after this conversation with Phoebe I met Maro's sister, Niki, and their 70-year-old mother, Maria. Affirming her mother's announcement that "all women want to become mothers," 35-year-old Niki, who had worked in insurance but was then unemployed, explained that while often "there are economic problems so they decide not to do it, I believe that all women want to become mothers. How can I tell you? It completes them [*tis oloklíroni*]." I pressed Niki, who was married and childless, "But you are a woman now, you don't feel complete?" "No," she replied. "I do not feel complete, how do you say? Full [*yemáti*]. Simply, the child is a mission [*proörismós*], a goal [*skopós*]. That you have formed a new life . . . I consider that this is the goal of the woman. Not only this. It's not the only thing, of course." Talking with Daphne, an unmarried high school teacher and feminist in her early thirties, helped me to recognize the significance of Niki's concluding sentence:

For my mother's generation . . . becoming a mother was the purpose of a woman's life. But for women my age or maybe younger – the *modern* woman, let's say – they work and they have a social life and they are involved with different activities. Maternity is something that could make you a *whole* woman . . . I think especially here in Athens, in the cities, they accept you if you don't have a child, but they admire you more, they accept you more if you are a working woman and you have your husband, your family, your house, *and* your children.

I came to discern a subtle yet crucial distinction between viewing motherhood as that which gives single-minded "purpose" to a woman's life – a view many now relegate to past generations – and the modern woman's attitude that motherhood is a virtuous goal which she works to achieve while engaged in other social roles and commitments.

In regarding motherhood as an achievement, Athenian women are well aware that their own goals for having children are not automatically obtainable. I was struck by how pragmatically these women regard the limits of choice. I was impressed by the political-economic perspective they brought to bear on obstacles they personally faced, and a bit envious of how many seem able to shrug off feelings of inadequacy for "failing" to meet their own and others' expectations. These women know of Greece's *ipoyenitikótita* (underfertility). They shake their heads in dismay that they live in a "country of aged people." The ideal that people should have bigger families "stays in the air," a friend told me.

Incessantly one hears in Greece the refrain, "What can I do?" (*ti na káno*). Anthropologists (e.g. du Boulay 1974: 95) have interpreted this as a move to avoid responsibility for an act whose outcome is attributed to the whims of *tíchi*, chance. Greeks appeal to a sense of fate (*míra*) to carry on in a world not under their control. They do not act because it is their fate to do so; rather, fate – which in modern settings can be shorthand for the emotional, moral, material factors impinging on (supposedly) otherwise rational action – allows them to cope with events that do not accord with their ideals. In addition, appeals to fate permit actors to manipulate circumstances behind the scrim of public scrutiny without upsetting dominant ideological order.

I heard Athenians utter the phrases "What can I do?" or "What can one do?" to accompany actions that do not meet social, often gendered, ideals such as delaying marriage or neglecting to have children. Economic trouble can serve as an alibi for choosing not to have children: "What can I do?" Couples who for physiological reasons cannot procreate, as well as others who may not want children, can hide what might be viewed as moral/character deficiency under the alibi of material scarcity. At the same time, when economic crisis is the most common justification Athenians offer for the country's low birthrate, women and men who nevertheless manage to have children are able to spin for themselves tales of heroic achievement and self-sacrifice. Mothers are exemplary women.

In a pronatal climate, childless women can call upon essentialized notions of maternal nature to portray themselves as proper women. For Phoebe, who decided not to bring a child into a tension-filled marriage, the realization of woman's maternal nature does not require childbirth: "I believe that within a woman exist feelings of motherhood. You will see this even in women who haven't had a child; it comes out in their behavior towards an animal, a dog, or a cat. It's a special behavior that seems somewhat like the feeling of motherhood." It is no coincidence to another middle-aged woman that she, after suffering four miscarriages and never having a child, has devoted her adult life to teaching school children. If "motherhood completes a woman," as both of these women said to me, the fact that "motherhood" is inside them anyway lets them off the hook for failing to produce children by this point in their lives.

The statement "motherhood completes a woman" mediates contradictions between a modern woman's ideal expectations for being a woman (which should include being a mother) and her lived reality as a woman (with or without children). It may be paradoxical but it is *not* inconsistent that 35-year-old Niki, after insisting that she is "not complete as a woman" shrugged off her childlessness by concluding, "What can I do?" By expressing a supposedly natural desire that all women (should) wish to become mothers they signal moral approval of motherhood, and in so doing are, to borrow from Michael Herzfeld (1985), both "being good at being" women and are being "good" women.

The notion that motherhood completes a woman also signals that reproduction is valued for *creating mothers*. Birthing and raising just one child is sufficient to transform a woman into a mother. This sort of reproductive arithmetic does not add up to population replacement. Then again, neither does it signal any lack of maternal sentiment, nor weakening of family values. Middle-class Athenian women want to be mothers to feel complete, but they do not want their social identities to be defined exclusively by motherhood. Nationalist politicians, wanting women to return to traditionally large families, have largely failed to recognize this.

Ethnicity and the Demographic Problem

When I asked women what the state offered by way of family support that might help them have additional children, children many profess to want, most replied with some version of, "the state does nothing." But Eleni, a publisher and mother of three grown children, responded further that the government, in reducing demographic concerns to questions of reproduction, sidesteps politically contentious issues of immigration. In the mid-1990s, Greek residents routinely witnessed on television thousands of Albanians – undocumented, destitute – corralled in shipyard warehouses outside Athens to await being packed onto military buses, driven north, and dumped at the border. Sensing my interest in her concern over escalating violence between residents and refugees, Eleni told me she was a member of a feminist group, the Greek Chapter of the European Forum of Left Feminists, who, directly motivated by the 1993 parliamentary demographic report mentioned above, were planning a public meeting on "Nationalism, Racism and Gender." "They're coming over tonight," she remarked. "Would you like to stay?" I positioned myself by the open window to watch this non-academic, well-read group of middle-class, age-diverse feminists assemble under a burgeoning cloud of cigarette smoke.

At this and subsequent meetings of the Forum of Left Feminists I attended in early 1994, activists discussed how the country's demographic situation constitutes a problem *not* because women are birthing fewer children, but because the nation-state and ideals for citizenship are conceived through racism and sexism (Anthias and Yuval-Davis 1992). A conflation of *ethnicity* and *national identity*, common throughout Europe, is promoted in Greece by the linguistic misfortune that these two distinct political concepts are subsumed under the same term, *ethnitikótita*. The adjective *ethnikós* refers to both national (citizenship) and ethnic (language, custom, religion) criteria. The 1993 parliamentary report (I received a photocopy from one of the forum members) acknowledged that successful repatriation of political refugees and the mass arrival of ethnic Greeks leaving homelands in southern Albania and the Pontus region of the Black Sea could have a "positive effect" on the Greek demographic situation: "Common cultural roots and Orthodox Christianity help greatly in their adaptation to and assimilation into Greek society" (Parliament of Greece 1993: 15). Nearly 15 percent of immigrants entering Greece in the 1990s are of Greek origin from Black Sea areas of the former Soviet Union (Bagavos 2001: 4).

Forum members are critical of an exclusionary, essentialist ideology consistent with Greek ethnic nationalism (opposed to civic nationalism based on shared principles or beliefs). Greeks often refer to their own ethnic population in positive terms as the Greek race (*i ellenikí filí*) (on metaphors of blood in Greek nationalism, see Just 1989; Herzfeld 1992). The parliamentary report claims that "other" immigrants, "chiefly Muslims from Afro-Asiatic countries ... create serious socio-economic problems" because "they cannot adapt to Greek society because of the completely different culture of Islam, which is not only a religion but a way of life" (Parliament of Greece 1993: 15). Nevertheless, forum members noted, "other" (non-Greek) immigrants fill an important role in the economy, taking up the lowest paying jobs Greeks disdain. Greeks favor Filipinas as domestics and nannies; as Catholic Christians, they are seen as "less other" than Islamic Africans or Albanians (Lazaridis 2000).

In a collectively written 1993 newspaper article, the Forum of Left Feminists challenged Parliamentarians, charging that their "report's direct incitement, that we should birth children in order to replace the economic migrants with a pure national labor force, is racist [*ratsistikí*], when a migration policy that would include the equal recognition of foreign migrants in Greek society with the same rights and obligations would be able – according to the logic of the authors of the report – to invigorate our country demographically" (Evropaïkó Forum 1993: 44). They argued, in other words, that if all immigrants were accommodated and welcomed, rather than excluded and mistrusted, they could solve many facets of Greece's demographic "problem" concerning labor and national defense. Reluctance to do so suggests that political concern is not about sheer numbers of the population, but about the future of "Greekness."

Acknowledging that racisms are specific to national and social context, these women argued that social and economic class divisions exacerbate racism against even Greek immigrants. While Greeks descended from merchant families in Cairo or Constantinople (Istanbul) tend to be wealthier and better educated than the average indigenous Greek and are visible participants in Greek society, Pontic Greeks from the Black Sea are poor, from rural backgrounds, and join the working-class ghettos established by Greek refuges from Asia Minor in the 1920s following a mandated exchange of populations between Greece and Turkey. At one meeting, a woman mentioned how common it is to hear Greeks identify individuals as "Albanian" by how dirty and ill-clothed they appear (see Seremetakis 1996: 489). Several generations ago things were different, forum members recalled. Because ethnic Greek and Slavic families migrating from Albania and other Balkan areas, particularly after the northern expansion of Greek national territory following the 1912–1913 Balkans War, came to settle in villages throughout the country they "became like natives" and were accepted (Seremetakis 1991; Panourgia 1995). Since the 1980s, most Slavic migrants, men outnumbering women, have come to Greece hoping to move on to America and view their labor and life in Greece as temporary. People today are thus more conscious of ethnic difference, the women speculated. Albanians have become the scapegoats for the ills of modern Greek society, blamed for crime, harassment, a drop in wealthy tourists (Panourgia 1995). The parliamentary report baldly states, "The demographic aging of the population leads to social decline with the weakening and degeneration of many institutions (family-child-motherhood), and with the appearance of the socially weak [immigrants] there is an elevation of criminality, narcotics and acts of arbitrary violence in general" (Parliament of Greece 1993: 32). Foreign immigrants are blamed for rising crime, drug abuse and violence that alternatively could be viewed as endemic to urbanization and a weak economy. In the terms of Omi and Winant (1994: 56), this is a racial formation, in which "race is a matter of both social structure and cultural representation."

In their meetings, forum members further addressed how gender and sexuality are enlisted as a technique of racism and nationalism. When the category of race or ethnicity delimits a nation's or a people's "own" women from "others," Eleni noted, racism is used to exploit women sexually. This, they agreed, is because women are figured in the parliamentary report and elsewhere as passive symbols of the nation (Anthias and Yuval-Davis 1992; Gal and Kligman 2000). The group discussed the systematic rape of Bosnian Muslim women by Serbian soldiers as a weapon of ethnic cleansing in the early 1990s, an act of defiling not only individual women, but also the nation for which they stand – and of cuckolding their symbolic husbands, Bosnian soldiers (Mostov 1995; Allen 1996; Gal and Kligman 2000). In Greece, the word for prostitutes, *pórnes*, is often synonymous with *Póntes*, or women from the Pontus region. *Smirniári*, or "woman from Smyrna," is another slang expression for "whore." Smyrna (now Izmir) is a city on the Aegean coast of Turkey whose Greek-speaking Christian population was relocated to the Athens area following the 1919–1922 Greek–Turkey War.

Women continue to be called upon by states to serve as the symbolic "bearers" of nations (Anthias and Yuval-Davis 1989). Quantitatively, women have been responsible, and frequently commended, for birthing new citizens and workers (Kligman 1998; Krengel and Greifeld 2000: 205; Kanaaneh 2002); hence, the Greek state pays modest pensions to mothers of four or more children (Paxson 1997). Qualitatively, women's nurturance and domestic labor "civilizes" nationally/ethnically identified children. Demographic calculations (how many children – and abortions – do women have?) codify a national identity that is born of women. When the strength of the nation-state is measured in terms of fecundity, as it is when demographics are reduced to fertility rates, a fertile *Ellas* (Greece) can be represented by – as it depends on – the fertile *ellinídha*, Greek woman. And when women are made responsible for reproductive practices, they are often held personally accountable for all accidents, errors, and failures to meet rational ideals (Tsing 1990; Gal and Kligman 2000). The demographic condition of a nation-state can be thus viewed, mistakenly, as the country's "woman problem" – the problem of a "barren state."

Conclusion: Rethinking "Barren" States and Population "Implosions"

Applying to Greece the notion of a "barren state," as journalists and nationalist politicians have done, is triply problematic. First, it overestimates the power of personal desire or choice in effecting behavior. Second, it feminizes reproductive responsibility and naturalizes women's maternal citizenship. Third, it reduces demographics to reproduction – skirting the xenophobia underlying migration issues. Greek Parliament members, nearly 95 percent of whom are men, overemphasize the centrality of women to reproductive practices in holding women's attitudes ultimately accountable for reproductive outcome, to the neglect of economic constraints, lack of childcare provisions, and the role of men (e.g. Gabriel, Chapter

4 in this volume). Moreover, the notion of a "barren state" as applied to Greece obscures a continuing and real maternalism that lays claim to even the most modern of women's desires and sense of womanhood, and it obfuscates the racial economy of demographics.

It is similarly instructive to question, as does Elizabeth L. Krause (Chapter 8 in this volume), the semantics of "population implosion." Implosion is an interesting metaphor, suggesting forces leading to a "violent compression" or "a collapse inward as if from external pressure." What might such forces be? Greek authors of the parliamentary demographic report suggest cultural forces, including a non-rational tradition that keeps women having abortions as well as a modernity that directs women away from producing large families. But it is precisely such a view, what Susan Greenhalgh (1995: 7) refers to as an "ideational" account of demographic forces, that overlooks the class, gender and ethnic formations that shape everyday experience. When we look at *these* forces there is no self-evident implosion. Take class: implosion exists only when reproduction is figured as a means of production, while Athenians themselves view it in terms of consumption. Gender: implosion, based on a quantitative view of Greek maternalism harnessed to pronatalism, exists only when motherhood is viewed as an exclusive identity (the idea that once a woman becomes a mother she may as well have several children), rather than as a personal achievement attained alongside other goals, and one reached with the birth of just one child. Race/ethnic nationalism: population implosion exists only when one imagines the reproduction – *replacement* in demographic argot – of a discrete kind of person.

To speak of implosion, then, is to entertain an ahistorical view of family, motherhood, and reproduction. It is a view that neglects a key feature of reproduction: as Marilyn Strathern writes, "the ideas that reproduce themselves in our communications *never reproduce themselves exactly*. They are always found in environments or contexts that have their own properties or characteristics" (Strathern 1992: 6, emphasis in original). And, as Kath Weston (2002) argues in *Gender in Real Time*, constructions of femininity and masculinity transform over time in response to these environments: one generation's view of womanhood and motherhood is not the same as another's. The implosion metaphor ignores the forward motion of time, leaning instead on a vision of reversed time, or what Athena Athanasiou (1999) calls "timeless time." At stake are meanings of womanhood, motherhood, Greekness. If dominant demographic discourse is ahistorical, everyday Athenian conversations are often explicitly historical. Middle-class urban Greeks elucidate both change and continuity between past and present, blurring distinctions between tradition and modernity, in narrating for themselves – and for their nation – considered, virtuous reproductive histories.

While calls to attend to the nation's underfertility have not significantly affected Athenians' reproductive behavior, they *have* pressed women to explain to others, if not also to themselves, why they have fewer children than they might like. Alarmist cries over Greece's "demographic problem" highlight women's self-consciousness about reproductive decision-making within socio-economic constraints. Middle-class women's sense that they must think hard about having children is significant because it at once *follows* the appropriately modern, rational model of the state-supported family planning imperative that couples should consciously prepare for children, yet *challenges* the assumption that this is simply a choice to be made, based on personal desire and/or appreciation of traditional values. These women's narratives call to mind Rayna Rapp's observation that the "individualism implied in the concept of choice" masks the "the structured situations over which individuals have very little control, but within which they regularly operate and compose their lives" (Rapp 1999: 226–227). By taking seriously these structured economic, social and cultural situations, well articulated by women I interviewed, I hope to convey an understanding of demographic conditions that begins from the complicated, relational and historically meaningful lives of people – parents, grandparents, aspiring parents, the happily childfree – rather than rationalized members of populations.

Acknowledgment

Many thanks to Carrie B. Douglass, Gail Kligman and Stefan Helmreich for their helpful suggestions regarding this chapter's organization and revision.

References

Allen, B. (1996), *Rape Warfare: The Hidden Genocide in Bosnia-Herzegovina and Croatia*, Minneapolis, MN: University of Minnesota Press.

Anderson, B. (2000), *Doing the Dirty Work? The Global Politics of Domestic Labour*, London: Zed Books.

Anthias, F. and Yuval-Davis, N. (eds) (1989), *Woman-Nation-State*, New York: St Martin's Press.

—— (1992), *Racialized Boundaries: Race, Nation, Gender, Colour and Class and the Anti-Racist Struggle*, London: Routledge.

Athanasiou, A. (1999), "Crafting Timeless Time: The Quest for Future in Constructions of Demographic Dystopias," paper presented at the 98th Annual Meeting of the American Anthropological Association, Chicago, IL.

Bagavos, C. (2001), "The Situation of Families in Greece, 2001," prepared for the European Observatory on the Social Situation, Demography and Family of the European Union, European Communities, 1995–2001.

Collier, J. (1997), *From Duty to Desire: Remaking Families in a Spanish Village*, Princeton, NJ: Princeton University Press.

Council of Europe (2001), *Demographic Yearbook, 2001*, Strasbourg: Council of Europe.

Dubisch, J. (1993), "'Foreign Chickens' and Other Outsiders: Gender and Community in Greece," *American Ethnologist*, 20(2): 272–87.

du Boulay, J. (1974), *Portrait of a Greek Mountain Village*, Oxford: Clarendon Press.

Emke-Poulopoulou, I. (1994), *To dhimoghrafikó* [Demographics], Athina: Ellin.

Evropaïkó Forum Aristerón Feministrión (Ellinikó Tmíma) [European Forum of Left Feminists, Greek Chapter] (1993), "Dhimoghrafikó: I yinékes ke páli énohes [Demographics: women are again to blame]," *Eleftherotipía*, December 12: 44.

Gal, S. and Kligman, G. (2000), *The Politics of Gender after Socialism*, Princeton, NJ: Princeton University Press.

Greenhalgh, S. (1995), "Anthropology Theorizes Reproduction: Integrating Practice, Political Economic, and Feminist Perspectives," in S. Greenhalgh (ed.), *Situating Fertility: Anthropology and Demographic Inquiry*, Cambridge: Cambridge University Press.

Halkias, A. (1998), "Give Birth for Greece! Abortion and Nation in Letters to the Editor of the Mainstream Greek Press," *Journal of Modern Greek Studies*, 16(1): 111–138.

Herzfeld, M. (1985), *The Poetics of Manhood: Contest and Identity in a Cretan Mountain Village*, Princeton, NJ: Princeton University Press.

—— (1992), *The Social Production of Indifference: Exploring the Symbolic Roots of Western Bureaucracy*, Chicago: University of Chicago Press.

Just, R. (1989), "Triumph of the Ethnos," in E. Tonkin, M. Capman and M. McDonald (eds), *History and Ethnicity*, London: Routledge.

Kanaaneh, R. (2002), *Birthing the Nation: Strategies of Palestinian Women in Israel*, Berkeley, CA: University of California Press.

Kligman, G. (1998), *The Politics of Duplicity: Controlling Reproduction in Ceausescu's Romania*, Berkeley, CA: University of California Press.

Krause, E.L. (2001), "'Empty Cradles' and the Quiet Revolution: Demographic Discourse and Cultural Struggles of Gender, Race, and Class in Italy," *Cultural Anthropology*, 16(4): 576–611.

Krengel, M. and Greifeld, K. (2000), "Uzbekistan in Transition – Changing Concepts in Family Planning and Reproductive Health," in A. Russell, E.J. Sobo and M.S. Thompson (eds), *Contraception across Cultures: Technologies, Choices, Constraints*, Oxford: Berg.

Lazaridis, G. (2000), "Filipino and Albanian Women Migrant Workers in Greece: Multiple Layers of Oppression," in F. Anthias and G. Lazaridis (eds), *Gender and Migration in Southern Europe: Women on the Move*, Oxford: Berg.

Margaritidou, V. and Mesteneos, E. (1992), "The Family Planning Centers in

Greece," *International Journal of Health Sciences*, 3(1): 25–31.

Mostov, J. (1995), "'Our Women'/'Their Women': Symbolic Boundaries, Territorial Murders and Violence in the Balkans," *Peace and Change*, 20(4): 515–529.

National Statistical Service of Greece (NSSG) (1992), *Statistical Yearbook of Greece, 1989*, Athens: NSSG.

—— (2002), *Greece in Figures, 2002*, Athens: NSSG.

Omi, M. and Winant, H. (1994), *Racial Formation in the United States: From the 1960s to the 1990s*, 2nd edn, New York: Routledge.

Panourgia, N. (1995), *Fragments of Death, Fables of Identity: an Athenian Anthropography*, Madison, WI: University of Wisconsin Press.

Papadopoulos, T.N. (1998), "Greek Family Policy from a Comparative Perspective," in E. Drew, R. Emerek and E. Mahon (eds), *Women, Work and the Family in Europe*, London: Routledge.

Parliament of Greece (1993), *Pórisma, Yia ti Meléti tou Dhimoghrafikoú Provlímatos tis Hóras ke Dhiatíposi Protáseon yia tin Apotelesmatikí Antimetopisí tou* [Findings, for the Study of the Demographic Problem of the Country and the Formulation of Recommendations for its Effective Confrontation], Athens: Parliament of Greece.

Paxson, H. (1997), "Demographics and Diaspora, Gender and Genealogy: Anthropological Notes on Greek Population Policy," *South European Society and Politics*, 2(2): 34–56.

—— (2004), *Making Modern Mothers: Ethics and Family Planning in Urban Greece*, Berkeley, CA: University of California Press.

Rapp, R. (1999), *Testing Women, Testing the Fetus: The Social Impact of Amniocentesi in America*, New York: Routledge.

Schneider, J. and Schneider, P. (1995), "Coitus Interruptus and Family Respectability in Catholic Europe," in F. Ginsburg and R. Rapp (eds), *Conceiving the New World Order: The Global Politics of Reproduction*, Berkeley, CA: University of California Press.

Seremetakis, N. (1991), *The Last Word: Women, Death, and Divination in Inner Mani*, Chicago: University of Chicago Press.

—— (1996), "In Search of the Barbarians: Borders in Pain," *American Anthropologist*, 98(3): 487–511.

Stivens, M. (1998), "Modernizing the Malay Mother," in K. Ram and M. Jolly (eds), *Maternities and Modernities: Colonial and Postcolonial Experiences in Asia and the Pacific*, Cambridge: Cambridge University Press.

Strathern, M. (1992), *Reproducing the Future: Anthropology, Kinship, and the New Reproductive Technologies*, New York: Routledge.

Symeonidou, H. (1990), *Apaskhólisi ke ghonimótita ton yinekón stin periohí tis protévousas* [Occupation and fertility of women in greater Athens], Athens:

Ethnikó Kéndro Kinonikón Erevnón.

Tsing, A.L. (1990), "Monster Stories," in A. Tsing and F. Ginsburg (eds), *Uncertain Terms: Negotiating Gender in America*, Boston, MA: Beacon Press.

Vaiou, D. (1992), "Gender Divisions in Urban Space: Beyond the Rigidity of Dualist Classifications," *Antipode*, 24(4): 247–62.

Valaoras, V. and Trichopoulos, D. (1970), "Abortion in Greece," in R.E. Hall (ed.), *Abortion in a Changing World*, vol. 1, New York: Columbia University Press.

Weston, K. (2002), *Gender in Real Time: Power and Transience in a Visual Age*, New York: Routledge.

–8–

"Toys and Perfumes": Imploding Italy's Population Paradox and Motherly Myths

Elizabeth L. Krause

The dominant assumption in Europe is that low fertility is a serious problem. My work challenges the common alarmist framings of contemporary demographic trends, specifically those that depict as an illness the fertility rate of Italian women, which at 1.2 is among the lowest in the world. Rayna Rapp (1999: 317) has observed: "Reproduction lies at the heart of a culture's representations of itself." As such, those of us studying topics linked to reproduction are historians of the present. What are the symbolic as well as material consequences of population politics? What kind of histories are demographers constructing and are social scientists reproducing in people's understandings of themselves and of the world when they/we depict populations as imploding? Furthermore, what does such language conceal?

Implode means "to burst inward"; it implies serious breakage. Consider this example: "when a vacuum tube breaks it implodes" (*Webster's Third New International Dictionary*). To be able to burst inward requires an outside. It requires fixed boundaries; nations and the European Union both have fixed boundaries – or, at least, controlled boundaries subject to surveillance as well as to policy. No wonder this language of implosion "makes sense."

To use the term "implode" in the context of population dynamics implies serious disruption, serious threat. It implies that something is deeply wrong.[1] Indeed, such phrases fuel fears and entice imaginings of a dying nation. The constant referent is the falling birthrate. This discourse of national decay is "a recurrent theme of nationalist discourse all over Europe" and masks as well as legitimizes other political agendas, including broad moralization processes, as Gal and Kligman (2000: 27, 29–31) point out. Such linguistic constructions pave the way for a fortress Europe in which xenophobia and racism become the order of the day (see Krause 2001: 594–598; 2005), in which aspirations of middle-class status seem inevitable, and in which rigid gender roles appear natural.

Headlines speak of "demographic desertification," of a nation that "is old and without babies," of "a crisis of births." Media reports on population trends in Italy juxtapose "empty cradles" with a growing "immigrant supply,"[2] encouraging a mood of anxiety toward non-European newcomers. Prominent Italian demographers in a recent book *Il malessere demografico in Italia* (*The Demographic Malaise in Italy*), draw on a metaphor usually reserved for bodily health. As such, the term malaise implies that the national social body is suffering from an illness. A demographic trend has become a national pathology. Indeed, some demographers speak of an "excess" of low fertility and the pending "deformations" in the age structure (Golini, Mussino and Savioli 2000: 7, 98). They ponder the dangers that transmogrified generational rapports may pose to "adequate social cohesion" (p. 99). The Pope has also contributed to the clamor. During a historic and controversial address to the Italian Parliament, he spoke about the "crisis of births" as a "*grave minaccia* – serious threat" that weighs on the future of Italy (Drioli 2002: 3). Such forecasts ooze with assumptions about what a normal, healthy society looks like, one based on a same-sex nuclear family with "rational" parents who, if all were well, would procreate two children.

Italy has received a good deal of attention in the mainstream US press. A *New York Times* article entitled "Population Implosion Worries a Graying Europe" framed low fertility as an "epidemic." The reporter located the etiology of this epidemic in women's practice of "choosing work and education over having children" (Specter 1998). The article invoked disaster as it described birthrates in many countries as being "in a rapid, sustained decline. Never before – except in times of plague, war and deep economic depression – have birthrates fallen so low, for so long." Another *New York Times* reporter characterized the situation as an "increasingly worrisome reality"; he visited a playground in Ferrara, Italy, filled with children and adoring parents, yet described there being "something wrong with the picture. Most of the parents were gazing at one, and only one, child" (Bruni 2002).

A sensibility of alarm spreads out across a terrain of uncertainty as it feeds into a politics of cultural struggle. The principle "fall guys" of this struggle, it turns out, are Italians of child-bearing age. A dominant framing of the problem suggests those men and, in particular, women are irrational family-makers (Golini 1991, 1994; Golini, De Simoni and Citoni 1995; Livi-Bacci 1994, Lori, Golini and Cantalini 1995; Volpi 1996). Another framing suggests that the perceived costs of having a child far outweigh the benefits, both in economic and non-economic terms, and hence having a child represents a lapse in rationality (Mazzuco and Ongaro 2003). One of Italy's most prominent demographers has even asked whether Italians' "hard refusal" to procreate might be similar to anorexic teenagers' refusal to eat food (Livi-Bacci 1994: 14). Without naming women, women are implicated.[3]

Rational family-makers would produce at least 1.7 children, according to a scenario that prominent Italian demographer Antonio Golini and his colleagues have proposed. This is still below so-called replacement level of 2.1 children, but it assumes some immigration. Golini *et al.* (2000: 102–103) view increases in Italian birthrates as crucial for creating a viable and hence "normal" population structure in the future.[4] To arrive at their scenario would require bucking the one-child family norm. A lot more women would have two and three children, and a whole lot fewer would have zero or one child. The most significant change would rest on those women without children: a decrease from the current estimates of 23 percent to 14 percent. Another large proportion of women – those with three children – would have to rise from the current 13 percent to 21 percent. I have argued elsewhere that the construction of the current low birthrate in Italy as a major population problem results in a sort of sneaky pronatalism. My ongoing research on this topic has revealed a move toward overt pronatalism complete with declarations and national family policies.

Fertility decline finds its roots in the nineteenth century. The regions with the earliest and most rapid decline were in the northern and central provinces of Piedmont, Liguria and Tuscany. By 1910–12, these regions had registered a decline in marital fertility of 25 percent, and they maintained the lowest rates through 1960–1962, according to Massimo Livi-Bacci (1977: 68). This aggregate work at the regional level tended to obscure important variations internal to a population, and the landmark study of Jane Schneider and Peter Schneider (1996) revealed the importance of class-based ideologies and practices for the timing of fertility decline. In Sicily, the gentry class began valuing and having small families at the end of the nineteenth century, the artisan class embraced a small-family ideology in the 1930s, and the peasant classes did so in the 1950s – all strategies to realize "respectability" (Schneider and Schneider 1991). Large to small families meant going from having between five and thirteen children before the first demographic transition to "two or, at most, three" thereafter (Schneider and Schneider 1992; 160; see Alter 1992, Kertzer 1993). By 1975, Italy's so-called "period" total fertility rate was 2.21 (Figure 8.1). In 1980, it had fallen to 1.64. By 1990, Italian women's fertility rate of 1.31 was reported along with that of Spanish women (1.39) to be "the lowest in the world" (Delgado Pérez and Livi-Bacci 1992). The trend took the public by surprise as both of these countries were thought to be Catholic and family centered, as well as relatively more patriarchal and less "feminist" than their northern counterparts.

Concern over declining fertility rates in Italy dates to the 1920s, when the dictator Mussolini promoted a demographic campaign that encouraged women to have numerous offspring to create a more populous and powerful nation as well as to populate Italy's colonies in Africa. The fascist demographic policy was overtly pronatalist: taxing bachelors, awarding prolific mothers, outlawing abortion,

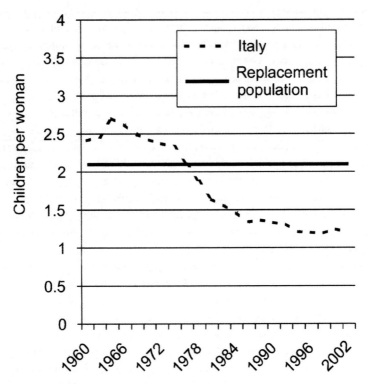

Figure 8.1 Total Fertility Rate, Italy, 1960–2002.
Source: Eurostat, Population and Social Conditions, Demography, Fertility Indicators, January 29, 2003.

banning contraceptives, restricting women's access to work. Ultimately, the campaign failed, as collectors of vital statistics continued to register a fall in the birthrates of Italian women between 1922 and 1944, the duration of the fascist regime (see de Grazia 1992; Krause 1994; Passerini 1987).

Demographers now seek to distance themselves from the overt pronatalism of the fascist years. They claim their primary concern has to do with a "deforming" population age structure and the social as well as economic challenges this may pose to society. Currently, of the 57 million Italians, 47.9 percent are between 15 and 49 years old, whereas 23.4 percent are over 60. Demographers forecast that by 2050, the Italian population will have declined to 38.2 million with 30 percent between 14 and 49 and 46 percent over 60. This is still a far cry from the most demographically "ill" localities whose age structures form an inverted pyramid (Golini *et al.* 2000: 31, 99). Population decline is common in the history of isolated areas. Witness, for example, the long history of "social malaise" and "hard life" as reflected in traumatic levels of emigration and trafficking in women wet-nurses (see in particular Dadà 1999).

This chapter draws attention to a particular moralizing effect of alarmist discourses. I seek to reveal what these strategies conceal with their heightened sense of the low birthrate as a problem. Such alarmist frames pressure women to procreate. I am not suggesting that women will give in to these pressures. But unlike the overt fascist campaign, which women and men largely resisted, this one is much more insidious. The clamoring over low fertility obscures the cultural expectations that prevent women from having on average more than one child – or from even daring to embark upon motherhood. The implosion-type stories conceal a major reason, I believe, that Italian women refrain from having the number of children that population scientists would deem "rational." In part, Italian mothers have on average one child not because juggling work with family has led them to "give up" on children, as is commonly implied.[5] Rather, a so-called culture of responsibility dictates a specific and intense set of expectations for Italian mothers (Saraceno 1996: 143–148). The *doveri di madre*, or motherly obligations, result from cultural struggles that connect with gender, class as well as ethnicity and "race." These struggles have become deeply connected to Italy's population paradox: while much of the world continues to worry about overpopulation, Italy and much of Europe ponder predictions of population decline.

Of Fieldwork, Women's Work and Family-making

I conducted ethnographic fieldwork in Tuscany, a region of central Italy described as having "broad and diffuse demographic malaise" (Golini *et al.* 2000: 225). I lived and worked in the Province of Prato for 22 months from October 1995 to August 1997, and returned there in June 1999 as well as in November 2002. The towns where I engaged in participant observation had a long history of integrated agriculture and industrial work.

For more than six months in 1996, during my second year of fieldwork, I toiled as an apprentice making sweaters. Tuscany's sweater industry was dominated by small to medium-sized family firms, and I believed locating myself in this sector would be a useful way to get a handle on the cultural politics of family-making there.

A politically active woman whom I call Carolina helped me secure my first apprenticeship. I worked for no pay (since I had a research grant) in a family-run sweater factory that made and sold high-end men's sweaters. After a couple of months, tensions resulted from my co-workers' view that their boss was exploiting me. I shared my problems with Carolina, and she offered a solution: come work for her. I accepted her invitation and assumed my station next to Carolina and her husband, a retired state employee, in their family-finishing firm. They subcontracted with several larger *maglifici*, or sweater companies, in the industrial district of Prato. Our job was to finish the sweaters with buttons and buttonholes. A room of the house was designated for this intensive labor. I received a small hourly wage and, in addition, a delicious hot meal, which contrary to the gendered division of labor in most Italian households, Carolina's husband prepared daily. Perhaps it was one victory in Carolina's ongoing struggle to create a democratic household.

The Province of Prato is significant as a research site for examining fertility dynamics for several reasons. First, it exists within Tuscany, a region where the average number of children per woman was 1.0 as of 1995. Second, Prato is not demographically extreme in terms of its age structure and hence in this respect represents a practical case study. The textile-based economy of Prato and its environs has made for a rather dynamic demographic context relative to isolated towns. In the 1950s and 1960s, peasants from the South and from Tuscany's hinterlands were drawn to the area's booming industry. Since the early 1990s, the area has attracted immigrants from outside Europe, the largest group being from China, and in 2002 Chinese women's births accounted for 11 percent of the total in the hospital of Prato.[6] The vibrant economy along with the immigrant population make for a less demographically "compromised" area, hence with only "moderate malaise," as Golini and his colleagues describe it (Golini *et al.* 2000: 225). Third, the Province of Prato itself consists of a territory where women have historically been workers in the global economy and hence issues of women's work have long been, and continue to be, of central concern and import.[7] The popular press and demographic experts often frame Italian women's participation in the labor force as new. Indeed, Delgado Pérez and Livi-Bacci (1992) hypothesized that the "massive entry" of Italian as well as Spanish women into the paid workforce in the 1970s was a primary force behind recent sharp declines in average births per woman. Such arguments discount the importance of women's work before the 1970s.

In the Province of Prato, the significant and historic role of women in the straw hat industry exemplifies the cyclical yet often hidden history of Italian women in the labor force. This hat industry was predominant in the area from the mid-1800s well into the 1930s. A tourist guidebook of Tuscany from 1904 observes: "Prato of today has of course its praiseworthy modern enterprise and industries: the women are picturesquely busy at every street corner with straw plaiting; there is a good trade in woolen cloths" (Sheldon and Newell 1904: 46).[8] Ortaggi Cammarosano (1991) notes a disappearance of working women nationwide from official statistics between 1871 and 1891. In 1871, a category called "unspecified employment" contained over 4 million women. State functionaries eliminated this category ten years later, and grouped these women as housewives, a category that leaped from 393,839 persons in 1871 to 3.7 million by 1881. Writes Ortaggi Cammarosano (1991: 158): "Hundreds of thousands of women from the lower classes who added some form of productive work to their household duties in order to balance family budgets now figured, in statistical terms, simply as '*massaie*,' or housewives."

Records from one provincial hamlet revealed that of 395 households in 1931, 86.4 percent of homes had at least one adult woman listed as having a profession, and the vast majority of those were *trecciaiole*, or straw weavers.[9] This aspect of a globalized rural economy was based on domicile labor involving women who often came together in household workshops. These weavers' labors were crucial to household, local and global economies, yet their work was highly devalued, especially by the men, as one report on women's work from 1893 stated.[10]

And now on to a story that explains the title of this chapter.

Of Toys and Perfumes

A popular Italian song from the 1930s, "*Balocchi e Profumi*" or "Toys and Perfumes," comments on the cultural expectations of motherhood as it warns of the consequences that await the self-centered, consuming, overly sexed mother (Figure 8.1). I heard the song on two memorable occasions while doing fieldwork in the Province of Prato. The first time, I was sewing buttons on sweaters while working in a home-based workshop with Carolina, a powerful and outspoken woman in her mid-fifties. Politically active in local government, Carolina was the mother of three children, two sons and a daughter in their twenties, all of whom were then living at home. She and her husband's finishing firm provided one site for my ethnographic fieldwork. We broke for lunch each day around 1 o'clock. There in the kitchen above an heirloom chest hung a portrait of a woman hunched over a lap of straw plaits. Carolina had painted her grandmother in a moment of fashioning the plaits into attractive straw hats. Carolina sang of a "shop window aglow with toys and perfumes," and of a mother who ignored her child. She laughed about her tone-deafness and recalled her grandmother really singing the song as she wove the straw plaits.

The second time, I was throwing a music party at the farmhouse we rented fall 1996 to summer 1997. A guitarist friend played "Toys and Perfumes," and most of the dozen Italian guests sang along. One of those guests, anthropologist Massimo Bressan,[11] took me aside and said with insistence, "This song is important!" I tracked down the words of the song with the help of the guitarist, Maurizio Geri. A performer of Tuscan folk songs as well as Django Reinhardt-style swing (Geri 1997), Geri had found the lyrics in an obscure little songbook by E.A. Mario (dated 1930) after years of casual searching.

The song's parable of motherly immorality and the price of transgression begins with a vivid description of a mother and her little girl entering a boutique, where the mother buys only powder and cologne for herself and ignores her child. The mother's indulgences continue in the second verse, where we learn of the woman's bourgeois tastes: "the living room rich with pillows of silk." The child watches as her mother "offers her ripe lip to sin." In the third, and last, verse, the exiled child

Balocchi e Profumi	**Toys and Perfumes**
di E. A. Mario	
1930	
Edizioni E. A. Mario, Napoli	

I.

Tutta sfolgorante è la vetrina
  piena di balocchi e profumi . . .
Entra con la mamma la bambina
  tra lo sfolgorio di quei lumi . . .
— Comanda, signora? —
— Cipria e colonia Coty . . .
  — "Mamma!"
  — mormora la bambina
  mentre pieni di pianto ha gli occhi
  — per la tua piccolina
  non compri mai balocchi . . .
Mamma,
tu compri soltanto i profumi per te!"

II.

Ella, nel salotto profumato
  ricco di cuscini di seta,
porge il labbro tumido al peccato,
  mentre la bambina indiscreta
dischiude, quel nido
pieno d'odor di Coty . . .
  — "Mamma!"
  — mormora la bambina
  mentre pieni di pianto ha gli occhi
  — per la tua piccolina
  non compri mai balocchi . . .
Mamma,
tu compri soltanto i profumi per te!"

III.

Esile, agonizza la bambina . . .
  Or la mamma non è più ingrata:
corre a vuotar tutta la vetrina
  per la sua figliuola malata . . .
— Amore mio bello,
ecco i balocchi per te . . .
  — "Grazie"
  — mormora la bambina!
  Ma il capo già reclina,
  e già socchiude gli occhi . . .
Piange la mamma, pentita, stringendola al
cor!

I.

The shop window aglow in a whirl
  brimming with toys and perfumes
The little girl enters with her mamma
  amidst the glow of that luminous room
May I help you, ma'am?
Sure Coty, face powder and cologne . . .
  "Mamma!"
  murmurs the child
  her eyes welling up with tears
  "for your little one
  you never buy toys . . .
Mamma,
you buy only perfumes for yourself."

II.

She, perfumed in the living room
  rich with pillows of silk,
offers her ripe lip to sin
  while the indiscreet little girl
discloses that nest
full of the smell of Coty . . .
  "Mamma!"
  murmurs the child
  her eyes welling up with tears
  "for your little one
  you never buy toys . . .
Mamma,
you buy only perfumes for yourself."

III.

Exiled, the child agonizes . . .
  the mother is no longer neglectful:
She runs to empty the entire store window
  for her ill, darling little girl . . .
My beautiful love
here are the toys for you . . .
  "Thank you,"
  murmurs the child!
  But her head already reclines
  and her eyes already shut . . .
The mother cries, repents, squeezing the
child to her heart!

Figure 8.2 *Balocchi e Profumi* (Toys and Perfumes)

grows sick from agony and neglect; her mother finally attends to the child but it is too late. For the irresponsible, neglectful mother, the lyrics suggest the most severe of punishments: the death of her child. This mother paid a heavy price for her fleshly and material indulgences.

Carolina had flavored her version of the song with irony rather than moralizing, for she viewed positively young women's *egoismo*, or self-centeredness. She reasoned that thinking about themselves prevented women from falling so quickly into subordinate, self-sacrificing roles of mother and caretaker. Certainly, her critique of the current low birthrate is a quiet one in the loud voices that clamor on about the "problem" of the *bassissima*, or very low, level of fertility.

The story portrayed in "Toys and Perfumes" prefigures the current culture of responsibility that surrounds Italian motherhood. In other words, the song serves as a moral trope against which subsequent notions of responsible motherhood are constructed. This trope erases the history of women as workers and idealizes them as mothers. It is to the persistent consequences of this moralizing trope that we now turn.

Of Culture and Responsibility

During the second year of fieldwork, I joined a group of women who met for coffee each morning after dropping off their children at the elementary school where my daughter attended first grade. One morning an unkempt man approached our table:

> "What do you all do here?" he asked. "You're incredible. Why, you meet here every morning."
>
> "*Si prende un caffè insieme* – we have a coffee together," replied Chiara, the mother of three who finished sweaters in her home. "In this way, we're better able to face the day."
>
> "What *mestiere*, or trade, do you do?" he continued.
>
> "*Mestiere di mamma* – the craft of motherhood," replied Anna, a mother who worked in the giftshop trade.
>
> "*Mestiere di mamma*?" the man repeated. "I've never heard of mothering as a trade, a profession."
>
> "You've never heard of it?" she asked in disbelief. "It's as old as the world!" (Fieldnotes, 28 February 1997)

The mothers discussed various aspects of the craft of motherhood during the eight months we met informally over coffee. These women taught me about the meanings and demands specific to the central Italian variety of the culture of responsibility. Raising children has assumed particular weight and character in the postwar setting of upwardly mobile Italy. Many people in the rural–industrial crossroads where I worked flaunted newfound wealth, as manifested through presentations of self and children, yet they simultaneously embraced selected aspects of the peasant past, as expressed through certain eating and healing practices.[12] In either case, the time, energy and thought invested in feeding, educating, clothing and healing children – from infants well into adulthood – was immense, and the implications for middle-class respectability were heavy.[13] In this chapter, I develop only one example: clothing children. It relates to the presentation and maintenance of the child and provides a sense of how Italian women, in particular, experience the culture of responsibility. While this example involves peculiar cultural practices rooted in Prato, I am convinced that similar examples of the culture of responsibility can be found elsewhere in Italy. With William Blake, I maintain that the world presents itself most lucidly in grains of sand, and for those granules I look to the details of daily life.

As I participated in daily life, I was continuously struck by the cleanliness of the houses, the neatness of the children, the precision of their clothes:[14] the delicate collars trimmed with lace or finished edging; the fine fabrics perfectly laundered and ironed. Granted, I was a graduate student who had lived for the previous three years in the very casual western desert city of Tucson, Arizona, so while I, too, juggled my roles as researcher, mother and wife, my standards of presentation with regard to my 4-and-a-half-year-old daughter were far below those of my Italian consultants. Indeed, as fieldwork progressed, I became increasingly self-conscious about my own parental habits of dressing and fussing over my daughter.

Children wore smocks where my daughter attended public preschool and first grade during 1995–1997. Parents found it helpful and convenient because "*ci vuole tanto a vestire un figliolo ogni giorno*," or it takes a lot to dress a child every day. In other words, a lot of domestic labor was required to ensure clothes not only matched (fabric as well as color was important), but that they were perfectly clean, orderly and ironed – a necessity in a place where everybody air-dried laundry on lines or drying racks. Dressing on Sundays, especially for outings, was important *per fare figura*, so that one makes a good impression.

Central to understanding the attention and energy that went into dressing children was the concept of *fare figura*, or to make an impression, or *fare una bella figura*, to make a good impression. The emphasis on *fare figura* is well known in Italy. Any observant tourist to Florence or Rome will have noticed the well-clothed Italian shoppers on weekdays or the even better-clad promenaders on Sundays. Obviously fashions change, and in the eight years of my research I have noticed a turn toward casual dress – though as of fall 2004 it remained a studied and stylish version of casual. Italy is a densely populated peninsula, and most Italians live in close proximity with one another. Individuals have a great deal of daily contact with others, whether in the piazza, at the market, the *bar*, the hairdresser's, a friend's or relative's house, or in line at the city hall or bank (an Italian adult spends on average twenty-eight days per year waiting in line). I suggest making a good impression has a specific meaning in the Prato area, where there is a convergence of intimate knowledge of the textile industry, heightened awareness of the fashion trade, and keen memory of social inferiority. After all, Prato's wealth emerged out of trade in rags and recycled fibers. Prato is located just 20 kilometers northeast of Florence and has long been in the cultural shadow of its Renaissance rival.

My initiation into the local norms of dressing a child and the quotidian art of laundering came through Nicoletta, the widow whose apartment I lived in, with my husband and daughter, the first year of my fieldwork. Nicoletta had migrated from rural southern Italy with her husband and two daughters to the industrializing periphery of Prato in the early 1960s. Nicoletta's family epitomized the demographic transition to low fertility. Her octogenarian mother had six children; she had two; neither of her children have had or intend to have children. At the time of my laundry "lesson," I received some pointers as well from Luisa, then 41, Nicoletta's oldest and married daughter:

> Luisa caught a glimpse of me as I finished hanging out laundry on the patio. From the stairs bordering Nicoletta's flower garden, she asked, "Did you finish already?"
>
> "Well, yes," I said proudly. "I'm that fast."
>
> Nicoletta walked over and cast a disapproving glance as she caught glimpse of stains on my daughter's drying T-shirt. The stains were months old. She took the shirt and said, "I'll show you how to get them out." She scrubbed the stains with a special bar of laundry soap.
>
> "Like this," she said. "*Se no, non fa figura* – If not, she won't make an impression. *I bambini italiani portano vestiti bianchi bianchi* – Italian children wear white, white clothes."
>
> I tried it. The soap in my hand felt as slippery as a fish. Luisa came in, and I pleaded, "Don't watch me." I took a sleeve of the shirt and rubbed it with soap. My hands felt awkward. I laughed. She laughed at me.
>
> "Take the whole shirt!" Luisa instructed, bemused by my incompetence.
>
> I started to jump around. "Let's do gymnastics!" I was much more comfortable moving my whole body than my wet hands. The soap slipped, the wet shirt moved against me. I lacked coordination in hands-on everyday laundering. What a curiosity I surely was. A 33-year-old woman who could hardly keep a bar of laundry soap under control and who could not get her child's shirt white.
>
> Nicoletta could. When she was finished, the colors of the imprinted teacups were still vivid and the shirt was bright white. She became the laundry magician, a legend in my daughter's memory. (Fieldnotes, 9 December 1995)

Strong social pressure favored white clothes. They showed that you had the resources and the decency to keep your child not only in clean clothes but also in well-ironed, white ones. The responsibility for carrying out this domestic work rested largely on mothers; even those women I knew who employed domestic help oversaw the laundering. The power of whiteness surely went beyond color. As a hue, white is symbolically often associated with purity, honor, virtue and even beauty. Richard Dyer (1997) observes generally about whiteness in modern times, "To be white is to have expunged all dirt, faecal or otherwise, from oneself: to look white is to look clean" (Dyer 1997: 76; see also pp. 64–68). In central Italy, it was as though morality became grafted onto the child through clothing, and the mother was ultimately responsible for this purified presentation of self. As Italians who had migrated from the impoverished South and who had vivid memories of anti-southern prejudice from native Tuscans, Nicoletta and Luisa may have felt acutely the "necessity" to demonstrate their morality through the whiteness of clothes.

Similarly, their need to socialize me into the dominant norms of laundering and of mothering derived from the fact that my presence and my habits reflected on them. I was a foreign newcomer to the neighborhood and as such an outsider whom the neighbors initially viewed with suspicion. Hence, it was important for Nicoletta's and Luisa's reputation that I learn how to be a respectable member of the community and to make sure my daughter donned not only clean clothes but stainless, white ones.

The presentation of the child echoes in the commonly stated dictum *stare dietro a un figliolo* – literally, to stay behind a child, to follow them, to guide them. As time passed, I began to feel strange about leaving my then 5-year-old daughter to dress herself, something she had been doing since attending preschool in Tucson, where her morning routine involved putting on whatever fanciful combination of clothing she so desired. Even mismatched clothes were celebrated as a show of the child's independence, choice and creativity in her Tucson preschool context. But in Prato, even my daughter began to notice that the children did not dress themselves. One evening when I returned from my volunteer shift at a community pizzeria to fetch my daughter from a friend's house, the mother of the other child got out my daughter's coat and helped her put it on. My daughter usually put on her own coat – at least she used to. I was suddenly finding her expecting me to dress her, to choose her clothes, just as she saw her little Italian friends' mothers doing for them.

Children internalized the importance of precision as a value. When we met my daughter's first friend, Irene was standing on the other side of a rock wall in a large yard with a vegetable garden and a field with grapevines and olive trees. She was casting us a curious but careful glance, made all the more powerful by her appearance: her dress was stylish and perfectly clean, and she herself was statuesquely groomed.

One day I was teaching the girls to do figure eights with their bikes in the dead-end street next to a soccer field. The game ended after a power struggle over the rules of play, and my daughter pedaled her mini-mountain bike over to a rocky parking lot. "You shouldn't ride your bike there," Irene said. "It will ruin the tires."

My daughter continued riding, her bike's large tires moving through the rocks. "I'm not like you," Irene said. "*Io sono una bambina precisa* – I'm a precise child." (Fieldnotes, 19 September 1996)

It struck me that a 7-year-old girl had already internalized the value of being precise and exacting. Irene's mother, Carlotta, was a good teacher. She was very disciplined in terms of how the house was kept, the time of day and day of week when she gave Irene her bath (Saturday evenings around 7 o'clock), and how orderly Irene's clothes were kept: the carefully selected and perfectly ironed dresses in her closet would have met the standards of the most well-kept boutique. As Americans, our Italian friends told us we were *disinvolti*, or laid back, in terms of our hands-off parenting style and our casual way of dressing.[15]

The emphasis many central Italian mothers put into dressing their children, I suggest, is linked to their heightened consciousness of fashion, to a culture that values stylistic presentations of self, and to the specific peasant-cum-artisan/entrepreneur social experience so common in Prato. Style, and the style of children, become important vehicles for expressing social identity. As Pierre Bourdieu (1984: 172) has pointed out, "social identity is defined and asserted through difference." The difference being asserted much of the time is one that creates distance from that most hideous of inferior social locations: *miseria* or poverty.

Carlotta, the mother of only-child Irene, explained to me the pressure she felt to have everything – clothes, food, house – in perfect order. She and her husband felt ambivalent about the possibility of having a second child. The couple through the 1990s managed a family sweater firm. Carlotta, then 38, her husband, his brother and mother worked within the firm; various stages of sweater-finishing were outsourced to other small firms or individuals. The family lived in a graciously restored farmhouse: Carlotta, her husband and daughter occupied one floor, and the widowed mother-in-law and her eldest bachelor son the other. The *maglificio*, or sweater firm, was located in one wing of the home. A theme of social status and public displays of it emerged one day as Carlotta and her mother-in-law spoke to me about their lives. I jotted down the talk:

"Everything has to be a name brand. Last year Irene (then gearing up to enter third grade) had a backpack that cost 30,000 lira [US$18.00]. All the kids looked at her, so this year I spent 130,000 lira [US78.00] and got her a Sailor Moon backpack, the type used in middle school. Otherwise you're looked upon as *genterella*" [or a low-class or disrespectable person].

"Ah," her mother-in-law chimed in, "they're all really *genterella*."

"Of course they are," said Carlotta. " But everybody wants to cover it up, to show the next person up." (Fieldnotes, 28 June 1997)

This passage suggests that Carlotta sought to avoid a sense of social inferiority for herself as well as her daughter.[16] Social status powerfully shaped Carlotta's sense of personal identity and self worth. With such an emphasis on the acquisition of expensive material goods, coupled with a culture of responsibility in which a great deal of attention is placed on the details of laundering, ironing, clothing, feeding, healing and educating, the thought of more than one child seemed beyond reach. It is worth noting that demographers' official surveys cite Italian women as those with the largest gap between children desired (an average of two) and those actually had (an average of one) (Delgado Pérez and Livi-Bacci 1992).

Such displays of fashion and style validate bourgeois, or middle-class, consumer values, and I would argue that the acceptance of *fare figura*, of making an good impression, can be connected to a broader hegemonic project that benefits a ruling political-economic elite. Yet all of the elite do not participate in the same way, and this reflects the way in which one's style cannot be reduced to one's class position (Mouffe 1981: 231). Consider that in my fieldsite the adult daughter of the best-known noble family was chastised (behind her back) by working-class and middle-class parents for the sloppy way she dressed her children and the messy house she was reputed to keep. She was not participating in the stylistic performances that those of the newly moneyed classes found so important.

The acute attention to dressing children exemplifies "contradictory consciousness" (Gramsci 1971: 333) because for working-class mothers to live up to bourgeois Italian-style notions of self-presentation, these presentation regimes require tremendous amounts of work on the part of women. And yet at the level of every day, these practices become "necessary," part of the "common sense" required to send children out into the world of social relations. Differences between classes in the capitalist world of consumer culture become transmuted "into distinctions of virtue and merit," as Eric Wolf pointed out (1982: 389–390; see also Wolf 1999). "Success is demonstrated by the ability to acquire valued commodities; hence, inability to consume signals social defeat." Ability to consume signals social victory. Ensuring social victory in a new moneyed context rests on both parents, but the performance of it rests most heavily on women.[17]

When one examines the details of daily life and the culture of responsibility, it is difficult to make sense of claims that "the interests of women are intrinsically at odds with the interests of babies and with the population" (Golini *et al.* 2000: 104). Here, the interests of women refer to contemporary women's pursuit of education, careers and leisure activities. In an effort to diffuse their blame-placing on women, the researchers portray the demographic crisis as the manifestation of a "profound and generalized crisis of values that does everything but support procreative choice." They suggest that "women though not only women but also couples . . . remain imprisoned within the play of social pressures and the drive toward individualism" (Golini *et al.* 2000: 104). Such strategies deny the demands of the culture of responsibility and the struggles that women have waged toward gender equality within and beyond their doorsteps.

Of Civilizing Motherhood

Sociologists Marzio Barbagli (1996 [1984]: 387–92) and Chiara Saraceno (1996: 143–48) trace the rise of these *doveri di madre*, or motherly obligations, to modernity and namely to the birth of the privatized, "modern" family to the 1600s; characteristics of this modern family only become fully realized among the bourgeois and aristocratic classes in the 1800s. Among the Italian popular classes, the modern family develops much later – well into the twentieth century (Saraceno 1996: 144–45).

The modern family form represented a break from the patriarchal model, which began to unravel in the last decades of the eighteenth century. Hierarchical social distance between husband and wife lessened as it did between parents and children. The transformation acquired a class character, moving first through the intellectual bourgeoisie (late 1700s and early 1800s), then catching hold among the aristocrats (1850s to early 1900s), next affecting bureaucrats, merchants, artisans and industrial workers, and finally transforming social relations among the agricultural classes. The change followed this class-based course, according to Barbagli, because of a crisis of the *ancien regime* and accompanying transformations in the political-economic system. Barbagli (1996: 26) suggests that just as the rigid asymmetries between classes were diminishing, so too were the asymmetries breaking down within households. The peasant classes eventually followed suit, and by the postwar era, as agricultural reforms took hold and the peasant sharecropping system unraveled, the formal patriarchal family gave way to more egalitarian models (Saraceno 1996: 145).

These egalitarian models, however, have not been fully realized particularly in terms of gender equality. In fact, the culture of responsibility reflects one aspect of the double burden in terms of professional and domestic/affective work that rests on women. Saraceno argues that the modern family, as a unit of sentiment and of education, finds its core meaning in two interdependent figures: the mother and the child. This model identifies the woman as mother not only in the biological sense but also in affective and educative terms; she is expected to participate in educative and moral projects (Saraceno 1996: 145).

New norms for childrearing accompanied the modern view of the family. New attention was given to bodily comportment, moral and intellectual education, medical practices, hygiene and dietary norms. These standards brought about new expectations for mothering. The practice of giving children over to wetnurses, for example, became recast in terms of "indifference, frigidness, and vanity on the part of mothers" (Saraceno 1996: 146; see also Dadà 1999). These very themes were echoed in the popular song "Toys and Perfumes." The refrain describing the little tearful girl who murmurs, "for your little one you never buy toys," cast against the self-indulgent mother who neglects the girl's health reminds that responsible mothers are self-sacrificing ones.

In short, new regimes for childrearing were part and parcel of a "civilizing process," a term now broadly associated with the work of Norbert Elias (1994). The point I wish to make is that the burden of socializing children according to the norms and morals of this "civilizing process" was largely placed on mothers. Indeed, it still is.

Of Confronting Class "Necessities"

Women who face the culture of responsibility and who adhere to its dictates are caught in the "fissures" of a class structure that they do not comfortably fit into (after Comaroff and Comaroff 1991: 58).[18] The early-twentieth-century *signore*, or elites, had access to far greater resources than average women who today emulate in part their standards of hygiene, education, clothing, feeding and childrearing. Those elite women had a lot of domestic help, including wetnurses from poor villages, so as to continue their society lives (Dadà 1999: 26).

The new-moneyed Province of Prato is a sort of mimetic place where people joked that you live for your house rather than having a house to live in, and where commodity acquisition served to distance oneself *and* one's children from the "hard life" and its *genterella*, or low-class folks. New-moneyed people there knew well their closeness to *genterella*. In many cases, these adults of child-bearing age were the sons and daughters of one-time peasants, peasant-weavers turned sweater-makers, or southern Italian migrants. One day while taking a *passeggiata*, or walk, with my longtime confidante Luisa, we passed by the large house of a relative – half of which nobody lived in. Luisa thought it showy. She said, "*Si nasce nobile, non si diventa nobile* – You're born nobility, you don't become nobility" (Fieldnotes 14 November 2002). Her statement illustrated how people become caught in class fissures as they try to one-up their class background.

I suggest the ideologies of class that shape the culture of responsibility impinge not only on mothers but on would-be mothers as well. Attending to domestic tasks and keeping husbands presentable (shopping, laundering and ironing clothes) already kept such women running. The unpaid domestic work that such women performed for the benefit of their husbands revealed consent to gender and class ideologies rooted in old patriarchal forms. Patriarchy continued to be reproduced through what people did and said. The rigid patriarchal family form had disappeared but it had left visible traces. Yet women also derived power and respect from their well-nurtured and impressive men folk, just as Italian women have long since derived power from food (Counihan 1988; Krause 1999: 137–147, 255–262; Ochs, Pontecorvo and Fasulo 1996).

Women without children looked around them and took note of the expectations of motherhood. Many were hesitant to take the plunge. Some women emphasized they postponed marriage because they feared their boyfriends really wanted a substitute mother. A number of women who married but who claimed to have chosen not to have children pointed to their personality – of "being too nervous," of not having the "right character." I have space here only to say that this perceived character flaw raises the question of the constraints Italian women have on their ability to choose. Was the explanation of "nervousness" a painful consequence of conforming to middle-class expectations of modern motherhood that place a premium on order? I could not help but see some women's nervousness and fixation over cleanliness as connected with their personal histories of coming from subaltern classes or regions. These histories were common in the new-moneyed environs of Prato – even the new-moneyed peninsula of Italy. Women's sense of responsibility in terms of living up to what was expected of them commonly manifested itself in the form of a constant sense of being on-edge. I so often heard women say, "*Non ce la faccio più* – I can't do it anymore." It sounded like a mantra.

But, it was not everyone's mantra. In late December 1996, a university-age cousin of Luisa's invited me to go with her to the beach town of Viareggio for a dinner party. She had complained to me about her mother and that generation's fastidious and obsessive attention to the house, to the point that it almost became a pathology. So I was particularly struck when, in the middle of unwrapping sausages that the men were preparing to grill outside, the women friends poured themselves some champagne and toasted themselves: "*A noi ganzissime donne, perchè non si pensa sempre alla pulizia,*" or, "To us ultracool women because we don't always think about cleaning!"

Of Consequences and Adjustments

If we listen closely to the alarmist language of demographers and the media concerning Italy's "super-low" fertility, we may recognize something familiar: contemporary women sound an awful lot like the self-indulgent mother figure in "Toys and Perfumes." Recall Golini and his colleagues' assessment that women's interests "are intrinsically at odds with the interests of babies and the population" (2000: 104). In this version of the story, women in particular have become like that figure in the song: prisoners of rampant individualism. The alarm ringing suggests that not only are they neglecting to have a "rational" number of children, they are neglecting to sufficiently replenish the nation.

This chapter is intended as a historical corrective to the current project of myth-making now underway: specifically, that because women put their own "interests" before those of their offspring, realized or would-be, they are to blame for the demographic "implosion." Demographers and the media have repeatedly implied that women's work is antithetical to having children. So let us consider the effects of such alarmist language on the so-called perpetrators of low fertility themselves: the "native" women, especially those born between 1950 and 1975.

The alarmist language relies on imaginings of a historical woman who was a non-working, non-participant in local and global economies. This is a myth born of the liberal nineteenth century, ripened during the fascist era, and harvested in the postwar period: the myth that women didn't work "before" seems to have really taken hold among what Italians call the popular classes in the 1960s. This myth about how women "used to be" speaks loudly about what women's practices and performances should look like: dedicated only to being self-sacrificing mothers. These explanations persist even though it is well documented that Italian women in the nineteenth and early twentieth centuries had not only a conspicuous but a predominant role in industry, and birthrates were much higher than they are now. The notion that women are "naturally" mothers and not workers has become a tale that is being reseeded via these cacophonous depictions of Italy's low birthrate. In portraying women as non-workers, the alarmism solidifies the cultural space for a non-working *mother* figure.

This type of mother figure is essential to the politics of cultural struggle now ongoing in central Italy, and elsewhere, related to population dynamics. What is paradoxical about this situation is that while the rest of the world worries itself about too much population, much of Europe concerns itself about too little population. In both places, however, there is acute alarmism. This fact might signal to us that the field of population is a highly charged one and a site for normalization. When the Pope speaks about the grave birth crisis, he speaks from a specific political position. The Catholic Church remains opposed to birth control, including condoms and the pill, as well as abortion.[19]

Are women – and couples – caught in a prison of individualism? Or are they caught in a prison of social structures that demand they perform gender, class and whiteness in particular ways? Alarmist population rhetoric reinforces old tropes about women "naturally" being mothers. It conceals cultural struggles against patriarchal-ordered gender regimes that are implicitly related to Italy's population paradox. Alarms about demographic malaise erase the culture of responsibility that shapes the lived realities in which Italian women, as mothers, raise their children. In particular, the incessant talk of implosion casts women's daily activities related to *social* reproduction once again into the shadows. Finally, I have implicated alarmist demographic discourses as depicting Italian women as irrational family-makers. This is a not-so story; rather, these women are busy conforming to other normalizing gender role demands and adjusting to fissures related to their uneasy locations in shifting class structures as they figure out how they must, by "necessity," manipulate the symbols of a new-moneyed world to their and their children's advantages.

Acknowledgments

The research on which this chapter is based was made possible in part by funds from the following sources: Council for European Studies Pre-Dissertation Grant (1995), US Fulbright Grant and Renewal (1995–1997), Beth Dillingham Award, Central States Anthropological Society (1998), Final Project Fund Award from the University of Arizona (1999) and a Faculty Research Grant from the University of Massachusetts, Amherst (2002–2003). I wish to thank Carrie B. Douglass for her editorial suggestions as well as for her organization of the session "Barren States: The Population Implosion in Southern and Eastern Europe" in 2001 at the American Anthropological Association Annual Meetings, Washington, DC. I am grateful to Ana Alonso, Jane Hill, Mark Nichter, Susan Philips and Hermann Rebel for comments on earlier drafts of this chapter. I am indebted to my field consultants, who in respect to their privacy remain anonymous. I owe much to guitarist Maurizio Geri for playing the song and providing me with the lyrics, and to Chris Brashear for introducing me to Maurizio. A number of people clued me in to specific references, and they are due my thanks: Massimo Bressan, Giovanni Contini, Luciana Fellin, Manuela Geri, Mariangeles Soto-Diaz, Jackie Urla and Jonny Zibbell. I of course take complete responsibility for any shortcomings with the caveat that, as the late Daniel Nugent once said, any work is always "in progress."

Notes

1. See Bruni (2002).
2. All translations are mine. "Italia? Vecchia e senza bambini," *La Stampa*, July 25, 1997, p. 17. Thanks to Italian anthropologist Massimo Bressan for providing me with this article. "Culle più vuote, l'Italia cresce solo per l'apporto degli immigrati," *La Nazione*, June 27, 1997, p. 7. See also Drioli (2002).
3. Demographers use only women to track births and Total Fertility Rates. See, for example, the landmark Princeton Fertility Project (Coale and Watkins 1986).
4. The typical fertility rate cited for replacement of a given population is a TFR of 2.2; however, Golini *et al.* (2000) cite a rate based on complex demographic calculations, including immigration, that reflect their notion of what the minimum level of natality would be to avoid demographic "deformation" in the next 25 to 50 years.
5. An "explanation" about Italy's demographic dynamic first published in the *New York Times* now appears on a website of a women's organization as the

"truth" about the situation. In that article, a University of Bologna professor told reporter Michael Specter:

> women of Italy have the worst of both worlds. They now work for a living in record numbers, but tremendous obstacles remain for balancing work and family life. Far more than places like Sweden, France or even the United States, the Italian man still seeks a wife who will make his dinner every night and who takes complete charge of the family. Women responded by realizing that with only 24 hours in each day something has to give. Children seem to have become that something. (Specter 1998)

By chance in fall 2001, I came across this quote on the website of the Women's Environment and Development Organization. The authors of an article about Italian women's low fertility used the quote to explain why Italian women's fertility rates are so low. Two things struck me about the deployment of this quote. First, it implies that women are not investing in children. In practice, quite the reverse appears to be the case. They have fewer children but invest heavily in each one. This is where dominant notions about gender morality intersect with dominant schemes of middle-class respectability (Schneider and Schneider 1996). Second, even the women's group participates in the historical amnesia about Italian women as workers: the construction of the historical non-working woman figure, the idea of work as something novel for Italian women, is a myth. See the excellent critical work on this theme by Pescarolo (1995), Pescarolo and Ravenni (1991) and Ortaggi Cammarosano (1991).

6. Fieldnote, "02.11.10 breastfeeding, global." My thanks to Dott. Francesco De Ninno for facilitating interviews with several hospital personnel in the maternity ward in November 2002.

7. In Golini *et al.*'s (2000: 225) scheme, Prato falls in the category of commune most strongly industrialized and with the highest levels of employment, total as well as female. Of the "active" population, the official employment rate is 94 percent. Of the total population, 41.2 percent are employed. Of the total female population, 29.7 percent are employed. The numbers derive from Istat data from 1991.

8. Thanks to Peter McLaughlin for this reference from his library.

9. I consulted household records in the historic archive of Carmignano, which was then part of the Province of Florence: Archivio Storico di Carmignano, Foglio di famiglia, VII Censimento Generale della Popolazione, 21 Aprile 1931, Provincia di Firenze, Comune di Carmignano, Frazione di Comeana.

10. Thanks to Silvano Gelli (1996, 1998), who was doing archival research at the same time that I was, for his assistance in deciphering this document. Archivio Storico di Carmignano, Categoria III, no. 93; Fascicolo no. 13, Filza 2, Agosto 30 1893.

11. See Bressan (1997).
12. One thinks of Raymond Williams' (1977) notion of selective tradition. See Roseberry's insightful discussion (1989: 26–27).
13. For more on respectability as related to fertility decline, see Schneider and Schneider (1991).
14. Fieldnote, "97.01.19 stare in dietro."
15. Fieldnote, "09.19.96 bambina."
16. The noun *gente* means people, and the suffix *-ella* indicates a negative, a lack. In this particular context, the word suggests material lack and likely points to a peasant past, a time in which commodities and education were scarce.
17. See Kemp and Bono (1993) and Passerini (1996) for discussions of the feminist movement and gender struggles in Italy.
18. In the Comaroffs' ethnography of Nonconformist missionaries and Tswana peoples of South African, the missionaries are caught in these fissures, "suspended uneasily between the privileged and the impoverished" in nineteenth-century bourgeois British society. Also noteworthy for my argument is the authors' mention of emergent gender ideologies over the "woman problem": that "ladies of bourgeois class [were] ever more restricted to the roles of wife and mother" (Comaroff and Comaroff 1991: 69). This gender ideology seems to be making its way across Europe in the nineteenth-century; it seems to go hand in hand with the transition from protoindustrialism to industrial capitalism, at least in Europe, and in certain colonial contexts, such as South Africa. Perhaps encounters in the colonies were giving form to hegemonies in the metropole, as Stoler (1995) has convincingly argued about sexuality.
19. For the Church's official view of contraception and sex education, see http://www.vatican.va/, accessed June 12, 2003. In southern Africa, Roman Catholic bishops condemned the use of condoms to protect against the spread of HIV/AIDS; see "Church rejects plea on condoms," July 30, 2001, http://news.bbc.co.uk/1/hi/world/africa/1465326.stm, accessed June 12, 2003. See also Gunther Simmermacher, "The Condom Debate," *The Southern Cross*, July 18, 2001, http://www.thesoutherncross.co.za/editorials2001/editorial010718.htm, accessed June 12, 2003.

References

Alter, G. (1992), "Theories of Fertility Decline: A Nonspecialist's Guide to the Current Debate," in L.A. Tilly, J.R. Gillis and D. Levine (eds), *The European Experience of Declining Fertility, 1850–1970: The Quiet Revolution*, Cambridge: Blackwell.

Barbagli, M. (1996 [1984]), *Sotto lo stesso tetto: Mutamenti della famiglia in Italia dal XV al XX secolo*, 2nd edn, Bologna: Il Mulino.

Bourdieu, P. (1984), *Distinction: A Social Critique of the Judgement of Taste*, Cambridge, MA: Harvard University Press.

Bressan, M. (1997), "Culturali e istituzioni comunitarie nello sviluppo di un distretto industriale," PhD thesis, Università di Firenze.

Bruni, F. (2002), "Persistent Drop in Fertility Reshapes Europe's Future," *New York Times*, December 26: A1.

Coale, A.J. and Watkins, S.C. (eds) (1986), *The Decline in Fertility in Europe*, Princeton, NJ: Princeton University Press.

Comaroff, J. and Comaroff, J. (1991), *Of Revelation and Revolution, Vol. 1*, Chicago: University of Chicago Press.

Counihan, C.M. (1988), "Female Identity, Food, and Power in Contemporary Florence," *Anthropological Quarterly*, 61: 51–62.

Dadà, A. (1999), "Il lavoro di balia. Memoria e storia dell'emigrazione femminile da Ponte Buggianese nel '900," Comune di Ponte Buggianese: Pacini Editore SpA.

de Grazia, V. (1992), *How Fascism Ruled Women, Italy, 1922–1945*, Berkeley, CA: University of California Press.

Delgado Pérez, M. and Livi-Bacci, M. (1992) "Fertility in Italy and Spain: The Lowest in the World," *Family Planning Perspectives*, 24(4): 162–173.

Drioli, I. (2002), "Le 'tavole' del Papa conquistano il Parlamento," *La Nazione*, Quotidiano Nazionale, Prato, November 15: 3–5.

Dyer, R. (1997), "Coloured White, not Coloured," in *White*, New York: Routledge.

Elias, N. (1994), *The Civilizing Process*, Oxford: Basil Blackwell.

Gal, S. and Kligman, G. (2000), *The Politics of Gender under Socialism*, Princeton, NJ: Princeton University Press.

Gelli, S. (1996), *Q.M.P. Le Epigrafi nel cimitero di Poggio A Caiano: Testimonianze di Storia poggese (1884–1954)*, Signa: Tipografia Nova.

—— (1998), *Movimento Cooperativo e Lotte Sociali nel Territorio Orientale del Montalbano (1872–1922)*, Quaderni di Ricerche Storiche 5, Signa: Tipografia Nova.

Geri, M. (1997), *Maurizio Geri Swingtet. Manouche e Dintorni*, Robi Droli.

Golini, A. (1991), "Introduzione," in R. Palomba (ed.), *Crescita Zero*, Scandicci (Florence): La Nuova Italia.

Golini, A. (ed.) (1994), *Tendenze demografiche e politiche per la popolazione. Terzo rapporto IRP sulla situazione demografica italiana*, Milan: Il Mulino.

Golini, A., De Simoni, A. and Citoni, F. (eds) (1995), *Tre scenari per il possibile sviluppo della popolazione delle regioni italiane al 2044*, Rome: Consiglio Nazionale delle Ricerche/Istituto di Ricerche sulla Popolazione.

Golini, A., Mussino, A. and Savioli, M. (2000), *Il malessere demografico in Italia*, Bologna: Il Mulino.

Gramsci, A. (1971), *Selections from the Prison Notebooks*, New York:

International Publishers.

Kemp, S. and Bono, P. (eds) (1993), *The Lonely Mirror: Italian Perspectives on Feminist Theory*, London: Routledge.

Kertzer, D.I. (1993), *Sacrificed for Honor: Italian Infant Abandonment and the Politics of Reproductive Control*, Boston, MA: Beacon Press.

Krause, E.L. (1994), "Forward vs. Reverse Gear: The Politics of Proliferation and Resistance in the Italian Fascist State," *Journal of Historical Sociology* 7(3): 261–288.

—— (1999), "Natalism and Nationalism: The Political Economy of Love, Labor, and Low Fertility in Central Italy," PhD dissertation, University of Arizona.

—— (2001), "'Empty Cradles' and the Quiet Revolution: Demographic Discourse and Cultural Struggles of Gender, Race, and Class in Italy," *Cultural Anthropology*, 16(4): 576–611.

—— (2005) *A Crisis of Births: Population Politics and Family-Making in Italy*. Belmont, CA: Thomson/Wadsworth.

Livi-Bacci, M. (1977), *A History of Italian Fertility*, Princeton, NJ: Princeton University Press.

—— (1994), "Introduzione," in A. Golini (ed.), *Tendenze demografiche e politiche per la popolazione: Terzo rapporto IRP sulla situazione demografica italiana*, Milan: Il Mulino.

Lori, A., Golini, A. and Cantalini, B. (eds) (1995), *Atlante dell'invecchiamento della popolazione*, Rome: Consiglio Nazionale delle Ricerche.

Mazzuco, S. and Ongaro, F. (2003), "La bassa fecondità tra costrizioni economiche e cambio di valori. Focus City Report di Padova," paper presented at the workshop, Il contributo degli studi qualitativi per la comprensione dei comportamenti familiari e rirpoduttivi, Padua September 19.

Mouffe, C. (1981), "Hegemony and Ideology in Gramsci," in T. Bennett, G. Martin, C. Mercer and J. Woollacott (eds), *Culture, Ideology and Social Process: A Reader*, London: Open University Press.

Ochs, E., Pontecorvo, C. and Fasulo, A. (1996), "Socializing Taste," *Ethnos*, 61(1–2): 7–46.

Ortaggi Cammarosano, S. (1991), "Labouring Women in Northern and Central Italy in the Nineteenth Century," in J.A. Davis and P. Ginsborg (eds), *Society and Politics in the Age of the Risorgimento: Essays in Honour of Denis Mack Smith*, Cambridge: Cambridge University Press.

Passerini, L. (1987), *Fascism in Popular Memory: The Cultural Experience of the Turin Working Class*, Cambridge: Cambridge University Press.

—— (1996), "Gender Relations," in D. Forgacs and R. Lumley (eds), *Italian Cultural Studies*, Oxford: Oxford University Press.

Pescarolo, A. (1995), "I Modelli del Lavoro Femminile: Continuità e Mutamento nei Percorsi e nei Valori," Istituto Regionale per la Programmazione Economica della Toscana (IRPET), Pontassieve: Centro Stampa.

Pescarolo, A. and Ravenni, G.B. (1991), *Il Proletariato Invisibile: La Manifattura della Paglia nella Toscana Mezzadrile (1820–1950)*, Milan: Franco Angeli.

Rapp, R. (1999), *Testing Women, Testing the Fetus: The Social Impact of Amniocentesis in America*, New York: Routledge.

Roseberry, W. (1989), *Anthropologies and Histories: Essays in Culture, History and Political Economy*, New Brunswick, NJ: Rutgers University Press.

Saraceno, C. (1996), *Sociologia della Famiglia*, Bologna: Il Mulino.

Schneider, J.C. and Schneider, P.T. (1991), "Sex and Respectability in an Age of Fertility Decline: A Sicilian Case Study," *Social Science & Medicine*, 33(8): 885–895.

—— (1992), "Going Forward in Reverse Gear: Culture, Economy, and Political Economy in the Demographic Transitions of a Rural Sicilian Town," in L.A. Tilly, J.R. Gillis and D. Levine (eds), *The European Experience of Declining Fertility, 1850–1970: The Quiet Revolution*, Cambridge: Blackwell.

—— (1996), *Festival of the Poor: Fertility Decline and the Ideology of Class in Sicily: 1860–1980*, Tucson, AZ: University of Arizona Press.

Sheldon, A.R. and Newell, M.M. (1904), "Chapter Two, Prato: A Medieval Journey," in *The Medici Balls: Seven Little Journeys in Tuscany*, New York: Charterhouse Press.

Specter, M. (1998), "Population Implosion Worries a Graying Europe," *New York Times*, July 10: A1.

Stoler, A.L. (1995), *Race and the Education of Desire: Foucault's History of Sexuality and the Colonial Order of Things*, Durham, NC, and London: Duke University Press.

Volpi, R. (1996), *Figli d'Italia: Quanti, quali e come alle soglie del Duemila*. Bagno A Ripoli (Florence): La Nuova Italia.

Whitaker, E.D. (2000), *Measuring Mamma's Milk: Fascism and the Medicalization of Maternity in Italy*, Ann Arbor, MI: University of Michigan Press.

Williams, R. (1977) *Marxism and Literature*, Oxford: Oxford University Press.

Wolf, E.R. (1982), *Europe and the People without History*, Berkeley, CA: University of California Press.

—— (1999), *Envisioning Power: Ideologies of Dominance and Crisis*, Berkeley, CA: University of California Press.

–9–

"We're Fine at Home": Young People, Family and Low Fertility in Spain

Carrie B. Douglass

The cultural iconography of Spain – bullfights, the arrogant gypsy woman Carmen, sangria, flamenco and sun – still evokes a romantic vision for an Anglo-American public. The advertising slogan, "Spain is different," initiated during the Francoist 1970s to bring tourists to Spain, still brings wry smiles to the faces of older Spaniards. For northern Europeans and Americans, "Spain," along with the rest of the Mediterranean countries, was opposed to the rational, economic, productive, Protestant and individualistic North. Since at least the time of the nineteenth-century Romantics, the "Mediterranean" has represented passionate, sensual, consuming, Catholic and relational culture.

A large, multigenerational and close family has been another stereotype of difference attributed to these cultures. The image of the large southern European family was probably due to the central role and public place children had in these societies. Northern Europeans took "the noisy presence of children on the streets, the attention they received from parents, and the active role they took in rural and urban populations as signs of unusually high fertility and big families" (Delgado Pérez and Livi-Bacci 1992: 162).

Whereas Spaniards may have rejected most of the other stereotypes that outsiders have of Spain as erroneous, the large extended family, made up of parents, grandparents, children, siblings, cousins, nieces and nephews, has been a distinguishing characteristic for all the national communities of Spain. In contrast to northern Europe, part of Spaniards' individual identities has been as a member of a large multigenerational family. Images of Sunday dinners in restaurants with large tables crowned with grandparents, surrounded by their children and in-laws, while hordes of grandchildren of all ages scurry about, are ubiquitous. Summer vacation homes filled to the brim with siblings and their children (all cousins) populate Spanish film and literature and real life. Scores of studies and surveys attest to the importance and pleasure that these families bring in Spain (Alberdi *et al.* 1994; Corell and Cañas 2001).

Thus, it came as a shock to many Spaniards when in 2000 the National Institute of Statistics (INE) announced that the 1999 Spanish birthrate, 1.07 (children per woman), was the lowest in the world, in fact in the history of humankind (Bosch 2000). The 1.07 figure was dramatically below the 2.1 figure needed for population replacement. For years, during the 1990s, Spanish friends of mine had been noting that daycare centers were closing, children's clothing stores were folding, and toy stores were going out of business. However, for a country that in 1970 had had, with Ireland, the highest birthrate in Europe (TFR 2.8), this news, the lowest birthrate in the world, was a surprise. "I always thought family was really important in Spain!" exclaimed perplexedly one informant, a 28-year-old female law student.

Paradoxically, as valued as the traditional Spanish family is, it will disappear if the Spanish birthrate continues to hover below 2.1. I remember speaking to one woman who described returning to Galicia from abroad to spend summer with her adult siblings in the family house on the coast. She spoke eloquently and with delight of her sense of family and of how much her 15-year-old daughter enjoyed being with all her cousins. Later we spoke about the low birthrate among Spaniards. I pointed out that families of one child like hers would later result in families with no aunts and uncles and no cousins. My friend looked at me as if shell-shocked.

Ironically, the very generation that is most implicated in the low fertility rate (those Spaniards between 20 and 35 years of age) seems most surprised by the low birthrate announced in 2000. Perhaps this is because most of these young people still live at home, ensconced in a web of family relationships. Still living in the parental home, still as children, the family, of course, seems important to them. Natal families are the source of their affective and material well-being. In this chapter I want to consider these young people and their understanding of their roles in the phenomenon of declining birthrates. To do this I will review the recent history of fertility in Spain and explain my fieldwork project. Then I will review the political, economic and social "causes" of the plunging Spanish birthrate before I look at what young Spaniards have to say about their postponing marriage and still living at home.

History

Although Spain experienced the first demographic transition slightly later than some other European states, Spain's history of fertility has had a typical European trajectory. By 1920 the Spanish birthrate was 3.8, down from a high of 4.74 in the mid-nineteenth century (Reher 1996: 237). The Spanish state has always been highly differentiated by region, and this was certainly true of the demographic transition. Catalonia was the first area to see the birthrate fall at the end of the nineteenth century, whereas some other areas, Castilla la Vieja and Leon, for example, did not experience low birthrates until after the 1920s, or even until after the civil war (in 1939) (Reher 1996).

During the 1930s, the Spanish birthrate continued to fall. The years of the Spanish civil war (1936–39), with all the physical and emotional disruption this caused, accelerated the descent and this was followed by a decade of instability. The end of the civil war ushered in the conservative, Catholic, forty-year fascist dictatorship of General Francisco Franco. The imposition of social policies, laws and values crafted by the Generalísimo, who had "saved" Spain from the secularizing and liberal ideas of Europe, coincided with the closing of the first demographic transition.[1]

The Spanish birthrate began to rise again in the decade of the 1950s and continued to do so for almost twenty years. These were the years of the Spanish "baby boom," corresponding to a rise in economic prosperity and a rise in the standard of living. The survivors of the Spanish civil war, encouraged and coerced by gender and social policy of the conservative Spanish state, continued to have higher numbers of children for a decade even as populations in northern and central Europe had begun to reduce their number of children to below replacement levels. As stated above, in 1970, along with Ireland, Spain still had the highest fertility in Europe. From the perspective of northern European fertility, Spain did, indeed, seem "different."

However, beginning in 1975, the year of Franco's death and the return to democracy, Spanish fertility began to behave in a way similar to most of the other western European countries (albeit a bit later). It began to drop – precipitously. The very generation born into the society created by the Spanish civil war began a trend of lower fertility. Recall that in the mid-1970s the Spanish TFR was at 2.8; by 1981 it went below replacement level (2.1) and continued to fall for twenty years, until 2001 (Figure 9.1).

Although demographers were well aware of these fertility phenomena and had been tracking them for years, the general population in Spain seemed oblivious to these trends. It wasn't until the end of the 1990s when the media began announcing the low fertility statistics, and their possible implications, that the general public, somewhat stunned, began to notice them and become aware of the change in the Spanish family structure that they had wrought.

The media emphasized two preoccupations with respect to the impending population implosion. On the one hand, newspapers in some regions with a deep sense of historical identity and nationalism (i.e. the Basque Country, or Galicia) saw the drop in the birthrate as a threat to their very existence. Some regions responded by offering tax incentives to couples to have children. Galicia published a birth watch in the newspaper, keeping constant tract of the number of births

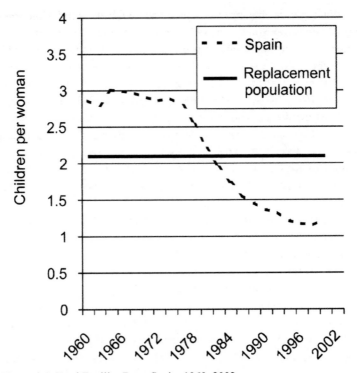

Figure 9.1 Total Fertility Rate, Spain, 1960–2002.
Source: Eurostat, Population and Social Conditions, Demography, Fertility Indicators, January 29, 2003.

produced there. On the other hand, other media tended to emphasize population projections that showed that the old would soon outnumber the young, thus posing problems for pensions and the labor force. Who would support the long-living Spaniards in their old age?[2] Furthermore, demographers project that Spain will lose one-quarter of its population in the next fifty years (United Nations Population Division (UNPD) 2000)). Most solutions to these problems implied opening doors to more immigration in order to replace the needed workers.

Until the late 1990s Spain had had little experience with immigration. Spain itself had been a labor-exporting nation (most of which went to northern Europe or to several specific countries in South America) from the late 1950s to the early 1970s. However, by the late 1990s, illegal immigrants risked dying as they struggled to cross the Straits of Gibraltar in order to reach work opportunities in Spain. Immigrant Others were streaming into Spain for the first time from North Africa, sub-Saharan Africa, Eastern Europe and South America. Violent culture clashes, especially with Moroccans, were occurring in phenotypically homogeneous Spain, unused to such visible numbers of non-Spaniards. Many Spaniards were not receptive to suggestions of taking yet more immigrants in order to solve their pending labor shortage. In a survey 54 percent of young people said they think immigration is bad in the long run for Spain (Escárraga 2000) and almost half of the Spanish interviewed elsewhere said they were not tolerant of foreigners ("La Mitad de los españoles . . ." 2001). In 2002, newspapers announced with satisfaction and relief that the birthrate had gone up, to 1.24, although headlines also alluded to the fact that this increase in births had been due to immigration (i.e. births to immigrant women) (EFE 2002).[3]

Fieldwork

I undertook intensive fieldwork on this topic in four Spanish cities. I explored how people understand their life cycle decisions, especially emphasizing the agency of women. In general young Spaniards do not leave home until marriage and marriage has been postponed until near 30 years old on average. What are the arguments that people use to justify the prolongation of this stage of life? What are the dynamics of living at home in their late twenties and thirties? Is there any impetus to leave home?

My project was based on interviews, in the form of focus groups. Given my long association with Spain and my many years of fieldwork there (1983, 1985–86, 1989, 1992), I completed this research during the fall of 2000. I worked with two age groups. First, I organized groups and taped interviews with a category of informants I called "*young people*." This group included individuals ranging in age and situation from 18-year-old university students to 35-year-old married couples. The second group of people was (ostensibly) "*the parents*" of the "*young people*." This group included parents ranging in age from 45 to 65. Most of the interviewees were broadly middle class. It is educated middle-class people who are leading the fertility decline.

Lifestyles and values within Spain vary dramatically by geography, by urban or rural location, and most importantly by *nacionalidades* (nationalities, or ethnic groups). These *nacionalidades* are divided into historical and cultural administrative units called Autonomous Communities. Consequently, it is important to look at several different areas of Spain in order to be able to talk about the whole. The Autonomous Communities in the north have the lowest birthrates, some of which do not even reach 1.0 TFR: Asturias has a birthrate of 0.85, and Galicia has 0.92. The birthrate in the south is the highest but nevertheless only varies between 1.33 (Andalusia) and 1.51 (Murcia) (Instituto Nacional de Estadística (INE 2001). Nowhere in Spain is the birthrate above replacement level. Since fertility grades from extremely low in the north to slightly higher in the south, I chose to interview in a swath across the center of Spain. I wanted to visit the periphery as well as the center of Spain. Consequently, I chose four interview sites: Madrid (with 3 million+ inhabitants, the capital of Spain), Zamora (65,000 inhabitants, in rural

Castile), A Coruña (200,000 inhabitants, in Galicia on the Atlantic coast) and Valencia (760,000 inhabitants, on the Mediterranean coast). These cities were large urban centers (and provincial capitals) that spanned Spain, and thus were representative of the places that are moving the demographic numbers. I was not interested in the exceptions but rather the rule.

I tape-recorded conversations between many groups of young people and older parents, as well as engaged in spontaneous conversations with individuals. Each group was composed of eight to ten people of about similar ages. The same questions were posed to each group. In these conversations the participants expressed many opinions and debated among themselves. Rarely was there complete consensus. Nevertheless, I was impressed at the consistency of the responses. I also spoke to social demographers, social welfare workers, government administrators and academic experts about many other aspects of Spanish population decline. In my conversations with young people, I was especially interested in their long stay in the parental home (compared to northern Europe) and the parent–child dynamic thus produced.

Causes

When low birthrates are reported in the Spanish press, journalists quote experts from the various research institutes who give lists of reasons "why." Spanish experts on demography say that the reasons for the rapid decrease in the birthrate are the improved quality of life, improved education, an increase in contraceptive use and the speed of the country's social changes (Zaldivar and Castells 1992). Others point to the massive increase of women in the workforce and high unemployment, causing economic insecurity and a reluctance for youth to leave the parental home (Iglesias de Ussel 1998). According to others, the most important reasons given for the decrease in the birthrate are the drop in the nuptiality rate, the increased number of single people in the population and especially the high mean age of women when they have their first child (Bosch 1998). In 2000 the Spanish National Statistics Institute (INE) president listed the main factors affecting the decision to have children: level of education, marriage and religious belief (Bosch 2000). Sociologists have attributed the decline in birthrates to such economic factors as unemployment, low salaries and unaffordable housing (UN Wire 2000).

In these lists, political, economic, social and gender role changes are conflated, rather than teased apart. Moreover, it is assumed that the connections between some of the reasons and the data are self-evident. Although Spanish birthrates had been falling slowly since the late 1960s, 1975 marks the year when they began their spectacular dive from the European high to the European low. Consequently it is important to review the social changes that began to accelerate in 1975, upon Franco's death and the return to democracy.

Political Changes

From a political perspective the Francoist rule had been characterized by strong state intervention in all areas of economic and political life. The Constitution of 1978 paved the way for vast political and social changes. Certainly the Spain of 1970 and 1990 were galaxies apart. In 1970 the country was still under the iron grip of an arch-conservative Spanish leader, born in the nineteenth century, and supported by the military, the Church and the landed gentry, all still dragging behind them their nineteenth-century conservative ideals. Nevertheless, even in 1970, festering under the anachronistic surface of Franco's "official" Spain was the young, well-educated, well-traveled "baby boom" generation, products of the "Spanish [economic] Miracle" of the late 1950s and 1960s. This was also an urban generation, as Spain had passed from a primarily rural, agricultural population to a majority urban population in the mid-1960s.[4] This was a young, politically aware and politically active generation, who did not live the civil war, only its consequences. This generation, attuned to and longing for "Europe," was ready to take over Spain.[5] The majority of the Spanish people had effectively "modernized" even if the government had not. For many, Franco's death marked an already dead way of life. Consequently, when Franco died, residing within most Spaniards were many pent up desires: desires for democracy, Europeanization, higher standards of living and new roles for women. The political and social changes to come seemed to occur rapidly, but much of the population was already living in the already longed-for New Spain.

Gender Role and Other Social Changes

This brings us to a second great social change in Spain since the mid-1970s: the radically transformed role of women. Anthropologists writing in the 1980s about fieldwork in the 1970s wrote much about gender and women's status, exploring the so-called honor and shame complex.[6] We were fascinated with the asymmetrical public relationship between men and women, as well as the dynamic of the public–private opposition (Pitt-Rivers 1966; Brandes 1985; Gilmore 1987, 1990). As in many areas of the Mediterranean, it was believed that women had a stronger, lustier sexual drive than men and thus could not be responsible for their own sexuality. It was the responsibility of men to contain women. Thus grew up a social organization where women were contained and associated with the home and domestic sphere. Any women loose in public places were suspect and full of shame. Men avoided the feminization of the domestic sphere and parked themselves "in the street" – the bar, the plaza – always, however, suspicious of their women's whereabouts and motives. Although women were imagined by outsiders as oppressed and domesticated, Spanish men were painfully aware of female power (over them). As mothers and keepers of the house, women had real power there, which is why many Spaniards often referred to their society as a matriarchy.

During the Franco dictatorship women were encouraged to develop themselves within the domestic sphere. Educators created the ideal of the "true Catholic womanhood," based on models from the sixteenth century. True womanhood was self-abnegating, saintly and modest (Morcillo 2000). Chastity was stressed. Special relevance was given (by the government, by law and by the Church) to the role of "mother." The Francoist regime advanced a doctrine of the *perfecta casada* (perfect housewife) and *angel del hogar* (angel of the home), all the while promoting an "aggressive, pronatalist policy" (Nash 1991). Nonetheless, Spanish women had very few, and very unequal, public roles. They were constrained by a legal system that put them under male authority. Birth control, abortion and divorce were not allowed. In this ideology, female education was not important. Women often worked, but usually at service jobs, and only until marriage. In 1965 only 5 percent of married women worked (Miret-Gamundi 1997: 185). Children arrived soon after marriage because children, traditionally, were the very purpose of marriage (de Miguel and Escuin 1997).

However, the families that anthropologists studied in the 1970s did not reproduce this gender system. The children of these families left rural Spain for urban centers, and the daughters of these mothers took seriously their mothers' admonition: "Don't do as I did." Those daughters went to school, entered the university, got careers, and, in the majority, have had only one child.

Although by the end of the dictatorship gender roles were already changing, things exploded at the advent of democracy. The feminist movement made its first appearance in 1976, only two months after Franco died. The 1978 Constitution gave women equal rights under law.

In the 1970s women began filling the university classrooms and by 1987–88 there were more women in the university than men (Hooper 1996). Advanced education, and the time needed to get it, was another reason for postponing marriage. Education level correlates with low fertility. Women with fewer than five years of education have 2.72 children on average. For women with a secondary education the average is 1.37. Women with higher education and/or training have fewer than one (0.72) (INE 2000).[7] Increased educational attainment also affects labor force participation.

The percentage of Spanish women working doubled in twenty years, although at the present time the rate of women's labor force participation remains low compared to that of other European countries.[8] However, the difference between the generations is telling. Women in the workplace between the ages of 25 and 44 went from 13 percent in 1964 to 68 percent in 1988 (Carrasco and Rodríguez 2000). Not even having children was a cause for stopping work. Thus, married women employment has increased more rapidly than single women (Cebrián, Morena and

Toharia 1997). Working women on average have 1.0 child; those who dedicate themselves to the home (*labores de hogar*) have 1.97 (INE 2000).

Although studies show that married women, even if they hold outside jobs, do the large majority of the childcare and domestic work, men, especially young men, now say they expect to contribute to the domestic chores and childcare (de Miguel and Escuin 1997). The new norm of women working in the public sphere has led some Spaniards to conclude that "low fertility" is due to these young women behaving in a "masculine way" by displaying *egoismo* (self-centeredness, selfishness). Motherhood is still defined by *sacrificio* (sacrifice), not *egoismo*. Thus, according to this way of thinking, low fertility is a result of women's *egoismo*.

Furthermore, soon after the return to democracy, birth control, divorce and abortion were legalized (in 1978, 1981, 1985 respectively). Through these means women's roles in marriage became more equal to those of men. Certainly for women and couples, free and unfettered access to birth control pills and other contraceptives, which previously had been limited to condoms, abstinence and coitus interuptus, coincided with not only the drop in the birthrate, but also the postponement of marriage and a rise in the age of first-time motherhood.[9] Moreover, the sexual double standard has fallen, and women enjoy premarital sex without any social repercussion.

All of this was in spite of the enormous influence of Catholic doctrine in this overwhelmingly Roman Catholic country. Catholic doctrine proscribed sex outside of marriage and declared that within marriage sex was for reproductive purposes only. Although Spain remains a profoundly Catholic country culturally, belief and practice have been losing ground in a process of "galloping secularization" since the Second Vatican Council (1966). Among young people under 35, only half consider themselves believers and only 22 percent attend mass once a month (Hooper 1996: 143). About 42 percent never attend mass; almost 61 percent claim they are not religious; 14 percent of the population call themselves atheist (Europa Press 2001). Although most children are still baptized, that may be the last time they are in church until they marry.

Religious practice and belief also correlate with fertility. Practicing Catholic women have 1.29 children; non-practicing Catholics have 1.01 children; non-believers have less than 1 on average (Cañas 1999).

Certainly, since the early 1970s young women seem determined not to repeat their own mothers' life trajectories. Almost all anthropological literature on gender roles in Spain up through the early 1980s emphasized that to be an adult, both men and women had to be married and have children. This was especially true in the case of women. Motherhood was the longed-for social goal, celebrated in song, sayings and life. Suddenly in one generation this single life-goal evaporated for most women. Now to be a parent, to be a mother, is one of several goals, which ideally should be attained in the "proper" sequence of getting an education, finding appropriate job, experiencing freedom and consumer society, leaving home and living as a couple for several years before finally having children (Puyol 1997). In surveys and polls, young people often state that the couple is the point of marriage – not children (de Miguel and Escuin 1997: 160). This new understanding of the life cycle is a change in the value system. Postponing marriage and children is due not only to opportunity costs and economic restrictions (as many imply) but also to a change in aspirations and expectations, of woman as well as of men. The desire of these men and women to form a family competes with other desires that are equally, or more, important: desires of lifestyle, of consumption and of self-actualization, as we shall see.

It is interesting to note the difference in men's and women's responses to some questions in my interviews. When I asked young people if they wanted to live the life their parents had, young men overwhelmingly said, "Yes." They thought their fathers had had good lives. Young women, on the other hand, almost unanimously said that they did not want to live the life of their mothers. One 26-year-old woman said, "I don't want to live like my mother, who was always serving others." This was said, remember, while she lived at home studying at the university and her own mother continued cooking, cleaning and caring for her.

Part of the dilemma many young women may have with motherhood is that, despite the vast social changes in women's lives since the 1970s, the definition of "mother" has not changed (see Sánchez and Hall 1999). She is still the self-sacri-ficing, self-abnegating angel. Others have noted that this may cause women to have special difficulties reconciling working and having a family and has lead them to wonder if Spanish mothers are "culturally inclined to stay at home" (Fernández Cordón and Sgritta 2000). Although in my conversations almost all young people adamantly expressed the idea that it was perfectly fine for a woman who has a child/children to work, in polls more than half the general population says it is not a good thing for a mother with small children to work (Informe Juventud en 2000).

One of the oft-mentioned distinguishing characteristics of Spanish low fertility is that marriage is the principal gateway to having children. Unlike in the countries in Northern and Central Europe, in Spain and the other countries of Southern Europe, the number of children born out of wedlock is low: only 12 percent (Fernández Cordón and Sgritta 2000). However, since 1980 nuptiality rates have fallen by half. Most social demographers believe this is due to postponement of marriage (although almost 19 percent of 40-year-old women have never married). Cohabitation, while accepted as a social possibility, is not widely practiced. Only about 2.6 percent of Spanish couples cohabit (Congreso 1997). Moreover, it is considered a pre-marriage step, not a rejection of marriage (Alberdi *et al.* 1994). Many young people told me that they would definitely want to live with their partner before marriage, but at least until now social and parental pressure pre-cludes this from happening on a wide scale. One man, a 33-year-old civil engineer who had studied abroad for several years, returned home to live and work, living in his parents' home with a younger brother, age 29. This economically independent engineer has a fiancée (*novia*) and plans to be married "soon." Asked if he would like to live on his own, he answered that it wasn't worth the struggle with his parents, especially his mother.

As couples postpone marriage until late and childrearing until even later, the years of optimum fertility shrink. The mean age of childbearing is 30 years in Spain. In several Autonomous Communities the average age of first-time mothers is over 30. Spanish women between the ages of 30 and 34 have the major portion of births (Cañas 2002), and have the highest fertility rates of this age group in the EU (and the lowest fertility among young women).[10] Although my own data and many social surveys show that men and women say that their ideal number of children is two, in many cases there is often not "time" to have two children (Informe Juventud 2000). Moreover, the desired number of children changes over time as couples confront new social and economic challenges. Nor are couples always in agreement about the number of children desired. One 35-year-old woman with one child told me that it was her husband who didn't want any more children. He said that at 37 years old he "just couldn't do it [raise another child] again." So he went out to have a vasectomy. She was heartbroken.

In conversations with several groups of older women, the topic of why older daughters could not get pregnant or why they miscarried often came up. This was an obvious topic since I was talking with them about fertility. There were all kinds of speculation: too long on birth control pills, low male sperm count or stress.[11] It is important to note that almost all of these older women thought their daughters lived a more stressful life than they had. The mothers spoke positively about their daughters' careers and work but, these women seemed to be saying that working and having one child is more stressful than their own lives with three or four children but not working outside the home.

The daughters, on the other hand, voice different reasons for low fertility. In the 2000 Encuesta de Fertilidad (Fertility Survey) about one in four Spanish women said they have fewer children than they would like due to economic restraints (INE 2000). The women who chose this answer, of several offered, implied that they could not afford to have more/any children. Economists also point out that Spain is the EU country that gives the least economic help and social protection to families (Nogueira 2002).

Economic Causes

Many economic reasons are given to explain the low birthrate. Such things as high unemployment, low salaries and unaffordable housing are always mentioned by demographers. Spain was especially hard hit during the restructuring of its economy and the world recession of the 1980s. The economic conversion from a protectionist capitalist system under Franco to a competitive economy compatible with the new global system resulted in recession. Unemployment soared. It went down during a period of economic growth (1987–92) and later rose again when Spain's economy foundered in the 1990s. During these periods youth unemployment was many times higher than that of the general population. Obtaining the first job was especially difficult. Even now, Spain has the highest unemployment rate in the European Union, hovering around 14 percent (Agencias 2000). Nevertheless, during the period when unemployment figures were low, birthrates continued to plunge. Unemployment, coupled with low salaries and unaffordable housing, are arguments inevitably invoked to explain why the majority of young people in Spain continue living at home with their natal families until their thirties.

Housing in Spain is expensive. Prices began to rise in 1984 and later soared. Interest rates are high and mortgages are paid off relatively quickly (usually less than fifteen years). Housing has been an area of spectacular speculation and investment, witnessing average price rises of more than 15 percent annually through 2000. Construction of public housing is low. Nevertheless, 85 percent of Spanish families own homes.

Sociologists assume that these negative economic conditions keep Spanish youth living at home, when, of course, "naturally" they would much rather leave the parental house if they could (Leal Maldonado 1995; Fernández Cordón and Sgritta 2000). Several unexamined assumptions characterize this argument. Certainly it was extremely difficult for young people to find jobs in the 1980s and in their minds, this continues today. It is almost a mantra, repeated over and over, that it is difficult to find a job.

The job search, however, is complicated by the fact that young people do not want just "jobs," but rather jobs that they have studied for (at university or technical school), in other words, careers. Moreover, they want what they specify as "stable jobs" (*un trabajo estable, un trabajo fijo*), which means a permanent job with a future, a job for life. Other researchers have noted this prerequisite of a *trabajo estable*, as well as the generalized preference for a position in public administration rather than the private sector, due to more perceived security. In one poll 49 percent of those surveyed said that, if given a choice, they would prefer to work for the state (de Miguel and Escuin 1997: 79). Thus, many young people will remain in the parental home studying for civil service exams or waiting for a position to open up. A temporary job, part-time job or a job that is not in one's true career is not worth leaving home for.

Another cultural restriction is that most middle-class young people prefer jobs in the same city in which their family lives. Regional and national identities play a role here. Although in my interviews most young people said they would go to another part of Spain to get a job, the reality is that they do not. This is a new phenomenon. In the 1950s and 1960s there was much internal migration as the poor and jobless from the south and rural areas throughout Spain left native villages and migrated to jobs in cities or abroad. That migration was the catalyst for Spain's urbanization. Now, however, "underemployment" is a middle class, urban phenomenon. Since the late 1970s, as Spain has undergone a period of political reinvention of its "historical" identities (Catalan, Basque, Andalusian, etc.), people are reluctant to leave their region of identity – even to find work.

A final point worth mentioning is the lingering bias against manual labor in Spain. This often translates as a reluctance to cross class lines when looking for work. "Job" also means a job with the appropriate social status. One academic demographer commented that most middle-class parents want their children to have "good" jobs (as doctors or lawyers), even if the son or daughter would make less money than in a blue-collar job (as electricians or technicians). Therefore, the many recent immigrants in Spain take jobs in agriculture and construction that Spaniards don't want.

The other economic argument that both demographers and young people themselves offer for not leaving home is the dearth of affordable housing, but "housing," like "jobs," is also a cultural construction. Unaffordable housing contributes to the low birthrate because Spaniards of all ages think married life should begin in a home they own (versus rent). Spanish young people don't want to marry until they can buy a home, and, furthermore, furnish it completely. For their parents this was not necessarily so. During the 1960s 47 percent of people rented and people did "not perceive any necessity of buying a dwelling to live in" (Miret-Gamundi 1997: 193). Now engaged couples often spend several years of their engagement living in their respective parents' homes while they pay off the mortgage of a home they are buying.

Moreover, only 15 percent of the housing market in Spain is rental, which is the lowest in the European Union (Hernán Montalbán and López Maderuelo 1995). Spain, however, has the highest ownership of second family homes in the EU. Almost a quarter of the population has a second family home (often a vacation home), with the result that many homes sit empty most of the time (Leal Maldonado 1995). These homes are often used only a few days a year. As we shall see, young people find a use for these second family homes, but they do not live in them.

Likewise, newer and more culturally acceptable housing (with modern facilities and design) in the desired center of urban areas is very expensive and often unattainable for young people (de Miguel and Escuin 1997). Most Spanish young people expect to move out of their parents' home and into a home of similar quality. They don't want to move down.

Marriage is the only appropriate reason accepted by both generations for leaving the parental home, which explains why cohabitation forms only a small part of Spanish social life. Marriage as the gateway to leaving the parental home also explains the lack of young people sharing a rental property as roommates. The desire to leave home is simply not strong enough to motivate young, unmarried people to find more economical forms of housing. For example, one university student, a single man within a year of graduating, told me in front of his parents that, "Even if I get a job earning a lot of money, I probably won't leave home."

A further economic reason that has contributed to lowering the birthrate is, ironically, the overall rise in the quality of life since 1975. As the Spanish economy modernized (1960–80), Spaniards have become consumers. Part of the pent-up desires that were released when Spain buried its fascist government and rejoined the democracies of Northern Europe was the full-blown development of consumer society. A telling example of this process is the fact that in 1980 there were only 33 shopping centers or malls in Spain. By the year 2000 there were 386 (Nogueira 2000). Spaniards not only entertain themselves by becoming consumers of material goods and services, but also travel and consume experience, like all young Europeans. The infamous morality of "thrift" and "austerity" of the 1940s and 1950s (Morcillo 2000) gave way to an orgy of spending and buying in the 1980s and 1990s. Young people repeatedly told me that marriage (and especially child-care) would put a damper on their ability to go out, to travel, to go skiing, to "enjoy life." One 32-year-old man, a salesman and father of a 6 month old, told me that his generation did not want to miss out on the things his parents' generation had. There still seems to be a pent-up desire for consumerism, which in young people trumps the desire for their complete independence.

In addition, most young people express a desire to "live as a couple" for "a few years" after marriage. When I inquired what they meant by "to live together as a couple," most explained that they wanted to be able to live free of the responsibility of children so they could spend money on themselves and their own consumption.[12] This was often said in order to contrast their relationship with that of their parents' marriages, which often saw children arrive nine months after marriage.[13] When people finally marry, couples wait on average three years before having children (Castro Martín 1992).

The above cultural prerequisites explain another trend that has appeared: that of the adult child living in the parental home. As stated earlier, the majority of Spanish youth live at home until marriage. Marriage has been postponed and the age of marriage has risen to 30 years. This very late *emancipación* ("emancipation" – leaving home and becoming economically independent) on the part of young Spaniards has coincided with the impressive decline of Spanish births. Thus, one of the cultural "twists and turns" (Kreager 1997) of the low Spanish fertility, after the long postponement of marriage itself and the cultural norm of not having children outside of marriage, is the extremely long dependent period of youth. Sociologists and demographers blame this delayed emancipation on economic factors, as well as the new gender roles and political conditions. To summarize: the implication is that Spanish youth would leave home earlier if they could, but they are prohibited by needing to prepare themselves for jobs, the tight job market, high unemployment and the lack and prohibitively high cost of housing.

This may have been true in the 1980s but twenty years later, what once had been an economic impediment, has changed to a cultural preference. "Why should we leave? We're fine here. We live in a five-star hotel!" Young people I spoke to expressed this sentiment – with the same wording – over and over to me all across Spain. Thus, one of the most striking aspects to an American about Spanish fertility decline is how it is linked to and made possible by the "Spanish family." Many Spanish youth live at home until they are 30 or 35 (or more) and, what's more, their parents want them to. Their parents recruit them to live at home and put many pressures on them to stay until marriage. One researcher wonders if "the coziness of the family nest prevents young people from adapting themselves better to changing conditions of the labour market and to changing their preferences in relation to housing" (Fernández Cordón and Sgritta 2000: 9). Another asks, "What factors can lead to a young person remaining single and under the parental home until almost thirty years old? Is it the love at home or the hostility outside?" (Miret-Gamundi 1997: 195).

In the rest of this chapter I want to explore the phenomenon of adult children living at home in Spain and propose it as one of the interesting and differentiating characteristics of Spanish low fertility.

"We're fine here. We live in a five-star hotel"

"To many Spanish families, it must appear that their children will live with them forever!" (Miret-Gamundi 1997: 183). According to Informe Juventud 2000, only three of every ten young people at age 29 are economically independent of their parents. This is less than in 1990. Seemingly, "young people can't manage to leave the nest" (Longhi-Bracaglia 2000).

For most people I spoke to there seems to be nothing pressing about leaving home. Many young people assured me that they wanted to leave home eventually, but not yet. To begin with, for this generation of Spaniards there are few family tensions. Compared to the strict patriarchal family of the early half of the century, Spanish families are now characterized by permissiveness (Alberdi *et al.* 1994). Democratic values are pervasive and acceptance of all lifestyles is the norm. Adult children are not trying to escape.

Moreover, parents see no reason for their children to leave home before marriage. Mothers, especially, said they wanted their children to leave "*por la puerta grande*" (through the front door, i.e. marriage). Since parents want their children to stay home until marriage, they have accommodated modern youth by making the family like Spanish democracy: open and accepting. In fact, very few rules or strictures are imposed on Spanish youth. Since most social life takes place in the "street" (i.e. outside the home), young Spanish people spend most of their free time out socializing. Cities in Spain are infamous for their night life. Teenagers and young people in their twenties go out several nights a week to discothèques and bars. To stay out till 7:00 a.m. or even later is common on weekend nights, even for teenagers. Meals are another instance of when young people come and go as they please. Most people said they would let someone know if they were not coming to dinner, but there was no obligation.

Another example of accommodation is that these young adults have virtually no domestic chores. I specifically asked questions about mutual responsibilities. Young women usually said that they made their beds and helped clean up the kitchen, but as long as they are in the parental home, most young people up to their thirties do not cook or shop for meals. One 29-year-old woman, who works full time in the modeling business, even had her mother buy her deodorant and other necessities for her. Mothers cook, clean, wash, iron and run errands. Several people agreed with what one interviewee told me: "My parents tell me that my responsibility is to study." Another 25-year-old, to generalized laughter, joked, "If they give me any [chores], I'll leave."

Money is another issue that surfaced in all the recorded conversations. I asked about money because I wondered how young people were paying for their active social lives in the "streets." It is not common or well considered in the middle classes for teenagers to have part-time or summer jobs. Many people told me they received a *paga* (an allowance). In one group, university students up to 26 years old said their fathers gave them a monthly *paga*. However, most people I talked to who were still living at home had some kind of part-time job: tutoring, private classes, working in a bar or working in a store. Older youths, around 30, had full-time jobs; 62 percent of young people who live at home work, while 20 percent are only students (Miret-Gamundi 1996). Those young adults with jobs sometimes give money to the household, more as a symbolic gesture than out of necessity or expectation. This seems to be more common in the memory of young adults aged 34–36; 25 year olds said they give small symbolic sums, while 20 year olds give nothing. Thus, most money earned in part-time or full-time jobs is spent on self.

Part of the parental strategy of keeping their offspring at home is not to make any financial demands on them, either overtly or covertly (through guilt).[14] One mother, a cleaner, bragged that her 21-year-old son was voluntarily giving money from his first job's paycheck to his father. Unbeknown to the son, the father was putting the money into a bank account in order to return it to the son when he finally marries.

The only restriction families put on young people's "freedom" was in the area of sex. With very few exceptions, young people told me that they could not have their lovers (girlfriend or boyfriend, *novia/novio*) in their rooms. Since according to sociologists the permissibility of sex outside of marriage has made possible the long postponement of marriage in Spain, I was interested in where sex was taking place. Spanish young people tend to opt for long-term relationships (*noviazgos*) (Iglesias de Ussel 1998), which in many ways approximate some aspects of marriage, such as inclusion at family celebrations and Sunday dinners. *Novios* of many years who are in their late twenties or early thirties must look for opportunities for sexual intercourse outside of the home. Where does sex take place for these youths? Everywhere the same list was given: the second family home, the house in the village or a hotel on weekend trips. Younger, and presumably less moneyed, people added to the list: the car, the parks and (in some cities) the beach. In the fall of 2000 I watched a television sit-com that referred to the plethora of condoms now found in city parks and night parking spots. These public sites of sexual encounters seem to be the only inconvenience of living at home.

Parents of Spanish youths want their adult children to stay home because it is a jungle out there. As evidence of the power of the market, these parents want their children to be "prepared" to get a job. Recall that their vision of the New Economy is that culturally acceptable jobs are scarce and competitive. So Spanish parents are willing and able to offer their adult children refuge. Spanish families spend a long time preparing their children to be "marketable," getting them ready to compete in the wage-labor market. Training and school are very important.

The university system itself is structured so as to allow people to remain in the category "student" for years. Over 30 percent of Spaniards go on to university (Hooper 1996).[15] The structure of the university is such that a student hardly ever fails out. If a student fails a final exam in June, he or she can retake it in September. If the student fails it in September, it is possible to retake the course (and the exam) several times. Although courses must be taken in a certain order, there is no minimum number of classes a student must have to be a "full-time" student in the university: to begin five courses in the fall, drop two and fail one is typical. It has no repercussion on one's final outcome at the university (except length of stay). One can spend years studying for a desirable profession. In one university, la Politécnica de Catalonia, the average time in university for a 5-year major is 8.65 years (Hooper 1996).[16] Then there are workshops, extra courses, language schools, summers abroad studying language and master's courses. After the university, students often spend years studying for the *oposiciones*, entrance exams, to state and civil service jobs. In the upper-middle classes 40 percent of 25 to 29 year olds are still studying (Hernán Montalbán and López Maderuelo 1995). All of this is without leaving home. Students almost always attend universities in their home town (or near it, in the case of a small village). In the meantime the "student" lives at home.

The young people I spoke to, in general, simply did not have to separate from their parents in order to feel treated as adults. Most people told me they felt completely understood and free to "be" who they were in their family home. Recall that the family is the one area of life that Spaniards say brings them most happiness. Informants were perplexed, and defensive at my questions. "Why should I leave? I'm fine here," they answered, throwing the onus back on me, the interviewer, to explain why this was even a question. In 2002, one 17-year-old male told me adamantly that he would never leave the family (I assumed he meant to live on his own). This was no different from the 24-year-old male with his own business and in a three-year *noviazgo*, who in 2000 said he had absolutely no desire to leave home. "*Estoy bien en casa!*" 'I'm fine at home!" Over and over I heard that phrase.

Although in every group I interviewed there were always exceptions to the rule, most young Spaniards saw no persuasive reason to leave the parental home. They were aware that at home everything was taken care of for them. They could tick off on their fingers the advantages: food, laundry, ironing and clean environment. They lived surrounded by televisions, videos, cars and computers. As my informants rhetorically asked me, "Why would I leave home? I live in a five-star hotel [*un hotel de cinco estrellas*]."

The metaphor of the hotel came out in many contexts and conversations. Parents also use this expression to ask me why their children would leave home – "They live in a five-star hotel!" Other times parents seem to complain to their children, admonishing them, that their home is not a *pensión*. Young people, when talking about their (lack of) responsibilities at home, would explain that their parents did not want their home to be just a *pensión*, a hotel that offers breakfast and dinner but no other relationships. "Don't just come here to sleep and leave dirty clothes," mimicked one.

When I asked if they wanted to leave home, many young people said, "Yes, but not yet." Or they "can't now." Many explained about the expensive "housing" or the difficulty getting "jobs." After talking about the cultural prerequisites of "housing" and "jobs," however, someone in almost every group would summarize by saying that young Spaniards could leave home but they don't want to. They seem to be putting into practice the wry Spanish expression, "Live off your parents until you can live off your children." In conversation after conversation, young Spanish people confessed to (and parents sometimes complained of) *comodidad* and *egoismo*, i.e. being addicted to comfort and being self-centered and selfish.

Earlier cohorts of Spaniards, *the parents*, who had come of age in the 1960s and 1970s, had married rather young compared to previous generations (Alberdi *et al.* 1994). Then, young marriage had been facilitated by urbanization, industrialization and a booming economy. Those generations of Spaniards had gone from home directly to marriage at an early age because, economists say, they could afford to do so. However, there was another factor. Informants of that age told me that they had married in order to be "free" (*libre*). Marriage in the 1960s and 1970s had symbolized "freedom" (*libertad*). Those generations had also stayed at home until marriage, thereby adhering to the traditional norm. But in those cases, marriage became their escape, especially for women, from the very authoritarian, patriarchal family structure that characterized Spanish families during the dictatorship. Marriage was equated with "freedom" in their minds. One woman, in explaining this to me, recounted the sensation of freedom she felt when she got married and did not have to conform to her father's time schedules for lunch and dinner. Children, the final step on the path to adulthood, soon followed, generally within the year.

The current generation of young people also used the category "freedom" to explain their decision. Young people now, however, said that they were *not* marrying, or leaving home, in order to be "free." Marriage is now seen as an impediment to their freedom. This impediment is not just being tied down relationally, but also economically. I questioned young informants about the term "freedom," and its definition. The young in city after city answered that they wanted freedom "to go out, to socialize, to travel." At home they are freer to consume experience (go out, socialize, travel) than they would be on their own.

Having children, especially, is believed to inhibit "freedom." Children, although desired by the majority of my informants, were described as *una carga* (a burden), or *una gran responsibilidad* (a huge responsibility). As the Spanish demographer Anna Cabré has said, "If they don't have children, it's because they don't feel like it . . . but this isn't said" (quoted in Rivière 2000).

These young adults view the world of work and marriage (independence) as responsibilities, which will hinder, in some ways, their ability live well. Even romantic relationships were not compelling enough to make them want to lose their freedom. As one woman noted, "We want freedom, but it's a comfortable freedom (*libertad cómoda*)". Another said, "*Somos muy señoritos a la hora de irnos, ¿sabes?*" (We are very "spoiled" about when we will leave, you know).[17]

Conclusion

At first glance, the low birthrate in Spain may seem to be a result of the same factors shared by all European countries: urbanization, secularization, new social roles of women, education, consumer society, opportunity costs and other economic instabilities. However, Spain's own "twists and turns" are more fascinating to contemplate. They, like the other examples in this book, belie a hegemonic model of the family and marriage that is imposing itself in a homogenous way.

Although headlines sometimes sensationalize the possible repercussions of below replacement level fertility, many Spaniards find it hard to imagine the autonomous, "sad and lonely" one-child family that these figures imply. After all, they are ensconced in a large web of family relationships: parents between 45 and

65 years old still living with (adult) children at home; young people up to 30 years old still living at home. It is the stable "traditional" family that has facilitated the low Spanish birthrate. Ironically, birthrates are higher in the northern countries, with their higher rates of divorce, cohabitation, birth outside marriage and women in the workplace.

Economic issues – lack of jobs and lack of housing – certainly impede the first step toward "independence" (leaving home), but as everywhere these issues are culturally conditioned. What distinguishes Spanish young people from some other European youth is their lack of hurry out of the parental home. Men and women have redefined adulthood as getting established in a career, or finding a *trabajo estable*. The appropriate job will bring the possibility of economic independence from the parents, but most young Spaniards do not act on that economic independence until they are ready to marry and buy a house. Only then will they leave the parental home. "Freedom," as defined as a lack of (economic and social) responsibility, competes with economic autonomy, and, of course, children. Most young Spaniards say they want children, yet in the correct sequence, and they want to savor every step along the way. Playing in the market comes first. The result has been to lower Spanish fertility rates to among the lowest in the world.

Notes

1. Spain did not take part in the Second World War. The civil war, which ended in 1939, had devastated the country – physically and spiritually. Rebuilding and stabilization took place during the 1940s. Franco, although a Fascist and an ally of Germany and Italy, kept Spain out of the world war.

2. Spain has the longest life expectancy of the countries represented in this volume: men, 75.9 years, and women, 82.8 years (United Nations Population Division 2003).

3. In 1999 4.7 percent of births in Spain were to foreign mothers. That year 15,000 more babies were born than in 1998. However, 17,815 babies were to foreign mothers. Statistics were not available yet for the years 2000 and 2001 but as immigration continued to grow (and the population continued to grow) in those years, it is possible that immigration will have even greater weight in the birthrate numbers for those years (Nogueira 2002).

4. The UN calculates that in 2000 78 percent of Spanish citizens live in an urban environment. Spanish calculations tend to be higher (around 85 percent).

5. Since the Spanish empire declined in the eighteenth century, and northern European countries acceded to political, cultural and economic domination of the world, "Spain" has felt left behind. The Enlightenment did not find fertile ground in conservative, closed, Catholic Spain. In the first half of the nine-teenth century, Romantic authors from England and France fled to the unin-

dustrialized Mediterranean countries in search of passion and authenticity. The French author, Alexandre Dumas, declared in 1846 that "Africa begins on the other side of the Pyrenees." Such was the Romantics' perception of Spain's backwardness. By the end of that century many members of the literary Generation of '98 were urging Spain to "Europeanize" as a solution to Spain's failures. The Spanish civil war and Franco's triumph and forty-year dictatorial rule re-emphasized Spain's difference from more democratic northern Europe. Although the Franco government had applied to join the EU in the 1960s, the petition was rejected. Not until after democracy was re-established was Spain allowed to join (1985). Although most young people in Spain now feel confidently "European", in the 1970s this was not the case.

6. Honor and shame never characterized the whole Iberian peninsula. Ethnographic work in the north and in urban areas, starting in the 1970s, always denied the ubiquity of this behavior code between men and women.

7. Women with fewer than five years' education make up less than 2 percent of women age 15–49; women with a secondary education compose 47 percent of that population; women with higher education are 32 percent of the fertile population (INE 2000).

8. In 1999, 37.5 percent of Spanish women were working. The EU average was 56 percent, with a high of 60.1 percent in Denmark and a low 35.4 percent in Italy (Ministerio de Trabajo y Asuntos Sociales y Instituto de la Mujer 1999 http://www.mtas.es/mujer/mcifras/principa.htm, accessed 5/15/2001).

9. Nevertheless, condoms are the most used method of birth control. More than twice the number of women depends on condom use (by men) than uses the birth control pill (42 to 20 percent) (INE 2000). Numbers of abortion are also extremely low in Spain compared to other European countries. According to INE, 1.7 percent of women between the ages of 15 and 49 have had a legal abortion (INE 2000). In the 1990s legal abortion in Spain averaged 5.5 per 1000 births. Compare to Italy (11.4), France (12.9), Sweden (18.7) and the Czech Republic (25) (Henshaw, Singh and Haas 1999).

10. In 1999 Spain and Italy had the highest mean age of women at childbearing (around 30 years), with France at 29.2, Greece 28.6 and Austria at 27.9 (EUROSTAT, in Fernández Cordón and Sgritta 2000).

11. No one ever mentioned that they thought that a woman in her thirties was possibly too old to conceive.

12. Divorce rates in Spain are the second lowest in Europe (Iglesias de Ussel 1998: 54), although they have doubled since 1993, to 14 percent of marriages (INE 2000). This rise in the divorce rate has impressed young people. Waiting several years after marriage to *adaptarse/acoplarse* (to get adapted or get used to each other) is also a way of not involving children in a possible divorce.

13. It should be noted that their parents' generation, who married between 1960 and 1975, married at an age almost ten years younger than the present generation (Delgado 1993).
14. Ironically I recorded several stories from the parental generations of sons going to work at age 12 or 14 (in the 1950s and 1960s) and handing all their money over to the parents.
15. A Director of Families, Minors, and Adoptions in Valencia told me that 65 percent of Spaniards start at the university.
16. An architect in Valencia told me that the average time for a student to complete architecture at the university in Valencia was twelve years.
17. This literally translates as, "We are very much like the pampered sons of the upper class landed-gentry at the hour of leaving".

References

Agencias (2000), "España sigue con el nivel de paro más alto de la UE," *El País*, Economía, October 4: 70.

Alberdi, I., Alvira, F., Cabré, A. *et al.* (1994), *Informe Sobre La Situación de la Familia en España*, Madrid: Ministerio de Asunto Sociales.

Bosch, X. (1998), "Investigating the Reasons for Spain's Falling Birthrate," *The Lancet*, 352 (9131): 887.

—— (2000), "Spain's Birthrate Drops to an All-Time Low," *The Lancet*, 355, (9198): 126.

Brandes, S. (1985), "Women of Southern Spain: Aspirations, Fantasies, Realities," *Anthropology*, 9: 111–128.

Cañas, G. (1999), "España es el país con el menor tasa de fecundidad del mundo, Según INE," *El País*, December 22.

—— (2002), "Las españolas son las europeas que más tarde tienen a su Primer Hijo," *El País*, edición impresa, October 9.

Carrasco, C. and Rodríguez, A. (2000), "Women, Families, and Work in Spain: Structural Changes and New Demands," *Feminist Economics*, 6(1): 45–57.

Castro Martín, T. (1992), "Delayed Childbearing in Contemporary Spain: Trends and Differentials," *European Journal of Population*, 8 : 217–246.

Cebrián, I., Morena, G. and Toharia, L. (1997), "Las transiciones laborales de las mujeres casadas en España, 1987–1996," *Información Comercial Española*, 760.

Congreso (1997), *Informe de la Subcomisión para Analizar la Situación actual de la Familia en España (154/2):* La Familia en España. Datos demográficos y estadísticos, 137, May 6.

Corell, M. and Cañas, G. (2001), "'El lujo' de tener hijos," *El País*, Sociedad, May 27: 32.

Cortés Alcalá, L., (ed.) (1995), *Pensar la vivienda*, Madrid: Agora.

Delgado, M. (1993), "Cambios Reciente en el Proceso de Formació de la Familia," *European Child and Adolescent Psychiatry*, 9: 123–153.

Delgado Pérez, M. and Livi-Bacci, M. (1992), "Fertility in Italy and Spain: The Lowest in the World," *Family Planning Perspectives*, 24(4): 162–171.

de Miguel, A. and Escuin, M. (1997), *ABC de la Opinión Española*, Madrid: Espasa.

EFE (2002), "La tasa de natalidad en España continua subiendo," *El Mundo*, Sociedad, October 15.

Escárraga, T. (2000), "El 30% de los jovenes españoles considera la inmigración prejudicial para la raza," *El País*, Sociedad, October 20: 30.

Europa Press (2001), "La mitad de los españoles cree que la sociedad es 'bastante' racista," *El País Digital*, January 25.

Fernández Cordón, J.A. and Sgritta, G.B. (2000), "The Southern Countries of the European Union: a Paradox?", paper presented at the seminar "Low Fertility, Families and Public Policies," organized by the European Observatory on Family Matters in Seville, Spain, September 15–16.

Gilmore, D.D. (ed.) (1987), *Honor and Shame and the Unity of the Mediterranean*, Washington, DC: American Anthropological Association.

—— (1990), "Men and Women in Southern Spain: 'Domestic Power' Revisited," *American Anthropologist*, 92: 953–970.

Henshaw, S.K., Singh, S. and Haas, T. (1999), "Recent Trends in Abortion Rates Worldwide," *International Family Planning Perspectives*, 25(1): 44–48.

Hernán Montalbán, J. and López Maderuelo, O. (1995), "Jóvenes y vivienda: conceptos, estrategias y políticas," in L. Cortés Alcalá (ed.) *Pensar la vivienda*, Madrid: Agora.

Hooper, J. (1996), *Los Nuevos Españoles*, Madrid: Javier Vergara Editor.

Iglesias de Ussel, J. (1998), *La Familia y el Cambio Político en España*, Madrid: Tecnos.

Informe Juventud en 2000 (2000), Ministerio de Trabajo y Asuntos Sociales y Centro de Investigaciones Sociológicas.

Instituto Nacional de Estadística (INE) (2000), *Encuesta de Fecundidad 1999, Resultados definitivos*, Madrid, Spain: see http://www.ine.es, December 21, 2000.

—— (2001), *España en cifras*: Población: Número medio de Hijos por mujer, p. 10, Madrid: INE.

Kreager, P. (1997), "Population and Identity," in D. Kertzer and T. Fricke (eds) *Anthropological Demography: Towards a New Synthesis*, Chicago: University of Chicago Press.

"La mitad de los españoles cree que debe restringirse la entrada de extranjeros" (2000), *El País*, October 22.

Leal Maldonado, J. (1995), "La cuestión de la vivienda o la vivienda como problema Social," in L. Cortés Alcalá (ed.) *Pensar la vivienda*, Madrid: Agora.

Longhi-Bracaglia, I. (2000), "Uno de cada dos jóvenes se va de casa después de los 29," *El Mundo*, Sociedad, October 20.

Miret-Gamundi, P. (1997), "Nuptiality Patterns in Spain in the Eighties," *Genus*, 53 (3–4): 183–198.

Morcillo, A.G. (2000), *True Catholic Womanhood*, Dekalb, IL: Northern Illinois University Press.

Nash, M. (1991), "Pronatalism and Motherhood in Franco's Spain," in G. Bock and P. Thane (eds) *Maternity and Gender Policies: Women and the Rise of the European Welfare States, 1880s-1950s*, New York: Routledge.

Nogueira, C. (2000), "Los centros comerciales se consagran los sábados como alternativa de ocio y compras," *El País*, Sociedad, June 19: 32.

—— (2002), "España es el país de la EU que menos ayuda a la familia, según Eurostat," *El País, edición impresa*, February 23.

Pitt-Rivers, J. (1966), "Honor and Social Status," J.G. Péristiany (ed.) in *Honor and Shame*, Chicago: University of Chicago Press.

Puyol, R. (ed.) (1997), *Dinámica de la Población en España: Cambios demográficos en el último cuarto del siglo XX*, Madrid: Editorial Sintesis.

Reher, D.S. (1996), *La Familia en España: Pasado y Presente*, Madrid: Alianza Universidad.

Rivière, M. (2000), "Anna Cabré, La investigadora de los españoles," *El País Semanal*, 1224, March 12.

Sánchez, L. and Hall, C. (1999), "Traditional Values and Democratic Impulses: The Gender Division of Labor in Contemporary Spain," *Journal of Comparative Family Studies*, 30(4): 659.

United Nations Population Division (UNPD) (2000), *Replacement Migration: Is It a Solution to Declining and Ageing Populations?* New York: UN, Dept of Economic and Social Affairs.

—— (2003), *World Population Prospects: The 2002 Revision Population Database*, New York: UN, Dept of Economic and Social Affairs.

UN Wire (2000), "Spain: Birthrate Falls Dramatically," http://www.unfoundation.org, *Women's International Network*, March 1.

Zaldivar, C.A. and Castells, M. (1992), *España Fin de Siglo*, Madrid: Alianza Editorial.

–10–

Making Family:
Depopulation and Social Crisis in France

Anna Lim

The demographic situation of France is serious. Public authorities are aware of this, and the government has recently proposed a new series of measures on behalf of large families. This strategy will be pursued in all sector-based policies likely to have a favorable effect on our demography. But family size is a matter for couples themselves to decide. All the state can do is ensure that the choices expressing their wishes and their freedom are more real and more responsible, in particular by providing better information about their consequences for society as a whole. The people of France must understand and choose. (Institut National d'Etudes Démographiques (INED) 1980: IX, Presentation of the general report on the demographic situation in France)

This chapter examines the development of French family policy in the context of demographic concerns over low birthrates in France, focusing in particular on the social and symbolic implications of that policy as birthrates dropped below replacement levels in the mid-1970s. While public officials had long been concerned with the low birthrates of the French, and thus had established an extensive family policy promoting higher birthrates as early as the 1920s, the drop below replacement levels led to new types of depopulation fears. This drop spawned the idea that families were not sufficiently reproducing to ensure the continuation of French society, and thus was taken as the incontestable sign of not so much a weak nation vulnerable to attack, but a society in crisis. Rather than place restrictive controls on the newly acquired contraceptive rights, French officials reinforced and expanded the already highly generous system of family benefits to increase birthrates. It was believed that the social promotion of families would reinforce social responsibility, leading to larger families, hence restoring French society to a healthy, socially productive state.

   It is widely acknowledged that France has one of the best social systems in the world and one of the most extensive, non-digressive systems of family benefits. I argue in this chapter that this is the case because family and children became the focal point of efforts to "save" French society. However, what constitutes a healthy, socially productive society came to be defined through ideas about family wherein certain families were deemed less apt than others to contribute. These distinctions were based not so much on class than on the cultural difference that certain families were said to embody.

The populations in the overseas departments in the Caribbean, namely Martinique and Guadeloupe (more commonly referred to as the French Antilles), were excluded from many of the new social advantages accorded to the family. Martinique and Guadeloupe are nevertheless part of France, and have been since 1946 when their colonial status was converted to departmental status. French Antilleans are hence full French citizens by birth, and in theory without distinction. Those laws and rights applicable in "metropolitan" (i.e. continental) France are supposed to be applicable in the French Antilles. Nevertheless, public officials argued that the full distribution of family benefits in the overseas departments would increase the already "overly elevated" birthrates and thus run counter to the larger goal of socially aligning these departments with metropolitan France. Because public officials claimed that the problem in these departments was the opposite of that in metropolitan France, a differential policy seemed justified. The problem may have been framed in terms of numbers (i.e. "overpopulation" and "high fertility"), but at issue were the social implications and consequences of large Antillean families, seen as wholly different from "French" families.

In addition to presenting the situation of French Antilleans vis-à-vis French family policy, this chapter examines foreign immigration policy, which became highly restrictive during the 1970s and 1980s concerning foreign entry into France, the acquisition of legal resident status by immigrants, and the acquisition of French nationality. The new controls primarily targeted immigrants from France's former colonies in Africa – with whom the term "immigrant" and particularly "illegal immigrant" came increasingly to be associated – rather than immigrants from other European countries. At this time, both in the media and within political debates, great attention was called to immigrant families, and in particular their cultural distance. It was feared that these immigrant families would not fully integrate and thus would threaten the stability of French society.

The situation of foreign immigrants complements that of Antilleans in unpacking the ways in which conceptions of family and fertility and the social symbolics of the "demographic problem," expressed through family, were used to define the constitution and future constitution of French society. The question raised by these policies is less whether social policy is able to meet the needs of an entire population or provide equally for all members of society. What is of interest to me here are the underlying assumptions and the social implications of that policy. I argue in this chapter that the increasing emphasis on the social promotion and social responsibility of families as a solution to the demographic crisis led to specific determinations about *who* would be responsible for assuring the future of French society and bringing French society out of its crisis. Furthermore, I suggest that the fears of depopulation and the sense of social crisis that seemed to be a response to the drop in birthrates below replacement levels were actually the outcome of a growing concern over how certain members of the population might alter the constitution of French society.

This chapter touches on questions concerning French conceptions of family and social belonging that I have been working through for some time now. At the time of writing I have been living in France for over five years, of which two and a half years were consecrated to ethnographic fieldwork and archival research in metropolitan France and the French Antilles as part of my dissertation research on family and French demographic policy concerning the overseas departments.

During the course of my fieldwork, I was often puzzled by the attention drawn to the specificity of the Antillean family and the way that policy-makers and metropolitan French with whom I spoke would talk about the importance of motherhood and family ties as particular markers of the Antillean family. In my day-to-day interactions with French metropolitans, the idea of family seemed equally important to them. In fact an enormous amount of time and attention seemed to be consecrated to the family, in both public discourse and the daily lives of metropolitan French: the high frequency at which families maintain regular contact – according to one survey, 50 percent of couples aged 25–45 visit their family at least once a week (Pitrou 1992 [1978]) – plus the persistence of lunch breaks long enough for children and parents alike to return home to eat together (even if this practice has become fairly obsolete), and the ritualized family vacation in August, when most of France seems literally to shut down. People also tend to rely heavily on family, the assumption being that the family should come to the aid of its members. While differences based on social class may exist, this assumption nevertheless crosscuts class lines (Pitrou 1992), with few possibilities for adaptive strategies when one is without family.

Family and membership within society (sometimes referred to as the "family of citizens") are intimately linked; not having family (in France) becomes a visible marker of not being French. In France, one of the most common forms of identification required in administrative matters is the *livret de famille* (family record). The *livret de famille* is delivered to each couple upon marriage. Unlike the birth certificate, which provides proof that one was born, at a certain place, and to specific people, the *livret de famille* situates one within the context of a family, noting children, siblings, marriages, divorces, etc. and is updated on a regular basis. This is not about biological relatedness, nor even about being born in France; rather it is about the presence of specific types of social relations centered on the family. I might add that current immigration laws make it extremely difficult to gain the right to reside or work in France in the absence of family ties. At the same time, having "too much" family, or having family relations that seem not to follow certain inexplicit yet culturally established guidelines, as in the case of Antilleans and certain immigrant populations, also become markers of difference, of non-Frenchness. These confrontations with French conceptions of family have led me to ask questions about the way that the processes of exclusion operate through the family and about the social role "family" plays within French society and the French nation.

This chapter begins with a discussion of the drop below replacement levels and the resulting vision of a society in crisis. It was precisely this sense of internal crisis that created a perceived need for the reinforcement of family policy and greater attention to family and the child, rather than the strict increase in population size through the promotion of immigration. In looking at the specific reforms to family policy, I highlight the state's insistence on social responsibility on the part of families and the idea that family policy was to promote all families equally. Next the chapter looks at the processes of exclusion. I present the reforms to immigration policy and nationality laws to show that immigrant families became increasingly seen as a social problem in and of themselves. Not only were they excluded as possible contributors to the depopulation solution, but also they were seen as running counter to it. I then turn to access to family benefits, which in the case of immigrants was limited by increasing legal constraints, and in the case of French Antilleans, by differential policy. I discuss how access to family benefits, in French terms, became associated with the right to social membership, and how differential access served to exclude certain groups from that right.

Demographic Crisis and the Reinforcement of Family Policy

In 1974, birthrates in France dropped below replacement levels (see Figure 10.1). The drop was signaled to public officials immediately, leading to a frenzy of concern and meticulous calculations of birthrates by month. Low birthrates had been a major preoccupation of policy-makers since the turn of the century, and with the legalization of contraceptive methods in the late 1960s, birthrates were being monitored even more closely for fear of negative consequences. While contraceptive rights had been hard won precisely because of fears of depopulation, when birthrates dropped below replacement levels, contraceptive rights were not retracted. Rather, emphasis was placed on "family," that is the social responsibility of families to *choose* to become larger.

Why the emphasis on family? What concerned policy-makers was the fact that the drop in birthrates could not, as in the past, be accounted for by political or economic factors, such as war, revolution, or economic crisis. Demographers determined that the new decline was due to social causes, that is changes in attitudes. Families were not being prevented, by some external force, from having the babies they desire; they were simply not desiring them (INED 1978). The drop below replacement levels

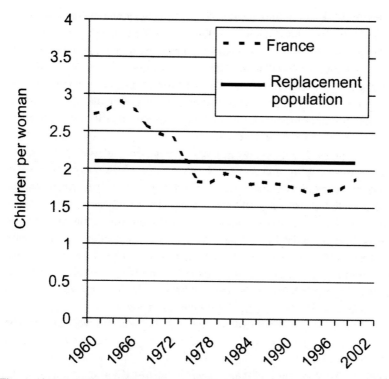

Figure 10.1 Total Fertility Rate, France, 1960–2002.
Source: Eurostat, Population and Social Conditions, Demography, Fertility Indicators, January 29, 2003.

then appeared even more dangerous. It meant that families themselves were responsible for the non-assurance of the continuation of French society.

Scholars began talking about the "family in danger" and the dissolution of the family. Public officials presented apocalyptic visions of France: a France unable to sustain itself if couples don't change their attitudes and don't start having more babies. Jacques Chirac, not yet President of the Republic, but nevertheless former Prime Minister, claimed in an interview presented in the national newspaper *Libération* (October 30, 1984), that France would become an empty country in twenty to thirty years. In the words of a campaigning President Mitterand, the French population was condemned to disappearance (declaration to the Socialist Party, June 21, 1979, cited in Le Bras 1991: 66). Michel Jobert, Minister under Presidents Pompidou and Mitterand spoke of "autogenocide" in an interview in the national newspaper *Le Monde* (March 24, 1976).

France, however, is far from disappearing – statistics show that the actual population of France is and was steadily growing (the total population size for metropolitan France was 39,848 million in 1962 and 52,599 million in 1975). Whether or not the situation was as serious as public officials claimed, the drop marked a significant shift in public discourse on family and the perceived role of family policy. On the one hand, it pushed demographic issues fully into the public realm as a *public concern*. It also led to the idea that the family itself needed to be saved. This diverged from earlier family policy which promoted higher birthrates because population size was equated with national and military strength. As President de Gaulle stated just after the Second World War, France needed 10 million beautiful babies to become a great nation once again.

Beginning in 1975, under the presidency of Giscard d'Estaing (1974–81), revising family policy to save the family became one of the central agendas for policy-makers. The reforms under Giscard d'Estaing focused primarily on encouraging families to have a third child by offering additional benefits to families of three or more children: a compensatory family allowance, supplementary tax deductions, housing assistance, higher benefits rates, and longer maternity leave. These measures were inspired by the idea that having three children versus two children meant the assurance of population replacement (2.1 children). Furthermore, demographers had determined that French couples were not refusing to have children (as was the case in some countries facing low birthrates), but were simply limiting their number of children to two. Policy-makers even came to label the family of two children a "French particularity" – and one that needed to be fixed (INED 1970: 44).

Overall, the family of three children became glorified, the implication being that a return to large, "traditional" families would mean a return to family values, and vice versa. The high rates of divorce, cohabitation and postponement of marriage were highlighted as contributing directly to the low birthrates of the French. Nonetheless, when birthrates dropped below replacement levels, the government did not tighten family laws. In fact, it was primarily during this time that laws concerning marriage, divorce, paternal authority and affiliation (particularly concerning legitimacy) became more and more relaxed. Rather, the government emphasized the social value and social necessity of large families. The point was to restore the family as the central site of production of those social values that permit social cohesion and that ensure the proper functioning and stability of society itself.

The emphasis on the third child, however, met with quite a bit of criticism because it seemed to insist on a single, moralizing model of family. A large wave of sociological studies appeared that attempted to document the diversity of the domestic sphere, and at the same time, highlight the failure of policy to take into consideration the "real" situation of families.

Family policy under President Mitterand (1981–88), who succeeded Giscard d'Estaing, fell in line with these new discussions of family. Rather than privileging a single family model, policy-makers revised policy to spread more equally family benefits among all types of families. While the Mitterand government claimed to want to reform family policy, it in no way removed benefits for having children, and in no way challenged the idea that children were a cost to couples that needed to be reimbursed by the state. Like Giscard d'Estaing, Mitterand wanted to revise policy "in order to ensure an environment favorable to the family and to the birthrate" (Mitterand, cited in Lenoir 1991: 183). For the government under Mitterand that meant a massive increase of approximately 25 percent in family benefits, the revalorization of benefits for the second child, and a series of measures in favor of working mothers.

The increase in benefits for the second child in no way corresponded to a relaxation of the promotion of large families. Rather it reflected policy-makers' belief that family policy must respond to the needs of families of one or two children since "the difficulties encountered in the raising and education of the first and second child can discourage parents from having more children" (Ministre du Travail et de la Participation and Haut Comité de la Population 1980: 49). Furthermore, while Mitterand's stance toward women and work was considered neutral because it de-emphasized the idea that women should stay at home to raise children, the new measures were not neutral about *having* babies. Rather, they were designed to permit couples, or more precisely women, to better negotiate their *double* role: professional and familial (Fagnani and Gignon 1997). Over 35,000 nurseries/daycare centers were created to facilitate this double role. The primary idea was that one's professional life ought not be a deterrent to having babies. The goal of French family policy was to remove all impediments to having children. In May 1985, Minister Dufoix launched a campaign entitled "[Let us] Open France to children," the goal being to "heighten public awareness in general and incite our fellow citizens to welcome children. Integrating the 'child' dimension in all thought processes, in all decisions is essential to our future" (INED 1985: VIII–IX).

The reforms were not simply about encouraging children and creating a "favorable" environment for having children, but also addressed what constitutes the family. Not only did family forms outside of the nuclear family model become more acceptable in policy terms, but also the family as a whole was redefined legislatively (see Rubellin-Devichi 1985). What we find is the progressive dissociation of conjugal relations and parenthood. The legislative reforms increased parental responsibilities outside the context of marriage relations such that *the child* – not the couple or marriage – came to define family (Hantrais and Letablier 1994). Despite divorce or separation, despite negligence or refusal or the impossibility of assuming full parental responsibilities, the child exists and becomes the living and legal proof of the existence of "family." At the same time, however, we find the development of laws and policies designed to protect the child from the family itself (see Donzelot 1977). The diversity of families was only acceptable within certain culturally-established guidelines that would permit the production of a healthy society. The State had to assure likewise the structures that would help bring families back in line.

It is important to note that policy-makers also avoided making the drop in birthrates a problem strictly about or with women. Their discourse emphasized instead "couples" and even more so "families." While "families" and "couples" may have translated in real terms to "women," this emphasis away from women was critical. The message was that raising birthrates was not about trying to keep women in the home, or preventing them from self-fulfillment through professional activities, it was about saving the family, which was above any of its constituent members, women included. While women may play a privileged role in the production of babies, it is not strictly women who produce children or potential citizens. It is the family that produces children (even if the child "makes" family), and then with the assistance of the state, turns them into citizens. The state saw its duty as ensuring that families, however they were coming to be defined, were protected and promoted.

More generally, the reforms under Mitterand sought a return to the original idea behind family policy and family allocations of favoring *all* families equally, the belief being that "the Nation must recognize all children as having the same value . . . whatever their rank or the resources of the parents" (Ministre du Travail et de la Participation and Haut Comité de la Population 1980: 23). The system of family allocations was also simplified in order to render it more comprehensible, and hence more accessible to the larger population. According to policy-makers, it was only by understanding their rights that families could benefit from them and would be more willing to accept the duty of having more children. Seeing family policy as a sort of "contract of confidence" between the state and families (ibid.: 22), policy-makers believed that financial incentives in the form of family allocations would be ineffective if families were not also well informed about the demographic situation, their role in it, and that of the state. The Family Code even stipulates that six hours per annum of instruction on the demographic situation in France be required in school.

Depopulation and Immigration Reform

The framing of the "demographic problem" in terms of replacement levels added to the sense that its resolution could be achieved only through the family, by having babies. The very idea of replacement levels implies a closed system where certain persons are considered legitimately reproductive and others are not. Immigration became in some respects irrelevant in resolving the social crisis.

In 1974, at the same time that policy-makers became aware that birthrates had dropped below replacement levels, the government called for the *temporary* suspension (yet to be lifted) of primary immigration. It also set up stricter controls on family re-unifications (the right of family members to rejoin their spouse or parent already residing in France). In the years that followed, a number of measures were also taken to expel "illegal" immigrants and make it more difficult to obtain "legal" status. Other measures were proposed, notably the full removal of the right to family re-unification, but were rejected because of their possible violation of constitutional rights.

Furthermore, in 1973, nationality laws concerning marriage between French citizens and non-French citizens were modified such that "marriage does not bring about, by right, any effect on nationality" (Article 21–1 of the Civil Code). Prior to this change, French nationality had been automatically conferred to the non-French spouse upon marriage. And in fact, since the First World War, nationality laws had been fairly open concerning the granting of French nationality to foreign parents raising their family in France. Fearing social disharmony, public officials felt it unwise to permit these new arrivals to remain "foreign" while living in France (Fulchiron 2000). At that time, it was believed that the granting of French nationality would link foreigners to France and facilitate their adoption of the Republican values attached to French citizenship. It was also believed that this would ensure homogeneity of nationality (and hence of citizenship) within the couple, and thus result in greater certitude that their children would be raised "French" (Fulchiron 2000). After 1973, French nationality had to be requested by the non-French spouse and certain delays respected in order to assure the legitimacy of the marriage. If French nationality was no longer automatic, it was perhaps because marriage was no longer seen as sufficient assurance in the transformation of non-citizens into citizens.

Note that, in France, nationality and citizenship tend to be equated; possession of French nationality is seen as carrying with it both the rights and obligations of citizenship. The suspicion of fraud that developed around marriages between citizens and non-citizens, or rather "foreigners," arose primarily from concerns that foreigners sought to acquire the rights conferred by French nationality without accepting the obligations of citizenship, that is adherence to French cultural values. In that respect, "foreigners" would remain, in practical terms, "non-citizens," and thus risked disrupting the system by disengaging citizenship from nationality.

The reforms to nationality laws seem consistent with the changing conceptions of family, where marriage was perceived less and less as the basis for the constitution of French families. Since the child was becoming the defining feature of family, homogeneity of nationality/citizenship within the couple may have been considered less important in the production of French families. Nevertheless, nationality laws concerning children were also being challenged.

In 1986, a series of discussions ensued over reforms to nationality laws concerning the acquisition of French nationality by birth. The proposal concerned the dissolution of automatic rights to French nationality for children born of foreign parents, where one of the parents or the child him/herself had been born in France or on French soil (the principle of *jus soli*). These measures would have affected primarily, and most severely, immigrants from Algeria and French West African countries because of their particular former colonial status (see Silverman 1992). While these measures were rejected,[1] discussions of access to nationality and the social consequences of granting French nationality to immigrants entered thoroughly into public debate. At stake was the issue of who could and ought become French citizens. Particularly in the case of "foreign" children born in France, the proposed measures suggested that the fact of being born and raised in the French cultural system, of attendance at French schools – often seen as the key site in instilling Republican values – was no longer sufficient in the production of French citizens.

While the reforms to policy regarding immigration were clearly due to a number of complex factors (i.e. increasing economic crisis brought on by the problems in the Middle East, problems of unemployment, and increasing social unrest with numerous strikes and protests), shifts in immigration have been cited as the crucial element. By the 1970s, immigration had become much less European, and far more non-European (i.e. primarily North African and West African). As the ethnic and cultural composition of immigration shifted, the issue of assimilation, upon which postwar immigration policy had been founded, was placed in question. Several scholars have argued that if integration and assimilation were seen as possible in the early years it was because those immigrating seemed already more "close" to French culture and thus more likely to blend "spontaneously" into French society (see Silverman 1992; Wihtol de Wenden 1988). The "new" immigration placed at stake issues of "ethnic balance" and brought on "fears of the social tensions which would ensue if this balance was not maintained" (Silverman 1992: 48). While the issue of "ethnic balance" was more clearly a concern of the political Right, the Left also pushed for stricter controls on immigration in the name of protecting immigrants' social rights, and for fear of creating immigrant "ghettos."

It is also argued that while postwar immigration had been predominantly that of unmarried male laborers, the new immigration was predominantly that of families, and thus associated with more permanent settlement. Despite the overall promotion of family and the fears of depopulation during this time, it was precisely when immigration became more familial and one of settlement that it fell under attack as posing a problem for society. Policy-makers focused heavily on the high fertility rates and family patterns of immigrants, with one administrator, Corentin Calvez, cautioning that this "would lead to the presence in France of an inassimilable island" of difference (Calvez 1969). Calvez's report sparked larger theories on the "threshold of tolerance" – that number of immigrants that society can support before fragmentation occurs (see Silverman 1992). The result was various policies to curb the development of large concentrations of immigrants and an ongoing attention to their fertility rates and family patterns.

Fears of fragmentation resulted equally from the belief that these immigrant families were less committed to France and to adopting Republican values for themselves and their children (Wihtol de Wenden 1988). While immigration was seen as more familial, and hence potentially permanent, the provisional nature of immigration was equally highlighted. The "new" immigrants were said to *envision* an eventual return home, and thus to maintain strong links – financial, social and cultural – to their home country, despite extended and even permanent settlement in France. The central issue was that immigrants were marking the French cultural landscape instead of being marked by it – they were settling more or less permanently in France, but not becoming "French."

While the drop below replacement levels drew overall attention to issues of family, the types of concerns that arose over "immigrant" families were markedly different than those over "French" families. "Immigrant" families were thought to threaten the very social cohesion that "French" families were said to ensure. As both birthrates and immigration became increasingly issues of national and social concern, thus meriting state intervention, a stronger line was drawn between the two. The demographic crisis was framed as an issue of "birthrates" (and hence of "family") and a question of "us," while immigration was framed as an issue of "social fragmentation" and a question of "them." Birthrates were seen as a problem emerging from within society, while immigration was seen as an external problem affecting society.

Framed in such terms, the envisioned solution required, on the one hand, aide to "French" families and their "responsibilization," and on the other hand, physical and symbolic expulsion of "immigrant" families. This separation called attention to immigrants in a way that made persons of more "visible" ethnic origins perpetual immigrants and hence perpetually outside the national community. It also made the demographic crisis an internal, social problem fixable only by those already considered inside the group. Little attention has been paid to the correspondence between these issues precisely because policy-makers defined them as wholly separate problems. I argue, nevertheless, that these issues remained intimately linked because of the role that family came to play in definitions of social citizenship.

Family Benefits and the Production of Citizens

With fears of depopulation, "family" became more central to questions about the constitution of society and the nation as well as one of the primary means through which difference was highlighted and created. Even if under Mitterand, the diversity of families was brought to the forefront of definitions of family, Antillean families and immigrant families were constructed as fundamentally "different" and therefore outside the parameters of those definitions. Though protection of the family and the social advantages accorded to the family may be more extensive in France than most other countries throughout the world (Bradshaw *et al.* 1994), the way that family benefits were configured as *social rights* protecting and assuring the proper development of social persons made central the debates concerning the capacity or incapacity of certain persons or groups to adapt to French culture and become full members of the community of citizens. The remainder of this chapter examines the conceptions of social membership expressed in French family policy and addresses the ways in which difference was constructed and in which differential access to family benefits served to reinforce processes of exclusion and marginalization.

As Parkes (1997) points out, in Britain (we might also add the United States), family policy tends to be associated with families and children "at risk," poverty and social problems. It is not seen as an aspect of social policy that concerns the entire population. In France, however, family policy is much more generalized. In fact, one of the key characteristics of French family policy is its longstanding adherence to providing social benefits based strictly on the number of children, regardless of income level. The reforms under Presidents Giscard d'Estaing and Mitterand maintained the principle of the all-inclusive distribution of aid to families, regardless of financial considerations. The point was not to *disadvantage* or *exclude* any family from the possibility of receiving family benefits. In fact, French family policy was seen as and promoted as a fairly comprehensive system, reaching practically the entirety of the population (Steck 1993: 11). Basic family allocations beginning with the second child were granted to all, whether French citizens or not, and disbursed automatically upon declaration of the birth. The goal of French family policy was to assist *all* families in their needs as families. While this all-inclusiveness may have been inspired by the need to raise birthrates, it was also an assertion of social solidarity and notions of equality (where equality of rights is seen as producing equality of condition), both fundamental precepts of French republicanism.

Dissociated from income level and questions of financial need, family benefits do not carry the stigma of poverty, nor is it seen as shameful to receive them. In fact, as Parkes (1997) points out in her chapter on social policy in France, suggesting to French people the removal of family benefits would be like suggesting the removal of public education. According to Parkes, the universality of family benefits seems imperative to the French because ideas of pronatalism are so deeply embedded in French cultural norms. I suggest that pronatalism has become the very expression of Republican values, and thus has served to link family benefits to basic civil or human *rights*, rather than to notions of *assistance*. In France, family benefits, like public education and universal medical care, are seen as part of the basic rights *entitled* by all members of society, and at the same time *necessary* to them in their development as social persons, hence as citizens. Family benefits are not strictly concerned with assuring that children are well fed, clothed, and provided with shelter, but also with assuring them access to education, leisure and cultural activities, seen as crucial in their proper social and cultural development.

This aspect of family benefits becomes particularly crucial in thinking about French nationalism. As Patrick Weil notes, French Republican law bases French nationality on the acquisition of certain "codes of sociability" (1998: 46). Unlike in other countries where nationality may be primarily an issue of filiation (as in Germany), in France, it is about place of birth, which then translates to one's socialization in French culture and one's adherence to Republican values (Weil 1998). The family, as a site not of filial ties, but of cultural values, becomes, like the national education system, one of the central agents in the production of French national identity, seen for the most part as singular and homogeneous (the "right to difference" has only recently taken hold in France). Family benefits become linked to the production of citizens by assuring the proper social and cultural development of children along the lines of Republican values. To take away family benefits or restrict access to them is seen as the equivalent of taking away the right to raise one's children under the proper material and cultural conditions that would permit these children to assume their citizenship as adults.

The reforms to family policy and the expansion of the system of family benefits so as to be more fully comprehensive were indeed about asserting the importance of family to the future of society and, by consequence, the responsibility of the state to the family and family matters, but can also be seen as part of a larger assertion about what and who ought constitute the French nation. Despite claims of universality, family benefits were not accorded equally throughout France; likewise, the large families that seemed so crucial to the rebuilding of society and the nation were not valued equally when associated with certain members of society, namely immigrants and the French populations in the overseas departments. If large "French" families were a sign of responsible citizenship, large "immigrant" and large Antillean families were associated with social irresponsibility.

The Case of Immigrant Families

Granted, access to family benefits was not limited to those with French nationality. Since the end of the Second World War, all persons legally employed in France were eligible for certain social services provided by the state, namely universal medical care and family benefits. And prior to the 1980s, all children born in France, regardless of the nationality of their parents, were eligible for family benefits since it was assumed that these children would become French citizens.

As controls on immigration became more restrictive, particularly in the regularization of visas for immigrants, so did access to family benefits (as well as other social services). The parents' legal status in France became increasingly important in the child's eligibility for family benefits. Furthermore, beginning in 1986, benefits were restricted to those children who, like their parents, could prove their legal status and extended, continuous residence in France. While the proposal of 1986 to remove automatic citizenship for those children born in France of foreign parents was rejected, this did not impede policy-makers from modifying the internal policies of the social security and family allocations systems to make access to these rights more restrictive with respect to immigrants. In 1987, as part of this modification, the types of acceptable visas opening access to social services were clearly defined by the Social Security Code.

Among those immigrants who were eligible for benefits, the bureaucratic delays brought on by constant proof of one's eligibility served in many cases as either a deterrent or a demoralizing struggle. Furthermore, the fact of going to the state to receive benefits meant that those families would be subject to possible controls by social workers and even public authorities if there was reason to believe that information on the family or financial status was incorrect (see Fassin 2000 on access to medical services). As Pitrou (1992) points out, it is precisely families in most need of financial support or other social services who are the most hesitant to take advantage of family benefits because of fears of being criticized as bad parents by social workers and the risk of having their children removed from their care. The repercussions would be even greater for immigrant families (i.e. possible expulsion).

Statistically, it is difficult to determine the effects of the new policies on immigrants. No material has yet been published on this subject. In fact, studies (whether governmental or scholarly) on inequalities in access to public health and social services have been rarely undertaken in France (see Fassin 2000). This absence is largely due to the creation in 1985 of a law restricting the collection of information on nationality, birthplace and ethnic origins, the goal being to limit the possibility for discrimination. Given that inequalities do exist in access to these services, the side-effect of this law is that it is extremely difficult, if not impossible in some cases, to investigate these matters.

Nevertheless, it is clear from government reports and overall public discourse that as greater attention was called to the demographic crisis and to the immigration problem, greater and greater attention was also accorded to the "difference" of immigrant families: their higher birthrates, their different type of family organization, their hierarchical gender relations and devaluation of women, their different marriage patterns, in some cases being polygamy, their different values in the raising of children, etc. These discussions not only reinforced negative stereotypes of immigrants (and of those who appeared to be of certain ethnic origins),[2] but also placed those persons in a position fundamentally at odds with French culture and society. The non-adoption of French family values was seen as a refusal to act in the best interests of society as a whole, and hence a refusal to defend the basic precepts of French republicanism.

The perceived difference (and persistence of difference) of immigrant families has thus at times placed the universality of family allocations in question. Immigrant rights to social services have been constantly debated since the 1980s. The popular belief that immigrants (both legal and illegal), with their large families, drain and abuse the system has been longstanding and still persists. Of course, (as I mentioned before) access to social benefits is assured for neither those without legal status in France, nor those with legal status given the heightened restrictions limiting access. Furthermore, since family allocations were intended to promote productive citizens who respect and adhere to Republican values, some administrators have suggested the suspension of family allocations to parents whose children raise problems at school or in the community (see Jelen 1993). While immigrant families are not always cited explicitly in these types of proposals, the reference is implicit. In France, delinquency equals the suburban youth population, which in turn equals immigrants.

Despite the growing attention to the protection of children and children's rights brought on by the natalist and familialist reforms of the 1970s and 1980s, the children of immigrants, seen as part of the "immigration problem," have often been excluded from those rights and services. Recall that on the policy level, "family" and "immigration" were dissociated – they were framed as different types of social problems requiring different types of solutions – even if issues of family were central in defining the immigration problem. Children of immigrants became the symbol of families unwilling to fall in line with French republicanism, and hence classed outside of the system of rights accorded to "French" children. While certain rights to family benefits are extended to immigrants and their children, it is worth asking to what extent immigrants themselves are able to conceive of family benefits as rights when, both collectively and individually, they are criticized for using these services.

The Case of Antilleans

With respect to Antilleans, the processes of exclusion did not operate through controls on entry into France, legal status, or nationality. As I mentioned earlier, Antilleans are full French citizens by birth. What we find is differential policy – families in the Antilles received benefits at substantially lower rates than families in metropolitan France (Table 10.1), and several categories of benefits were not applicable in the overseas departments. While those living in the Antilles did receive benefits beginning with the first child, compared to the second child for the Metropole, the high difference in rate distribution in no way made up for this advantage.

Table 10.1 Comparison of Family Allocations (Monthly Rates) between the Overseas Departments and the Metropole as of January 1, 1988[*]

	Overseas departments	*Metropolitan France*
1 child	103.25FF	0
2 children	391.25FF	558.82FF
3 children	753.00FF	1274.14FF
4 children	1205.25FF	1989.75FF
5 children	1390.25FF	2705.37FF
Each additional child	+ 90.25FF	+ 715.61FF
Each child over 10 years	+ 66.25FF	+ 157.08FF
Each child over 15 years	+ 99.50FF	+ 279.26FF

Source: INSEE, Familles de Guadeloupe 1988.

Note: * It is difficult to establish a comparison prior to 1988 since previous rates of benefits were not calculated on the same basis. Official conversion rate when the euro replaced the franc in 2001: 6.56FF = 1€.

The lower cost of living in the Antilles has at times been used to justify this differential policy. Cost of living, however, varies greatly from department to department, even in metropolitan France, yet no difference in rates has been made between metropolitan departments. Furthermore, Metropolitans who accepted civil servant posts in the overseas departments were awarded an automatic cost of living adjustment that increased their salary by 40 percent. Ironically, this adjustment was primarily based on the perceived *higher* cost of living in these departments and the fact that these individuals would be unable to access their rights to family benefits as would have been the case if they had remained in the Metropole.

The reason given by policy-makers for the differential distribution of family benefits was that the demographic situation in the overseas departments was the opposite of that in the Metropole. Policy-makers had long been trying to combat what they saw as the overly high fertility rates of Antillean women, which in their estimation was the primary cause of growing unemployment and poor social conditions in the Antilles. It is important to note that despite the popular belief that the average Antillean woman bears 10 or more children, actual statistics show approximately 4.2 children per woman in the 1970s.

Even prior to the reforms to French family policy implemented in the 1970s and 1980s, policy-makers were concerned with the consequences in the overseas departments of the already heavily natalist family policy adopted in the Metropole (see Baptistide 1972). Because of these concerns, beginning in 1968, several benefits were suppressed in the overseas departments (and yet continued to be disbursed in the Metropole): the prenatal allocation, maternity leave, the single-income family allocation, and housing allocations. The non-application of these benefits disadvantaged Antillean women, particularly lower-class women, compared to their metropolitan counterparts. In the Antilles, many women have raised their children alone (or at least with little financial or caretaking support from the father(s) of the children).

While benefits in the Metropole were disbursed according to a fixed monthly rate based strictly on the number of children, benefits in the overseas departments were based, up until 1988, on both the number of children of the beneficiary and the number of days that she had worked during the previous month. Even after 1988, when benefits in the overseas departments were adjusted as a fixed monthly rate, the rate remained substantially lower than in the Metropole. Likewise, while the criteria of exercising a professional activity to receive family allocations had been removed in the Metropole in 1975, this reform was not applied in the overseas departments until 1988. Because a significant portion of work available to women in the Antilles was seasonal work, agricultural work, or other forms of irregular employment, it was precisely when they could not work or had to work less that they also received less aid to raise their children. In 1975, a measure was added that opened up family allocations in the Antilles to include *unemployed* single mothers having at least two children in their charge. Family allocations however did and do not provide enough to raise a family independent of an outside income. In that respect, declaring unemployment to receive family benefits was often not a valid alternative for many women.

Overall, the reforms to family policy in the 1970s and 1980s were feebly applied in the overseas departments. Despite longstanding debates over these inequalities in distribution, it was not until 1996 that "global parity" was finally enforced, aligning the overseas departments with metropolitan France. The struggles of Antilleans may have been important in bringing about that change, but one must also ask if it was more precisely due to the fact that Antillean birthrates dropped in the early 1990s to 2.1 children per woman, hence not far above "French" birthrates. High birthrates could no longer be used as justification for differential policy. Likewise, the drop may have appeared, in the eyes of policy-makers, as the expression of responsible citizenship, which in this case would have been less babies rather than more.

The result, however, is that equality of rights becomes a reward for equality of condition, rather than equality of condition being an outcome of equality of rights. If the idea of family allocations had been to assure the well-being of families and children, and distribute aid equally since "all children are of equal value to the nation," then notions of equality did not fully apply to citizens in the overseas departments. Antilleans' membership within the nation remains conditionally based on their adherence to "French" norms, rather than being part of what defines those norms.

Policy-makers continue to argue that the demographic situation in the overseas departments necessitated, for economic reasons, differential policy. However the framing of the demographic problem in terms of "family" meant equally that much more was at stake than an eventual economic crisis brought on by the overload of an active population unable to find work.[3] Neither the idealization of the large family that appeared under Giscard d'Estaing, nor the acceptance of multiple family forms as under Mitterand applied to Antillean families. Whether living in the Antilles or in metropolitan France, Antilleans, like "immigrants," have been stigmatized by the negative image of large families, seen as wholly different in character than metropolitan families and as not conforming to Republican ideals. Though Antilleans living in metropolitan France were not excluded from receiving the same benefits as their metropolitan counterparts, *their* large families were seen as draining the system rather than being what the system was trying to promote. Large families then were not equally desirable for all parts of the population. Nor was the issue of overpopulation versus underpopulation simply geographic (i.e. Antilles versus Metropole), with large Antillean families, once in the Metropole, promoted as a positive contribution to the repopulation of the nation.

I might add that this unequal distribution of aid, well known by Antilleans themselves, has gone largely unmentioned outside a few scholarly works specifically focused on Antillean families (see Ancelin 2000; Attias-Dufont and Lapierre 1997). In the numerous publications that examine more generally French family policy and "French families," no reference is made to unequal distribution. This silence of course has only served to reinforce the notion (that is among Metropolitans) that family benefits are distributed unilaterally and equally, and thus uphold Republican ideals. While overpopulation in the overseas departments may have been, in the eyes of policy-makers, a real problem for which an immediate, active solution (in the form of differential policy) was deemed necessary, the adherence to claims of universality have not simply masked the inequalities but also led some to conclude (unjustly) that Antilleans have profited from an overly generous system of benefits that provides them a source of income simply by having more babies (see Baptistide 1972). Of course, the feeble level of recompense in the Antilles, particularly for larger families, was far from an incitement to having more children.

Conclusion

Birthrates in France have barely risen and remain below replacement levels (refer back to Figure 10.1). Interestingly, a common (yet somewhat joking) expression in France is: the more the French love their children, the fewer they have. This expression serves as a sort of self-critique that highlights the paradox created by the push for social responsibility and the efforts to raise birthrates. While the strong financial and social incentives to have more babies may have had little effect on "French" birthrates, family and children have nevertheless come to be seen as the very foundation of society that must be defended at all costs. As French demographer Hervé Le Bras has so insightfully stated:

> Without being dupes of natalism in their actual comportment, the French believe in it whole-heartedly. In opinion surveys, they declare themselves massively in favor of natalist policies. They plead for the child . . . [that is] of their neighbor . . . Perhaps, by dint of having it repeated, the natalist discourse has become the affirmation of social ties among the French, a sort of laic religion that permits them to express their attachment to the Nation. (Le Bras 1991: 14)

The policy reforms under Giscard d'Estaing and Mitterand were indeed attempts at rethinking the distribution of family aid so as to produce higher birthrates, but they were just as much about reconfirming the social importance of family, the state's commitment to family, and Republican notions of equality and universalism. The attention to family, however, has masked the processes of exclusion and marginalization precisely because the family was taken as, and put forth as, a non-discriminatory universal. In protecting and defending families and children, the state appeared to concern itself with basic human issues that defied notions of race, ethnicity, nationality, etc. Nevertheless, the framing of depopulation as a question of social responsibility on the part of families has served to make determinations about social citizenship and social belonging explicit. Calling attention to difference in terms of family permitted the exclusion of immigrants from access to French nationality and the configuration of Antilleans as partial citizens.

While I have highlighted in this chapter the way in which exclusion operates through the idiom of family, it is important to note that, in recent years, we have begun to find demands for greater social rights for those excluded under the "normal" structure of family rights and benefits that tend to be linked to membership within the nation. This includes fighting for the rights of those excluded by a system that sees "family" as the most (and at times only) legitimate social relation. Among these demands are: universal healthcare to include those with "illegal" status and numerous aids for the homeless and those in difficulty, often seen as "without family." The discourse of family has also been adopted by those fighting for immigrants' rights in general. One of the more popular, and effective, chants during protest marches in recent years challenges the distinction "French" and "immigrant" by invoking family: we are all children of immigrants.

Notes

1. They were eventually accepted in 1993, then overturned in 1998.
2. As immigration laws became more restrictive, greater numbers of persons who might have become citizens or legal residents were frozen under the status of immigrant or foreigner (the two terms being used interchangeably in France).

This also resulted in the growing use of these terms to designate anyone of visible "ethnic" origins.
3. Policy-makers were little interested in creating more employment in the overseas departments and in fact contributed to the decrease in the job market by withdrawing investment and closing down factories.

References

Ancelin, J. (2000), *Histoire de l'action sociale familiale dans les départements d'Outre-mer*, Paris: Comité d'histoire de la Sécurité sociale.

Attias-Donfut, C. and Lapierre, N. (1997), *La Famille providence. Trois générations en Guadeloupe*, Paris: La Documentation française.

Baptistide, J-C. (1972), *La Migration Guadeloupéenne vers la France (ou: Contribution à l'étude d'un mouvement de population organisé)*, PhD dissertation, Université de Rouen.

Bradshaw, J., Ditch, J., Holmes, H., Whiteford, P. and Ray, J-C. (1994), "Une comparaison internationale des aides aux familles," *Recherches et prévisions (Caisse nationale des allocations familiales)*, 37: 11–26.

Calvez, C. (1969), "Le problème des travailleurs étrangers," *Journal Officiel de la République Française, Avis et Rapports du Conseil Economique et Social*, March 27.

Donzelot, J. (1977), *La Police des familles*, Paris: Les Editions de Minuit.

Fagnani, J. and Gignon, M. (1997), "La politique familiale en France depuis les années 80. Des Préoccupations natalistes aux politiques de l'emploi," in F. Ronsin, H. Le Bras and E. Zucker-Rouvillois (eds) *Démographie et politique*, Dijon: Editions Universitaires de Dijon.

Fassin, D. (2000), *Les Enjeux politiques de la santé. Etudes sénégalaises, équatoriennes et françaises*, Paris: Karthala.

Fulchiron, H. (2000), *La Nationalité française*, Paris: PUF.

Hantrais, L. and Letablier, M-T. (1994), "Construction et déconstruction de la famille en Europe. Une analyse comparative," *Recherches et prévisions (Caisse nationale des allocations familiales)*, 37: 1–10.

Haut Conseil de la Population et de la Famille (2003), *La Fécondité en France depuis 25 ans*, report prepared by L. Toulemon, Paris: Haut Conseil de la population et de la famille.

Institut National d'Etudes Démographiques (INED) (1970), *Rapport sur la situation démographique de la France en 1969*, presented to Parliament by M. Joseph Fontanet, Ministre du Travail, de l'Emploi et de la Population, Paris: INED.

—— (1978), *Septième Rapport sur la situation démographique de la France*, presented to Parliament by M. Christian Beullac, Ministre du Travail, Paris: INED.

—— (1980), *Neuvième Rapport sur la situation démographique de la France*, presented to Parliament by M. Jean Mattéoli, Ministre du Travail et de la Participation, Paris: INED.

—— (1985), *Quatorzième Rapport sur la situation démographique de la France*, presented to Parliament by Madame Georgina Dufoix, Ministre des Affaires Sociales et de la Solidarité Nationale, Porte-Parole du Gouvernement, Paris: INED.

Institut National de la Statistique et des Etudes Economiques (INSEE) and Caisse des Allocations Familiales (CAF) Guadeloupe (1988), *Familles de Guadeloupe*, Pointe-à-Pitre: INSEE and CAF.

Jelen, C. (1993), *La Famille, secret de l'intégration. Enquête sur la France immigrée*, Paris: Editions Robert Laffont.

Le Bras, H. (1991), *Marianne et les lapins. L'obsession démographique*, Paris: Olivier Orban.

Lenoir, R. (1991), "Family Policy in France since 1938," in J.S. Ambler (ed.) *The French Welfare State: Surviving Social and Ideological Change*, New York: New York University Press.

Ministre du Travail et de la Participation and Haut Comité de la Population (1980), *Natalité: "Aspects financiers,"* Paris: La Documentation française.

Parkes, G. (1997), "Does France Still Have a Population Policy?" trans. C. De Luchi, in M. Cross and S. Perry (eds) *Population and Social Policy in France*, London: Pinter.

Pitrou, A. (1992 [1978]), *Les Solidarités familiales. Vivre sans famille?*, 2nd edn, Paris: Privat.

Rubellin-Devichi, J. (1985), "L'évolution du statut civil de la famille depuis 1945," in P. Laroque (ed.) *La Politique familiale en France depuis 1945*, Paris: La Documentation française.

Silverman, M. (1992), *Deconstructing the Nation: Immigration, Racism and Citizenship in Modern France*, London: Routledge.

Steck, P. (1993), *Les Prestations familiales. Que sais-je?*, Paris: PUF.

Weil, P. (1998), *The Transformation of Immigration Policies. Immigration Control and Nationality Laws in Europe: A Comparative Approach*, EUI Working Paper 98/5, Florence: European University Institute.

Wihtol de Wenden, C. (1988), *Les Immigrés et la politique. Cent cinquante ans d'évolution*, Paris: Presses de la Fondation nationale des sciences politiques.

–11–

Bodies Coming and Going:
Women and Fertility in Postmodern Ireland

Jo Murphy-Lawless

A Demographic Curiosity

At the beginning of the twenty-first century, Ireland is still attracting attention from demographers because of the unexpected speed, scope and shape of its demographic transition. It is also and unexpectedly the last European Union member to become a multiethnic society. As a result, there is a distinctly postmodern aspect to women's decision-making on childbearing, reflecting a diversity of needs and identities. This chapter deals with the rapidly changing background to these diversities and to the complex issues of women's decision-making on childbirth.

Historically, the shape of Irish demography evolved in an almost uninterrupted pattern of decline from the period of the Great Famine, 1845–49, into the 1970s. The Great Famine reduced the population from 8.2 million to just under 6 million in five brief years as millions of people either starved to death or emigrated. In relation to fertility and population, the Great Famine was the watershed that ushered in a period unique in Western Europe. While every other Western European country showed a steady increase in population into the twentieth century, Ireland's population declined in every Census between 1841 and 1961, when it fell to an historic low of 2.8 million. This haemorrhage was due to a peculiar combination of massive emigration and the Malthusian pattern of late marriage and high rates of celibacy practised by those who remained in Ireland. This can be illustrated by statistics from the four-year period between 1896 and 1900 when an astonishing 30 percent of men and 25 percent of women remained unmarried by the age of 50. Yet from the perspective of women who did marry, the most striking outcome of the post-Famine period comprised the extremely high rates of fertility within marriage. For example, in 1911, 81 percent of all births were fourth or higher order births; 50 percent were seventh or higher order births. These rates of fertility meant that Ireland had larger family sizes and a total fertility rate well above replacement level during the same period when the rest of Western Europe was experiencing the beginning of the neo-Malthusian shift characterized by a decline in marital fertility.

Ireland was the last country in the European Union to complete the demographic transition to below replacement fertility. In 1961, the pattern of high marital fertility was still pronounced, with 44 percent of all births being fourth or higher order births. The total fertility rate was 3.8 in that year. It peaked up towards 3.9 in 1971. Yet early moves towards convergence with the prevailing European fertility patterns were already taking shape. The 1970s were a period when the country was experiencing net immigration for the first time in well over a hundred years. This net immigration, comprising a significant proportion of young married couples, led to a widening of the pool of women of childbearing age. The numbers of women aged between 20 and 39 years of age were estimated to increase by 30 percent in that decade. This in turn led to Ireland's having the youngest population and largest population growth in the European Community,[1] with a population growth rate of 13 percent alone between 1971 and 1979. Yet this expansion in absolute numbers masked a radical shift in childbearing patterns as completed family size began to decline rapidly.

The total fertility rate drifted down throughout the 1970s and 1980s, and at their conclusion, the era of high marital fertility that had prevailed since post-Famine Ireland had ended. The total fertility rate was 3.4 in 1980. By 1986, it had fallen to 2.44. Only 25 percent of women were then giving birth to a fourth child or more (Murphy-Lawless 1987). Also by 1986, Ireland was once more in the grip of deep recession and had returned to a position of out-migration, with over 33,000 people, most of them young adults, leaving per annum (National Economic and Social Council (NESC) 1991). Overall between 1964 and 1997, total period fertility rates dropped from 4.1 to 1.94 (McCarthy and Murphy-Lawless 2000). Ireland had finally converged with the rest of the European Community in being below replacement level.

However, this convergence has actually proceeded little further. Not only does Ireland remain the EU member state with the highest level of fertility, there has been a slight but sustained upward movement in fertility since 1997. The sociologist Pat O'Connor (1998) has argued that Irishwomen are still finding sufficient power and identity in family and caring work to give childbearing a go, even if they are not choosing the older mode of unending fertility that once prevailed. The most recent trends seem to bear out O'Connor's argument. With an expanding and prosperous economy from the mid-1990s, the total number of births per annum began to rise once more for the first time since 1980. In 1999, the Irish Central Statistics Office predicted a total fertility level moving upwards as high as replacement level between 2000 and 2011 and a projected population increase to between 4 and 4.3 million (Central Statistics Office 1999). By 2002, the Irish population had risen to an unprecedented 3.93 million, a total which has not been seen since 1880. The total fertility rate rose more rapidly than the Central Statistics Office predictions, reaching 2.01 in 2002 (Figure 11.1).

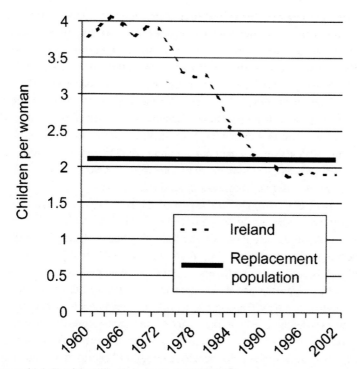

Figure 11.1 Total Fertility Rate, Ireland, 1960–2002.
Source: Eurostat, Population and Social Conditions, Demography, Fertility Indicators, January 29, 2003.

This upward movement reflected increased net immigration amongst other critical factors, an issue to which I will return in a later section of this chapter. Once more, Ireland has the highest population growth of any EU country due to having the highest birthrates of any EU country and due to the high rates of inward immigration. If Ireland has not quite returned to replacement level, these recent patterns indicate that the country remains a demographic curiosity.

Yet as the studies discussed in this chapter will indicate, women are making their decisions about childbearing in less than optimum circumstances, and O'Connor (1998) may be observing a phenomenon that is nearer its expiry date than current forecasts would suggest.

The Impact of Social Change on Women's Lives

The 1970s, 1980s and 1990s were a period of deep social change for women in almost every respect, as Irish society slowly grew away from the conservative Catholic ethos, enshrined in the 1937 Constitution, that had arguably over-determined women's actions for more than one hundred years. A principal agent of change was Ireland's entry into the European Community in 1972 and the consequent obligation to bring gender equality legislation on stream. This resulted in dramatically increased rates of participation in higher education and in labour market participation, including that of married women (O'Connor 1998). In turn, these were accompanied, albeit slowly, by a sea-change in women's perceptions of their roles in Irish society (O'Connor 1998). The fact that the steep decline in fertility in the 1980s caught demographers and planners completely by surprise was a disquieting element in this dramatically changed environment; a still strongly male-dominant public culture seemed not to comprehend that many women's definitions of their lives as solely wives and mothers were changing and that this would have an impact on related aspects in the social sphere.

By 1985, a concerted struggle on the part of the Irish women's movement to achieve reproductive rights was already fifteen years old. The total fertility rate had already fallen to 2.50, yet the notion of Ireland slipping below replacement fertility and the meanings this might hold for Irish society went largely unremarked. Instead the 1980s saw two embittered referenda campaigns, with mainstream politicians actively opposing and defeating a move to legalize divorce, and also successfully inserting into the Constitution a pro-life amendment to protect against legal abortion ever taking place. In the midst of this public hostility to women's autonomy and the return of mass emigration, women were making different choices and were rejecting the post-Famine ideology of "chaste motherhood and unregulated fertility" (T. Inglis, quoted in Murphy-Lawless 1993) that had resulted in such large family sizes in the past. However, the complexity of women's decision-making and their efforts to redefine their goals for themselves and to establish personal agency, were lost on a state that was in no hurry to amend restrictive legislation on their reproductive lives.

European Community membership helped to encourage a substantial reformation of legislation in the early 1970s with respect to issues like a clear entitlement to a weekly state allowance for all single mothers. Also, the marriage bar for women working in the civil service, which had required their retirement from their jobs upon marriage, was removed. But Irish women had to wait much longer for full access to all forms of contraception, with the last constraints being removed in 1993. Access to divorce did not arrive until the late 1990s (Murphy-Lawless and McCarthy 1999). Access to safe legal abortion remains very problematic.

In 1992, the infamous "X" case added new elements to an already difficult debate on abortion. The Irish Supreme Court overturned a High Court ruling that a 14-year-old girl, pregnant through sexual assault, could not leave the country to access a legal termination in Britain. The Supreme Court ruling took into account the 1983 pro-life amendment to the Constitution that guarantees the life of the unborn foetus as equal to the life of the mother. But the Court concluded that, in this case, there was a serious risk to the mother's life because of her suicidal state.

The Court also overruled the ban on her travelling outside the state to obtain an abortion. Subsequently, the government asked the country to vote on three cumbersome constitutional amendments to the previous pro-life amendment. This led to a very limited expression of a woman's right to abortion if her life were at risk, as well as sanctioning the right to information and counselling and travelling to abortion services abroad (Murphy-Lawless 1993). However, although the Supreme Court had called for enabling legislation for cases where the mother's life as distinct from her health is at risk, so that the law would state clearly the position on legal abortion being carried out in Ireland in these circumstances, there has so far been none. Women seeking a termination must continue to rely on the proximity of legal abortion services in Britain. A subsequent 1997 case drew attention again to this lacuna. In the "C" case, another very young girl, a victim of rape, was taken into state care for her own safety and was then permitted by the High Court to travel to England for an abortion, despite her parents' protests.[2] In 2002, there was yet another referendum on the pro-life amendment, with anti-abortion groups anxious to rid the Constitutional pro-life amendment of any ambiguity that could permit abortion in cases of suicide. The referendum was defeated but there are no current plans to introduce any legislation to clarify the 1992 Supreme Court ruling and the subsequent 1992 referenda. In the meanwhile so-called "abortion tourism" continues to increase annually. In 2001, over 7,000 women travelled to Britain in order to obtain an abortion, the highest total on record (McNally 2001).

The Celtic Tiger: Changing the Contexts of Women's Decision-making on Childbearing

In 1992, the Irish unemployment rate topped 18 percent and Ireland was still losing thousands of young people to emigration. By 1994, three critical events had taken place which changed the Irish economic context radically: the downloading of structural funds from the EU as a consequence of the Maastricht Treaty that completed Irish entry into the single European Union; the IRA (Irish Republican Army) and then the loyalist ceasefires of August 1994 which eventually brought about the Good Friday Agreement in 1998; and the series of nationally negotiated partnership agreements between government, employers, trade unions and the voluntary and community sectors to achieve growth and stability in the country's economy.

These events led to huge injections of investment funding. With a more stable island of Ireland and a greatly increased inward flow of foreign direct investment, centred especially on information technology, the Irish economy was transformed with extraordinary rapidity. Job creation levels between 1997 and 2000 surpassed the rate of job creation in the previous three decades (Department of Justice, Equality and Law Reform 1999). Women's participation in the labour market quickly grew to levels that matched EU rates, over 45 percent by 2000. However, this has not been matched by a significant expansion of family-friendly state policies.

So in this changed context, women have had to rely on the same strategies that characterise women's working lives in many other EU countries once they have children. It has been argued that the European female labour force exemplifies the feminization of work in a pattern where the majority of paid employment on offer to women is low-skilled and low-waged work (O'Connor 1998; Plantenga 1997). This creates problems for women in trying to reconcile work and caring duties in the home, as low-waged labour does not easily permit women to pay for childcare. Thus a common adaptation has been for women to opt for part-time work (Plantenga 1997). A large percentage of the Irish female workforce relies on low-paid, less skilled work. But women in this category with children also must rely on part-time work to deal with their childcare duties (Drew 1992). Drew (1992) and O'Connor (1998) argue that women must make strategic personal decisions about the reconciliation between workplace demands and childbearing. This argument is borne out by the 1991 survey of women's workforce participation by the National Economic and Social Council. That data indicated that there is an inverse relationship between women's full-time participation in the workforce and the number of children they have: the more children, the fewer hours they work (Callan and Farrell 1991). Many women see their decisions on limiting childbearing now determined by the additional costs and lost opportunity costs that prolonged childbearing and larger families entail (Coveney, Murphy-Lawless and Sheridan 1998; O'Connor 1998). Of course, this way of thinking about women's agency and opportunity could not even have entered into the Ireland of the mid-twentieth century, not least because women had no legal access to reliable fertility control.

In the changed climate of the Celtic Tiger economy, state measures to ensure equal social and economic access for women have not been evenly developed. A recent baseline study reveals that Ireland is one of the most unequal countries for women in Europe; despite recent unprecedented wealth creation, Irish women are the worst off economically of women from seventeen leading advanced economies and are least likely to have positions of power in either business or politics (Harvey 2002). Despite the flourishing economy, high rates of poverty continue and this has special ramifications for women, especially single parents, who are highly vulnerable to living in poverty (Harvey 2002; McCashin 1996). Concerted calls from employers' organizations, trade unions and women's community groups to create an appropriate state-funded framework for childcare, accompanied by intensive policy attention to the problem, have been sidelined by government inaction (Murphy-Lawless 2000). Paid childcare remains scarce and very expensive. Recent official data reveal that the average expenditure on paid childcare amounts to 97.47 euros per week (Central Statistics Office 2003b). If Ireland is compared with its EU neighbours in respect of childcare policies, it can be said to favour the model of "maximum private responsibility" (Callan and Nolan 1991); Ireland falls nearer to Spain, where official polices tend to ignore support for parents, than to Sweden, where there have been concerted efforts for many decades to support both parents in reconciling family care and paid employment (Folbre and Himmelweit, 2000).

In Ireland, housing costs also escalated substantially during the 1990s. In Dublin City, the average price for a three-bedroomed house has trebled since 1997; prices rose an additional 6 percent in the first six months of 2002 alone. It is reported that at least one in four young adult couples is now postponing starting a family to try to save money for a house (Irish Examiner 2002). The combined costs of childcare and housing suggest that there may be perceptible pressures on women in their decision-making about their fertility.

In the midst of these economic changes and political inaction, another curious development has emerged. Ireland has come to be seen as a hospitable option for people fleeing from collapsing societies of Eastern European and developing countries. In 1992, Ireland had 39 applications from people seeking refugee status. By 2002, there were 11,530 applicants who registered as asylum seekers while they waited for their claims for refugee status to be assessed under the 1951 Convention on Refugees. Nigerian citizens account for nearly one-third of all asylum applications, while Romanian citizens are the next highest single group of non-nationals (Haughey 2002).

A Supreme Court ruling in 1990, in the Fajujonu case, stated that any non-national, non-EU parent of a child born in Ireland has the right to apply for "leave to remain" as a permanent resident in Ireland if her/his child is born in Ireland.[3] Then in 1998, the historic Good Friday Agreement tried to resolve the status of Northern Ireland and return the administration of government directly to Northern Irish people. As part of the agreement, a clause was inserted copper-fastening citizenship for any child born anywhere on the island of Ireland. This automatic entitlement to citizenship contributed to a greatly increased number of non-nationals coming to give birth in Ireland. This represents a survival strategy in that many women are coming to Ireland already pregnant and prepared to endure life as exiles from countries which are collapsing socially and economically. If one of their children has Irish citizenship and if the mother or parents are permitted to stay in Ireland, they have perhaps better future economic opportunities than in the societies they have left. One in every four births in the three largest maternity hospitals in Ireland is now to a woman registered with the government as an asylum seeker. A significant minority of these women make the journey to Ireland alone and pregnant, echoing the outflow from Ireland of women seeking abortion abroad alone (Kennedy and Murphy-Lawless 2003). Their numbers have contributed to the increased Total Fertility Rate. Under the Fajujonu ruling, the right to remain in

Ireland had already been granted to 10,145 people as parents of Irish citizens. However, there are now serious question marks over their legal status and right to remain.

Understanding Irish Women's Current Experiences of Childbearing

Irish national Census data and annual vital statistics yield only broad figures for family formation in respect of age and geographical locations of women in relation to recorded births. National labour force surveys contain data on women's rates of participation in relation to marital status and family size. Small-scale but significant studies have been carried out on women's decision-making about abortion and contraception (Hyde 1996; Mahon, Conlon and Dillon 1998). But Ireland has never had the benefit of a detailed national fertility study, so national data on women's fertility disaggregated by indicators such as class, education and ethnicity is unavailable. The recently established statutory body, the Crisis Pregnancy Agency, charged with the task of reducing crisis pregnancies, has just commissioned work on women's decision-making, the results of which will come on stream in 2004.

In the interim, some sense of the range of issues comes through qualitative data from a series of research projects that I have undertaken in the last five years. The objectives of each project differed, but all of them explored various aspects of women's lives as mothers or potential mothers. This chapter presents data from those projects on the contexts and decision-making of five distinct sub-groups of women:

- young women who have career paths and who have not yet had children
- women who have returned to work after maternity leave
- women who left the workforce to care for small children and who are now trying to re-enter the labour market via second-chance education and training
- women from small towns or rural areas who are pregnant or have just given birth and are still in hospital
- women who arrived in Ireland as asylum seekers and who have given birth in Ireland.

Single Career Women Assessing the Problem of Work and Childbearing
Quantitative demographic methodologies measure cumulative actions. They cannot however capture meanings of those individual actions. By contrast, a great deal of methodological work within feminist inquiry is qualitative, an exploratory set of tools to enable us to get beneath the skin, to build an understanding about how women perceive the complexities of their lives, to see natural and social life from the viewpoint of where women are, and what we identify as producing our

experiences (Smith 1988). Young Irish women are negotiating complex multiple layers of identity as they take on adult life:

- their sexual identities
- their identities as workers and earners
- their identities as consumers
- and in choosing to have children or not, their identities around motherhood.

As part of a scoping exercise to explore these themes in 2000, I carried out case studies with women under the age of 30 who have come to adulthood in this most recent phase of the Irish demographic transition. I want to present data from one of these women in this section.

The woman is a university graduate with additional professional qualifications. She is a health care professional and works in a public health institution. Like the other four women in this exercise, she was asked about wanting children. She was aware that as a professional, she was in a strong position to pursue an excellent career of her choice.

However, she expressed her dismay that there is actually little support within the workplace on being pregnant and returning after the baby's birth, above that of the minimum statutory regulations. She described seeing her supervisor come into work after being off for her statutory fourteen weeks' maternity leave "grey every morning" with exhaustion and how this first alerted the respondent to the lack of sympathetic support and provision for women who have just given birth:

> That is something that surprised me, just seeing that. She [the supervisor] would be up every night with this small child and she was working full-time and supervising students. She's an incredible woman, extremely competent. But very shortly after I left [that job], she cut back to part-time and job-shared. But just the fact that she was doing that. She was in bits when she came in. Just looking at the workplace where I am now, it struck me as kind of ridiculous, really ironic. The whole ethos is of caring for people, but you don't get flexitime, I know that, for a longer maternity leave and shifts in schedules once the baby is born. Quietly, unofficially, people are a lot more flexible but at the same time the statistics have to be worked round and fixed up.

Of course this in turn leads to the culture of lying which we will encounter again below in relation to maternity leave. This young woman has been in a long-term relationship for several years. But she has begun to look at what she might do in relation to having children and has come to some deeply uncomfortable conclusions about how constrained she would be as a working mother:

> I've been thinking about this over the last while, the whole Celtic Tiger and the opportunities it has opened up. In a way these have been a double-edged sword because I was

just thinking about it and realized that compared with my mother, I have so far fewer options. Okay, she had to give up work when she married [because of the marriage bar]. But just in terms of property, it's a situation now where if I made the decision that I wanted to have kids, okay, I'd have a mortgage. But in the present climate, it would mean that I would have to work to have the kids and to have the background I would want and the situation I would want around that. I would have to work. In a way this is the exact opposite of what feminism fought for in your generation. Okay, it was great, you were fighting for women to be able to go out and work but now it's a situation where we have to and it's a sinister feeling that we're being kept there to feed this stupid economy and that we're being forced to stay there, like of course we're being forced to stay in the workforce, because they need the labour, they need the people. The scary thing about all this is that I would feel very much that if I were to go down that road [to have children] in the next few years, there are so few options, unless we moved down the country and lived in a shed, there would have to be two people in the house working. Okay, I might be able to negotiate and do job-sharing and part-time which is great and flexitime work. But the fact is the option isn't there to do what my mother did, to give us a good quality of life on one salary.

Her thinking illustrates the feminist analysis of the increasing pressure women are under to do it all, with no support from the state (in this case support over the issue of affordable housing). This is a pessimistic assessment coming from an articulate, highly skilled woman who has seen how older women in their respective work-places are struggling to cope and are concluding that the future presents a greater conundrum than ever for women on this issue. A forthcoming study for the Crisis Pregnancy Agency is expected to illuminate these themes in greater depth.

Women Returning to Work after Giving Birth

In an exploratory study I carried out for the national Employment Equality Agency on women returning to work after the births of their babies (Murphy-Lawless et al. 1999), there were a number of disturbing findings. The sample comprised thirty women who had permanent, pensionable employment in large-scale companies with rapidly expanding market potential. Each woman was married with a husband also in full-time employment. Twenty women were first-time mothers. The companies were

- a financial services provider
- an IT company
- a specialist manufacturing company.

Each employer offers a full maternity package to women: this includes pay to "top-up" the level of statutory maternity allowances to individuals' usual rates of pay; optional use of holiday and unpaid leave time to help extend statutory maternity leave of fourteen weeks at the time of the study (this has since been extended to eighteen weeks). Each company has a human resources manager who in interview indicated the company's full commitment to retaining women employees after maternity leave because of their value to the company as highly trained workers. In other words, this level of provision comprises the best maternity package women can expect under current regulations.[4]

Nonetheless, data indicated that:

- Women found difficulty adjusting work duties and hours to accommodate the physical changes of pregnancy.
- Just under half the sample concealed the true date of expectant delivery from their managers in order to maximize the amount of leave time they could spend at home after the baby's birth.
- Women with moderately serious to serious symptoms of pregnancy were reluctant to ask for the reallocation of duties to alleviate these problems. Their strong perception was that calling for more flexible arrangements to accommodate their pregnancy would compromise their position.
- Women who were breastfeeding encountered difficulties in relation to a sufficiently long maternity leave, lack of facilities for breastfeeding, and lack of support among colleagues.
- Half the sample recorded difficulty in accessing childcare and out of the fifteen who did not record difficulty, ten had older children indicating that childcare arrangements may be particularly problematic for first-time mothers.
- Despite demonstrating strong and continuing commitment to their jobs, women expressed concerns about the impact of their status as new mothers on promotion prospects.
- Several women indicated that the pressures of the dual burdens of work and new motherhood were too difficult to sustain on a full time basis and they were therefore withdrawing from the workplace.

Women drew attention to the fact that pregnancy and childbearing left them with something to prove in the workplace. In extended case study interviews, respondents stated their distress at the lack of policy attention to their situation as new mothers:

> I feel that this lying about the date of the birth of their child . . . everybody does it because there's no way you will take an extra month before hand . . . Imagine the baby is two weeks overdue and you have taken a month before, you lose six weeks out of the precious fourteen weeks and you have only eight weeks with the child.

> I think maternity laws should be changed in this country to reflect the demand of the parents. When one income is not enough to make a decent living, a society has to think

over its values. We are talking about the next generation here. We want them to be healthy and strong and for this the first steps should be breastfeeding and a protected, calm environment.

It is very difficult to find a trustworthy person to leave a baby with. Also, all forms of childcare are extremely expensive. After our mortgage, childcare costs are the biggest expense in our budget.

A more senior position became available during my second pregnancy in 1998 but I was advised by my senior manager not to apply as I would not be eligible because of commitments at home. This would "get in the way" of doing the job. I did not actually apply for this job.

I found that after my first pregnancy people in the workplace still treated me the same as before but after my second pregnancy things changed. I have recently accepted to take a redundancy package. This was not something I would have considered before my second pregnancy. Lack of child care in the workplace, no designated breast feeding/expressing areas plus not having the option to work either a three-day week or job-share has forced me to make this decision to leave.

What comes across is a sense of isolation and the feeling from the women that they must solve these problems on their own.

Women Returning to Second-chance Education and Training

Women continue to be over-represented among the lowest paid employees in Ireland (O'Connor 1998: 196–7). Leaving the workplace becomes a sensible decision if women face insuperable difficulties in maintaining home life for young children while working in settings of poorly paid low-skilled work, especially when safe affordable childcare is a rarity.

Yet this seeming "choice," which as Franks (1999) observes is not a real "choice," also means that in the long term women may face very real poverty, having fallen out of paid work altogether. In such circumstances, retraining and second chance education can present important opportunities for women to gain new skills to help them re-enter the labour market at a better level of pay. However, it is vital that such labor market initiatives include paid childcare. In a recent evaluation of a second-chance education programme set up to serve working-class women from two communities in one of the more isolated rural counties of Ireland, Donegal, women from this background explained what it has been like for them to try and engage in ongoing education, training and coursework, many of them for the first time in their lives, in order to improve their future chances (English and Murphy-Lawless 2000). Over half of the women involved in this project had children aged between 0 and 4 years of age; 50 percent of the women were in the 18–35 year age range. Only one-third of the women had completed second-level schooling. The majority of them felt they had had little choice about leaving school because their wages were needed to help support younger siblings. As one woman in her early thirties explained it:

> Education was very limited and very basic . . . From the age of 8, we were sent . . . to gather spuds in the harvest season so if it was wet, we could go to school. And I might have only been at school three months in the year . . . I was the eldest. I looked after the rest. I didn't look on it as work, do you know what I mean, I was just there for the rest of them and that's it. I did what had to be done and just took it for granted.

Most had followed a pattern of semi-skilled work in the catering and hotel industries, factories, shops and contract cleaning until their children were born. At that point it became difficult for them to sustain home and work, given low wages and no childcare facilities. Lack of support in the workplace for new mothers was a decisive factor in their withdrawal from paid employment:

> I enjoyed working in the hospital and I enjoyed working in the factory but when I got pregnant with my children, it wasn't the same. I found it very hard to keep up with the work and if you were off sick, you had to explain yourself why you were sick.

However, even with their recent involvement in second-chance education, two-thirds of the respondents stated that family responsibilities and childcare problems would prevent them from taking up longer-term courses that might provide them with better qualifications in the labour market. They stated that the principle problem was the lack of state-supported childcare facilities. None expressed regret at having children but all of them have negotiated difficult decisions about reconciling family and caring duties with other dimensions of their lives, including paid employment. At the same time, they feel they have lost out for themselves. Especially compelling were women's responses about their lack of self-confidence, once they had chosen to stay at home full-time with very young children. Thus they feel caught in enforced full-time motherhood as a consequence of a lack of supportive structures in education, training, family policies and childcare.

Women from Small Towns and Rural Areas Giving Birth

The Donegal case studies point to the problems experienced in rural Ireland which did not benefit greatly from the Celtic Tiger era and where there are geographic areas under great economic pressure with a very low employment base. Another pressing issue for women in rural areas is access to maternity services for those women who do become pregnant. The health care system in Ireland is under severe pressure at present (Wren 2003), with maternity services especially badly hit. This is yet another neglected policy area that impinges adversely on women and their decisions about childbearing, Midwives are leaving the profession because of poor working conditions and Ireland has begun to rely heavily on health care personnel from developing countries to make up shortages. With the closure of small rural hospitals, women in rural areas regularly have to travel long distances, up to 40 miles, to give birth. There is no community midwifery service for the postpartum period and women returning home can count on only one visit from the public health nurse. So there are critical problems of practical informed support for new mothers. I carried out a study in 2002 on women's needs and perceptions in a region of the country which has just lost two of its maternity units, forcing women to travel much further in order to give birth in hospital (Murphy-Lawless 2002).

There was a strong sense of women having to make do and muddle through, as with this young woman talking about the lack of support after she went home with her baby:

> The hardest thing I found was that for the twenty-seven days afterwards there was change in me, and there was change in the baby, and, you know, it says it in the book, but it doesn't ring true to you when you read it. And then I suppose, you don't like to put yourself out by asking things of nurses like i.e. "My stitches are sore," because you don't want to bother them, that kind of thing, you know when you go home you find out there's something wrong, you know, then you go to your doctor maybe two or three weeks after, and he says "This is all normal and you've kind of got an infection in your stitches or something" – d'you know what I mean?

Women spoke about how they "plod away," needing reassurance but trying to get through as best they can:

> But a lot of the girls will say, I think an awful lot of what we would look for is reassurance, just discussing your experience with somebody else, to know what's normal, and what to expect, and whether you should be concerned about something or you shouldn't. It's not so much coming to the hospital and everything is fine, I think it really is the going home bit, and being home, the wondering, and, you know, like, we'd say, like "Aw God I wouldn't ask that," and maybe you should see how tomorrow goes instead or whatever, like you know, and you just don't, you plod away and hope for the best.

Concern for overworked staff was a common reaction:

> The only thing is that, do they have the time to spend with you? You're always thinking, "They've somebody else to see," because they will tell you that they are overdone as well, they're being dragged everywhere, you know.

But some women were also able to identify that the lack of support in the community because of insufficient numbers of public health nurses was part of a wider political issue about resources for women:

It seems that the health authorities have lost the plot regarding women's issues.

If men had babies we would not be here, it's a crazy system here, it's the frustration that all of us feel, the frustration at the inability to get through to those in authorities, the health board. This is the reality of our lives, it's not some sort of a game we are playing, so I don't know.

I think there are going to be other health problems where women don't feel valued in the birthing process, and don't feel valued before and after and that is one main thing that has become clear to us since the removal of the maternity service is that people feel they are thrown out, they go home in a couple of days so other needs get overlooked, including mental health.

Women Asylum Seekers Giving Birth in Ireland

The situation regarding pregnant asylum seekers is becoming a deeply contested issue in Ireland. Ireland has not been a multiethnic society and the entry of perceived large numbers of people, principally from Africa and Eastern Europe, has met with a growing level of racism (Fanning 2002). As many asylum seekers are women who have gone on to give birth in Ireland, it was seen as vital to carry out a needs assessment study on their behalf.

Baseline data from sixty-one pregnant or newly delivered women who were registered as asylum seekers were collected in 1999–2000 (Kennedy and Murphy-Lawless 2003). Being an asylum seeker entails enormous insecurity, physically, emotionally and, above all, legally. These aspects make matters especially bleak for pregnant women asylum seekers. All maternity care is free and of the same calibre open to all women in the state, regardless of legal status. However, living conditions for asylum seekers are often poor. Generally they comprise hostels with meals provided from a canteen, or bed and breakfast accommodation paid for directly by the state, or private rented accommodation (with a state rent subsidy) which is in the poorer urban areas. Otherwise women are limited to a very small weekly cash payment from the state meant to cover all remaining personal needs. In the hostels, there were no cots for babies and, if women were on their own with no partner, they shared a bedroom with two or three other women and babies. The useful aspect of this was that it had the potential of providing a measure of support; 44 percent of the women were having their first baby and the lack of an extended family network was felt as a great hardship. Many women had left children behind them to come to Ireland. Disorientation, loneliness and social isolation were common reactions to their circumstances.

Another complication was their late arrival into Ireland vis-à-vis their pregnancy. Just under two-thirds of our sample were twenty-two weeks or more pregnant when they were first seen in hospital for their antenatal care.

Few had direct complaints about their physical levels of care in hospital, despite the many pressures on Irish maternity hospitals at present (see previous section).

But women reported practical problems such as lack of language support and lack of childcare to mind small children while attending the hospital. However, a minority of women found communication with medical and midwifery staff difficult and some questioned if this was because of their colour:

> When I was crying and in pain, I got no sympathy from the staff. I had to ask "Is it because I am black?"

And, despite the fact that women felt they had received good standards of physical care, they did experience isolation and fear during birth, especially where they had no family members with them:

> I was afraid, I was so afraid. My mother was not here. No one was here. I was afraid this child would die. I was so happy when I came out of hospital with my baby. I was crying all the time from happiness.

> I thought I was going to die giving birth, it was so painful. I didn't understand what was happening. They said when the baby's head was being born but I was too scared to watch it.

Coping without the extended family after birth was emotionally difficult. In the Irish health care system at present, there is almost no postnatal support available to women outside the hospital setting (see next section) and problems of isolation abounded:

> We were lonely and alone. We didn't know how to manage and I was very weak.

> When I came here, with no family and the climate was so different, I couldn't stop vomiting for the first few days I was here.

Some women were dealing with additional traumas as a result of rape, unwanted pregnancy and domestic violence. None of these could be easily responded to, even if they were known about by health care staff, because of the pressures on over-stretched public health services.

The negative impact on women facing an uncertain future was palpable. As a Nigerian woman who had left her family, including two children, behind her in Nigeria put it:

> We don't know what is going to happen. The future is bleak.

Another woman gave voice to an anxiety expressed by many:

> I'm worried about taking care of myself and my baby. I think about that all the time.

Where will they move me? If they don't put you in good accommodation, how can you do your best?

Current and Future Challenges for Women on Childbearing

In December 2002, the Celtic Tiger economy was announced officially dead by a government which produced a Budget to fit the global economic downturn. After nearly a decade of expansion, unemployment was once more on the rise. In January 2003, the Irish Supreme Court published a decision that in practical terms set aside the Fajujonu ruling of 1990, concluding that non-national parents of Irish-born citizens did not have an automatic right to apply for leave to remain. Although the Court said that decisions would need to be taken on a case-by-case basis, the decision potentially opens the way to deportation on a large scale with as many as 10,000 non-national adults and children could be affected by the decision (Donnellan 2003). Interestingly, the Chief Justice of the Supreme Court cited in his decision increasing pressures on the social services to underpin his argument that the common good of the state might have to prevail over the claims of a family unit with a child who is an Irish citizen (Donnellan 2003). To borrow Giorgio Agamben's (1998) phrase, women's "bare labour" is once again over-determined by the needs of the state in Ireland.

As Oaks (2003) has pointed out, young women in Ireland are currently receiving very mixed messages about the social value of motherhood. Oaks concludes "in contemporary Ireland, an appeal to uphold motherhood as a women's primary life goal is too limited to encompass the realities of many young, middle-class women's expectations and opportunities" (Oaks 2003). Women from working-class and minority backgrounds are seeing their chances very curtailed to be mothers and to have other life expectations. All women who give birth are facing strains in overcrowded and unsupported maternity health services. In Ireland the message to women remains that work for wages is the antithesis of motherhood. Motherhood under any circumstances is not particularly well supported by the state.

The Dutch economist, Janneke Plantenga (1997) argues that women across Europe have worked exceptionally hard to prove their commitment to engaging in paid work outside the home while still trying to deal with their unpaid caring responsibilities. But Plantenga also argues that with a market driven by the imperatives of deregulation, neither employers nor governments have matched this commitment:

> The lower activity rates of women, the large number of women filling part-time jobs and their unequal pay all point to gender-specific social assumptions about the responsibility for providing care. (Plantenga 1997: 94)

At the beginning of the 1990s, the sociologist Cynthia Cockburn (1991: 228) argued that in order to achieve true gender equality in society, the state urgently needed to redistribute resources "towards women as a sex and towards support for those caring for human health and reproduction." We have yet to see that perspective fully anchored into the health and social policy process for 21st century Ireland. Nevertheless, Ireland has edged back to near replacement level and still has one of the highest TFRs across the breadth of Europe.

Notes

1. Ireland joined what was then called the European Community in 1973.
2. The "C" case was complicated by the fact that the 13-year-old girl was a member of Ireland's indigenous minority ethnic community, the Travellers (see Oaks 2002).
3. If parents are granted "leave to remain" by the government, this does not mean that they are citizens, or even that they will be successful in any application for citizenship at a later point. It means only that they will not be deported.
4. Complaints from women about unfair treatment on the issue of maternity leave continue to account for half of the requests for information put to the Employment Equality Authority each year (Coulter 2003).

References

Agamben, G. (1998), *Homo Sacer: Sovereign Power and Bare Life*, Stanford, CA: Stanford University Press.

Callan, T. and Farrell, B. (1991), *Women's Participation in the Irish Labour Market*, Dublin: National Economic and Social Council.

Callan, T. and Nolan, B. (1991), "Concepts of Poverty and the Poverty Line," *Journal of Economic Surveys*, 5(3): 243–261.

Central Statistics Office (1999), *Population and Labour Force Projections, 2001–2003*, Dublin: Government of Ireland.

—— (2003a), *Vital Statistics, Fourth Quarter and Yearly Summary, 2002*, Dublin: Government of Ireland.

—— (2003b), *Quarterly National Household Survey, Childcare, Fourth Quarter, 2002*, Dublin: Government of Ireland.

Cockburn, C. (1991), *In the Way of Women: Men's Resistance to Sex Equality in Organisations*, London: Macmillan.

Coulter, C. (2003), "Half of Equality Agency's Queries Relate to Pregnancy," *Irish Times*, January 28.

Coveney, E., Murphy-Lawless, J. and Sheridan, S. (1998), *Women, Work and Family Responsibilities*, Dublin: Larkin Centre for the Unemployed.

Department of Justice, Equality and Law Reform (1999), *Equal Opportunities in the State-Sponsored Sector*, Dublin: The Stationery Office.

Donnellan, E. (2003), "10,000 Non-nationals Face Deportation," *Irish Times*, January 24.

Drew, E. (1992), "Part-time Working in Ireland: Meeting the Flexibility Needs of Women Workers or Employers?," *Canadian Journal of Irish Studies*, 18(1) 95–109.

English, M. and Murphy-Lawless, J. (2000), *Developing Neighbourhood Work and Second Chance Education in Two Donegal Communities*, Letterkenny: Second Chance Education Project/VEC.

Fanning, B. (2002), *Racism and Social Change in the Republic of Ireland*, Manchester: Manchester University Press.

Folbre, N. and Himmelweit, S. (2000), "Children and Family Policy: A Feminist Issue," *Feminist Economics*, 6(1) 1–4.

Franks, S. (1999), *Having None of It: Women, Men and the Future of Work*, London: Granta.

Harvey, B. (2002), *Rights and Justice Work in Ireland: A New Base Line Report*, York: Joseph Rowntree Charitable Trust.

Haughey, N. (2002), "Claims for Asylum Rise by 1,200 This Year," *Irish Times*, December 31.

Hyde, A. (1996), "Unmarried Pregnant Women's Accounts of their Contraceptive Practices: A Qualitative Analysis," *Irish Journal of Sociology*, 6: 179–211.

Irish Examiner (2002), "Soaring House Prices Force Couples into House or Family Decision," *Irish Examiner*, August 23.

Kennedy, P. and Murphy-Lawless, J. (2003), "The Maternity Care Needs of Refugees and Asylum Seekers," Feminist Review, special edition: Asylum and Exile, 73: 39–53.

McCarthy, J. and Murphy-Lawless, J. (2000), "Recent Fertility Change in Ireland and the Future of Irish Fertility," *Below Replacement Fertility*, Population Bulletin of the United Nations, special issue 40–41, New York: United Nations.

McCashin, A. (1996), *Lone Mothers in Ireland: A Local Study*, Dublin: Combat Poverty Agency.

McNally, F. (2001), "Figures say 7,000 will have Abortions this Year," *Irish Times*, November 9.

Mahon, E., Conlon, C. and Dillon, L. (1998), *Women and Crisis Pregnancy: A Report Presented to the Department of Health and Children*, Dublin: The Stationery Office.

Murphy-Lawless, J. (1987), *Fact Sheets on Fertility in Ireland*, Dublin: Health Education Bureau.

—— (1993), "Fertility, Bodies and Politics: the Irish Case," *Reproductive Health Matters*, 2 (November): 53–64.

—— (2000) "Changing Women's Working Lives: Childcare Policy in Ireland," *Feminist Economics*, 6(1): 89–94.

—— (2002), "Meeting the Changing Needs of Women in Childbirth," unpublished report for the School of Nursing and Midwifery Studies, Trinity College Dublin.

Murphy-Lawless, J. and McCarthy, J. (1999) "Social Policy and Fertility Change in Ireland: the Push to Legislate in Favour of Women's Personal Agency," *European Journal of Women's Studies*, 6(1): 69–96.

Murphy-Lawless, J. and Isis Research Group (1999) *New Mothers at Work*, Dublin: Employment Equality Agency.

National Economic and Social Council (NESC) (1991), *The Economic and Social Implications of Emigration*, Dublin: NESC.

Oaks, L. (2002) "The Transformation of Public Discourses on Irish Abortion Policy," *Women's Studies International Forum*, 25(3): 315–333.

—— (2003) "Antiabortion Positions and Young Women's Life Plans in Contemporary Ireland," *Social Science and Medicine*, 56: 1973–1986.

O'Connor, P. (1998), *Emerging Voices: Women in Contemporary Irish Society*, Dublin: IPA.

Plantenga, J. (1997), "European Constants and National Particularities: The Position of Women in the EU Labour Market," in A.G. Dijkstra and J. Plantenga (eds) *Gender and Economics: A European Perspective*, London: Routledge.

Smith, D.E. (1988), *The Everyday World as Problematic*, Milton Keynes: Open University Press.

Wren, M. (2003), *Unhealthy State: Anatomy of a Sick Society*, Dublin: New Island.

–12–

A Reflection on Barren States:
The Demographic Paradoxes of Consumer
Capitalism

Gail Kligman

Across Europe, "old" and "new," demographic concerns about low fertility trends have increasingly been replaced by pronounced anxieties about below replacement fertility.[1] As birthrates continue to decline or, in some cases, increase slightly, nevertheless to remain below replacement level (see, for example, Ireland and Norway), politicians, demographers and policy-makers alike grapple with fears about "demographic crises," "birth strikes," the "death of the nation," and "baby busts." Simultaneously, Europe's populations are graying, straining pension and health systems. To address projected demographic dramas associated with declining birthrates, Europe's leaders – supranational, national and local – are proposing various strategies ranging from female and family-friendly pronatalist policies to targeted immigration and return migration.

Statistics of low to lowest low fertility underscore the centrality of reproduction for Europe's polities, economies, and societies.[2] Social reproduction writ large is presently challenged by the perceived reluctance of citizens – notably women, and particular ones at that – to bear children or adequate numbers of them. Paradoxically, the birthplace of "modernity" seems to be sounding its own potential death knell. Declining infant mortality and birthrates combined with increasing life expectancy – hallmarks of the first demographic transition – are now viewed as potentially threatening to the very modernity that these same indicators previously heralded.

Myriad factors that vary in their historical and cultural configurations have contributed to the alarm raised by the so-labeled second demographic transition, itself a feature of the latter half of the twentieth century.[3] Among them have been women's increased educational attainment, labor force participation, consumerism and related postmaterialist values focusing attention on self-realization rather than self-sacrifice, as well as women's and men's changing roles in marital and partnership relations, in childrearing and in the meaning of motherhood and parenting more generally. The opportunity costs of childbearing have been further weighed against the decline in marriage, increase in divorce, single parenting, and inadequate or non-existent family services and support systems, ranging from tax breaks to child and health care. To these may be added economic insecurities provoked by postsocialist transformation, global marketization and increased labor migration (legal and illegal).[4]

As the chapters in this volume demonstrate, there is considerable variation in the overall trend of declining birthrates across Europe, with age, class, ethnicity and race being influential variables that shape and reflect different reproductive practices.[5] The contributors also demonstrate that interpreting below replacement fertility trends benefits from multidisciplinary analytic lenses: while demographic studies may shed significant light on generalizable trends and factors influencing them, they do not shed comparable light on the particularities of experience, of what changing reproductive practices mean, as ethnographic research does. These case studies thus "flesh out" certain aspects of the general trends, locating them in the embodied and meaningful experiences of the European women studied.

In general, as numerous demographic studies reveal and with which these concur, it is middle-class women who are accused of "not doing their part" or their "patriotic duty." Rural women tend to bear more children than do urban inhabitants. Cramped or unavailable urban housing often has a negative effect on fertility behavior, as does alcoholism (especially male). Women who are more highly educated tend to bear fewer children. Religion is another factor whose impact warrants further study. While Ireland's TFR has increased slightly in recent years, Italy and Poland, also strongly Catholic countries, have surprisingly low TFRs.

Economic uncertainty in Eastern Europe contrasts with relative prosperity in Western Europe. In the postsocialist states, as indicated in Chapters 3, 4 and 5 on Germany, Russia and the Czech Republic, post-emancipated women confront infrastructural constraints that make everyday life a challenge unfamiliar to those who grew up under socialism. Neoliberal policies have influenced the restructuring of health, education, and family supports, curtailing access to and availability of such resources.[6] The lure of market-dictated "needs" has exaggerated material desires and postmaterialist values. While women in Eastern Europe still bear children at younger ages than do women further west, they too are having fewer of them. Also, divorce and single motherhood have become more widespread, giving rise not only to changing family forms but to an increase in the feminization of poverty as well.[7]

In Western Europe, in countries where women-friendly and/or family-friendly policies have been more limited (e.g. in Ireland, Italy and Spain), women's greater labor force participation – whether full-time or part-time – higher education and consumption practices have contributed to tempering the number of children they have and when they have them. Elsewhere, in countries where welfare state or pronatalist, pro-family or women-friendly provisions have been more substantial (e.g. France, Greece, Norway, Germany), women and men face related concerns about negotiating family and career trajectories. However, where the state offers greater support to women and/or families, birthrates are slightly higher.[8]

East and west, middle-class European women and men alike have embraced postmaterialist values, prioritizing self-realization as a goal of adulthood. Images of self-sacrificing, selfless mothers have been replaced by those of self-interested, "selfish" women accused by public leaders and demographers of undermining their nations' futures (e.g. Spain, Italy, Greece). For many of these women, however, motherhood has changed, with mothers focusing on the "quality" of their children's lives as visible signs of modern, responsible mothering rather than on the number of children they bear and raise as defining their social value as mothers (e.g. Italy, Greece).

Clashes between "motherhood cultures" manifest themselves through different understandings of what motherhood means to women of different generations and different local and national cultures. What is selfish to some is modern and responsible to others. Despite the legal re-unification of Germany, its divided history in the twentieth century still shapes women's experiences of and thinking about motherhood differently in the former GDR than in the former federal republic. In Greece, where motherhood is believed "to complete" a woman's life, women are nevertheless delaying, if not eschewing, childbirth. As mentioned above, Greece is among an array of western countries in which age at first birth has increased in contrast to age at first birth in, for example, the postsocialist states.

Integrally related to changing motherhood cultures are changing attitudes toward children themselves. For many, children have become "consumer projects."[9] Middle-class parents, enjoying the benefits of postwar prosperity, wish the best and the most for their children, their nation's futures. The best and most are increasingly measured in material terms. To the extent that educational costs have increased over time as universal education has become more costly and western states propose privatizing higher education, so parents factor these concerns into their equations.

Being able to provide for one's children in the manner desired speaks to a redefinition of needs in the context of expanding global market economies and increased consumption, with women targeted as primary consumers. Not surprisingly, increased consumption and changing "needs" has had a tangible generational effect. Parents who by now had expected to themselves be grandparents increasingly find that their own children are still enjoying the comforts of home, prolonging their departures to begin their married lives (e.g. Italy, Spain).[10] Young men and women alike want to study and travel more, fulfilling their own lives and dreams before attending to those of others.[11]

Paradoxically, then, consumption and postmaterialism may contribute productively to expanding global markets and individual opportunities while simultaneously undermining social reproduction. The universalizing trend of global capital that seeks increased consumption and women as active consumers may contain an inherent reproductive contradiction. As feminism and changing labor force needs have increasingly brought women into "productive" labor (for personal and economic reasons), women have increasingly controlled their fertility behavior, bearing fewer children.[12] (Recall that birthrates are declining across the globe.)

Furthermore, women themselves are ever more mobile, often migrant, workers.[13] Historically, the mobility of labor, including women's incorporation into the workforce, did not preclude parenting. However, the chapters in this volume point to several trends that merit further consideration in the present-day economic context. First, the "modern" family of the second demographic transition is understood as a conjugal or partner-based family in which children are not required as constitutive of it. That is, couples no longer need nor necessarily want children, and second, if they do have children, they limit their number such that quality consumption opportunities are maximized.[14] Ironically, in another twist alluded to above, families in southern Mediterranean countries appear to be fostering the prolongation rather than reproduction of the nuclear family with their children staying home rather than seeking partners with whom to start their own families.

Barren States or Barren Nations?

The demographic vulnerabilities noted both in "old" and "new" Europe are themselves both old and new. Yet, constant in the concerns about the "demise of the nation," "birth strikes," "baby busts" and the like is who is reproducing. Demographic crises are not determined solely by numbers but by the social constitution of those statistics as well.[15] Discourses about demographic crises reflect differing views about who "should" bear children, often in opposition to who is bearing them. Such discourses classically invoke categories of otherness, be they of class, ethnic or racial distinctions. These "others" may come from within (e.g. the poor) or without (e.g. immigrants) and are frequently perceived to be one and the same (e.g. poor immigrants). Assessing Europe's current demographic trends, then, has as much to do with understanding why certain Europeans are or are not reproducing and the implications thereof for the future of the nation as it does with analyzing what various European welfare states propose to address the socio-economic problems produced by falling birthrates and aging populations.[16]

Indeed, it is against conceptualizations of "the nation" that anxieties about its demise emerge. Hence, in some respects, *Barren Nations* may be a more apt title for this volume, better capturing the underlying issues referenced in it. Unlike nations, states are "relatively centralized organizational structures with claims to sovereignty over a territory" (Gal and Kligman 2000a: 24). In the exercise of authority, state institutions "produce policies, regulations, laws, practices and discourses" that pre- and pro-scribe the parameters of participation in and support for the imagined community writ large that forms "the nation" (Gal and Kligman 2000a: 20). Nations, in turn, are "symbolic constructs, categories of identity or systems of social classification' (Gal and Kligman 2000a: 24).[17] Nations may be mono-ethnic or multiethnic/racial in composition as well as civic or ethnic in political, legal, and cultural orientation. The former (i.e. "civic" nation) embraces shared political obligations and rights; the latter ("ethnic" or "ethno-national") includes "shared origin, culture and blood" (Gal and Kligman 2000a: 24).

The rhetoric of demographic crisis masks the intimate intertwining of national, state, racial, ethnic, gendered and class interests. "Death of the nation" or related metaphors implicitly assume who "should" be reproducing rather than recognizing the legitimacy of who is. Such metaphors simultaneously signify that the nation's "proper" inhabitants are not reproducing whereas its "others" are reproducing too much.[18] Postcolonial and postsocialist immigration and integration draw attention to differentiated notions of the nation, of who is welcome and who is not, of inclusion and exclusion. To illustrate, in France (Chapter 10 in this volume), family policy has long been a site for understanding the nation and who benefits from the state's largesse. Yet, children from the former colonies are not viewed equally when the reproduction of the nation is at stake.

Not surprisingly, then, immigration and emigration are high on the list of contemporary demographic dilemmas. As Europe expands its political-economic union, its "internal" borders have become more porous and its "external" borders harder. Meanwhile, labor has become both more flexible and more mobile, radically challenging the social reproduction of "old" Europe's constituent nations (see Berezin and Schain 2003). It is not so much that European states are barren (just as it is unclear whether the current low fertility trajectory marks a long-term trend or is transitory), but that the historical or, to some, traditional understandings of "the nation" are increasingly at odds with demographic verities that are transforming the more familiar faces of Europe's nations.[19] Postcolonialism and postsocialism, as mentioned previously, have contributed importantly to diversifying Europe's nation-states. That very diversity and what it represents have provoked policy and public debates about impending demographic crises. Too many "others" are said to be draining the coffers of European welfare states that, in turn, are no longer readily sustainable in part because of various drains on them, ranging from economic to reproductive.[20]

In post-socialist Bulgaria (Chapter 6 in this volume) for example, limited options for "legitimate" economic improvement and postmaterialist personal fulfillment prompted many young people to leave for the long-desired West. The resulting brain drain was paralleled by a reproductive one. In contrast to their peers back home, Bulgarian émigrés in the United States not only pursued occupational opportunities but also began (re)producing Bulgarian-Americans. While the "nation" reconstituted abroad may contribute vitally to the Bulgarian state through remittances and other forms of economic activity, and culturally and "spiritually" to the sustenance of the Bulgarian nation, nonetheless, Bulgaria's lowest low fertility presents demographic challenges for the well-being of the nation-state itself.[21]

In the context of an expanding service economy, decreasing birthrates coupled with increasing longevity, global labor migration and the war on terror, it is not surprising that immigration policies and citizenship laws have, in many countries, become more restrictive.[22] Yet, at the same time, immigration and emigration are often, if paradoxically, presented as the means by which nations are being undermined (e.g. too many "undesired" immigrants draw upon strained welfare state economies and bear too many "undesirable" children) or by which nations may be saved (e.g. immigrants contribute through their productive and reproductive labor). To the extent that immigrant workers resolve labor force shortages (i.e. state-centered "needs"), they simultaneously, and again paradoxically, present reproductive concerns regarding rights to social benefits, citizenship, and the like (i.e. nation-centered "problems").

To address declining birthrates, politicians, policy-makers, demographers as well as enterprising mayors far and wide have posed various solutions. Some of these are meant to discourage reproduction by "others" by encouraging "locals" to bear children. For example, in the town of Coaticook, Quebec, the mayor has promoted family-friendly subsidies for local young couples willing to reproduce repeatedly. In contrast to much of Quebec where birthrates have dropped from 4 children per family to 1.4 per family, Coaticook boasts of a stable population "without the benefit of the Haitian, Vietnamese, Chinese and North African immigration that fills nearby Montreal" (Krauss 2004). Yet, in the small town of Teruel, Spain, its mayor has actively promoted selectively targeted preferential immigration policies to attract Spanish-descended Latin Americans and eastern Europeans – especially Romanians who speak a romance language – to reinvigorate the town's "aging and declining town population" (L'Express 2001; Clarin 2000).[23] Scotland has opted for a multifocused approach, both encouraging the return of expatriates and, in some towns, paying couples for each child they produce (Alvarez 2003).[24]

Attempts to "balance" the productive and reproductive demographic imbalances and tensions now challenging Europe are, to reiterate, both old and new. Debates about state provisioning, citizenship rights, immigration, emigration, childbearing and child rearing, are hardly recent (see, for example, Glass 1967). Yet, the context in which these issues are discussed has changed, underscoring that policies and everyday understandings of them as well as of the practices and processes with which they are associated are historically contingent. Decreasing birthrates and increasing longevity in an expanding global service economy shape the parameters of contemporary debates, whether among policy-makers or women deciding about their productive and reproductive interests. As feminist scholars, especially anthropologists, have long argued, reproduction engages both public and private concerns, "in part because states, families and other social actors all understand themselves as having much at stake in the control of childbearing and childrearing" (Gal and Kligman 2000a: 17).

The chapters in this volume explore various dimensions of Europe's demographic "crises." The majority examine why women and/or their partners often choose to postpone childbearing or to bear but one child or none at all and to do so in varying "family" forms. The chapters demonstrate that the ideals of responsible, modern motherhood, parenting and family arrangements have changed considerably in post-Second World War Europe. These changes have themselves been importantly shaped by the very aspirations and achievements of "modernity." Cultivating consumers and consumption has contributed to transforming individual, familial and societal "needs" and desires as individuals seek increasingly to pursue their own interests and explore the world in ever greater numbers. While birthrates are declining globally, in most of Europe – the focus of this volume – birthrates are uniformly below replacement level. Whether this trend is temporary or a long-term trajectory remains to be seen, as does the role, for example, of immigration either in relieving or in further exacerbating current concerns about the viability of European welfare systems and the nations they are meant to serve. Reflecting upon these interrelated issues, it seems appropriate to question the paradoxical relationship between neoliberal policies, expanding markets, and declining birthrates in the twenty-first century. As labor, production and profits migrate across the globe, do consumerism and "postmaterialist" values contain the seeds of Europe's reproductive demise? Yet again, the relationship between production and reproduction stares us starkly in the face. If the current low fertility trend persists, the reproduction writ large of European "nation-states" will depend in no small measure on their willingness and ability to incorporate newcomers fully. Perhaps feminist emphases on the centrality of reproduction – rather than the supporting role attributed it in classic social theory – have come of age.

Notes

1. The ideas expressed in this brief reflection are preliminary, suggesting issues that may warrant further consideration.
2. This is a point long argued by feminists (see, for example, Laslett and Brenner 1989, Ginsburg and Rapp 1995; Gal and Kligman 2000a, among many others).

3. On the second demographic transition, see Van de Kaa (1987); see, for example, Hobson, Olah and Morrissens (2004), Melegh (2002) and Szreter (1993) for critical assessments.

4. It is well beyond the scope of this summary reflection to review these issues and the literatures that pertain to them.

5. Recall that birthrates are declining all over the world, not only in Europe and Japan. The United States is distinctive although there are indications that its birthrates may differentially fall as well. To wit: between 2000 and 2003, the birthrate among people of Hispanic descent increased 13 percent; among Asian Americans, 12.6 percent; African Americans, 4 percent. For those who self-identified as "white," the largest group, the birthrate increase was 1 percent ("2 Minorities Spur Rapid U.S. Growth," *New York Times*, June 15, 2004: A14).

6. See, for example, Gal and Kligman (2000a: ch. 4), Haney (2002). Neoliberal policies have influenced restructuring in both eastern and western Europe.

7. See, for example, Emigh and Szelenyi (2001), Gal and Kligman (2000b), Fodor (2002).

8. For a review of feminist critiques of the welfare state literature and feminist contributions to theorizing the welfare state, see, for example, Gal and Kligman (2000a: ch. 4). There is a large literature on welfare states and demographic indicators. Among related discussions, see, for example Schoenmaeckers and Lodewijckx (1999) and Morgan and King (2001). I thank Judith Seltzer for calling them to my attention. See also Hobson *et al.* (2004).

9. See Krause, (Chapter 8 in this volume). On the changing value of children, see, for example, Zelizer (1985).

10. Although considered more a trend in Southern Europe, it has recently been noted in the United States, suggesting that lower US birthrates may be in the offing as well. See Lewin (2003); see also note 5.

11. As Douglass notes (Chapter 9 in this volume), among middle-class Spaniards of marriageable age, marriage is now often considered to limit individual "freedom" to pursue one's own interests.

12. Whether women are brought into the labor force equitably is quite another matter and beyond the scope of this reflection.

13. The literature tends to focus on women as migrant domestic workers (e.g. Hondagneu-Sotelo 2001; Milkman, Reese and Roth 1998). There is increasing attention to global sex workers (e.g. Kempadoo and Doezema 1998; Ehrenreich and Hochschild 2002). Women are also a large constituency of the world's refugees. See, for example, US Committee for Refugees (2000) *Refugee Reports*, 21: 2. See also Pesser and Mahler (2003) on migration and gender.

14. This recasting of "the family" is another dimension of the contemporary

variety of family forms that include single-parent families, divorced families and gay families. See also note 11.

15. It is beyond the scale of this brief reflection to rehearse the continuities and discontinuities between past and present, about which there is a large literature. These remarks are, to underscore, suggestive (see, for example, Teitelbaum and Winter 1998).

16. Data indicate that in Europe, the number of people active in the labor force is less than those too young to enter it and those who have exited it through retirement. Not surprisingly, this demographic trend presents enormous challenges for European welfare states. See, for example, Bernd Marin, "Sustainable Work, Wealth, Health and Welfare? European and U.S. Ways to Face the Aging Challenge," presented on June 9, 2004, in the Irene Flecknoe Ross lecture series, Department of Sociology, University of California – Los Angeles.

17. Again, there is a large literature on nations, states, the relationship between nations, states and population control. See, for example, Gal and Kligman (2002a) for a brief overview.

18. For an example of a demographic threat to the "American" nation, see Huntington (2004).

19. See, for example, Morgan and King (2001) and King (2002). I thank David Cook for the observation that "barren states" implies that states are reproductive agents, when it is people within their political borders who reproduce both notions of the nation and the nation's people.

20. These "others" tend to be foreigners, poor or both.

21. Immigration is not substantial and is thus not a pressing issue.

22. The war on terror has further intensified fears about foreigners seeking access to limited national resources, an observation that applies well beyond Europe. For a current example of changing citizenship laws, see Brian Lavery, "Voters Reject Automatic Citizenship for Babies Born in Ireland," *New York Times*, June 13, 2004. Although Ireland's birthrate is below replacement level, Irish voters supported a constitutional change, bringing Ireland in line with other European countries which do not automatically grant citizenship rights to those born in their territory.

23. I thank David Cook for bringing these articles to my attention. On Spain, see also Heer (2001). The title of his article is to the point: "Spain's Baby Bust: women are being asked to reproduce for the sake of the nation in Spain."

24. There are myriad examples of pronatalist and pro-family benefits, of which these are typical.

References

Alvarez, L. (2003), "Scotland Takes Action to Halt Drop in Population," *New York Times*, November 30: 4.

Berezin, M. and Schain, M. (eds) (2003), *Europe without Borders: Remapping Territory, Citizenship, and Identity in a Transnational Age*, Baltimore, MD: Johns Hopkins University Press.

Clarin (2000) "La nueva vida de 10 familias en un pueblito espanol," *Clarin* (Buenos Aires), December 19.

Ehrenreich, B. and Hochschild, A.R. (eds). (2002), *Global Women: Nannies, Maids and Sex Workers in the New Economy*, New York: Metropolitan Books.

Emigh, R.J. and Szelenyi, I. (eds). (2001), *Poverty, Ethnicity, and Gender in Eastern Europe during the Market Transition*, Westport, CT: Praeger.

Fodor, E. (2002), "Gender and the Experience of Poverty in Eastern Europe and Russia After 1989," *Communist and Post-Communist Studies*, 35(4): 369–382.

Gal, S. and Kligman, G. (2000a), *The Politics of Gender after Socialism: A Comparative-Historical Essay*, Princeton, NJ: Princeton University Press.

—— (eds). (2000b), *Reproducing Gender: Politics, Publics, and Everyday Life after Socialism*, Princeton, NJ: Princeton University Press.

Ginsburg, F.D. and Rapp, R. (eds). (1995), *Conceiving the New World Order: The Global Reproduction of Politics*, Berkeley, CA: University of California Press.

Glass, D.V. (1967), *Population: Policies and Movements in Europe*, London: Frank Cass.

Haney, L. (2002), *Inventing the Needy: Gender and the Politics of Welfare in Hungary*, Berkeley, CA: University of California Press.

Heer, J. (2001), "Spain's Baby Bust: Women are Being Asked to Reproduce for the Sake of the Nation in Spain," *National Post*, July 17.

Hobson, B., Olah, L. and Morrissens, A. (2004), "The Positive Turn or Birth-strikes? Sites of Resistance to Residual Male Breadwinner Societies and to Welfare State Restructuring," draft paper.

Hondagneu-Sotelo, P. (2001), *Domestica: Immigrant Workers Cleaning and Caring in the Shadows of Affluence*, Berkeley: University of California Press.

Huntington, S. (2004), *Who Are We? The Challenges to America's National Identity*, New York: Simon and Schuster.

Kempadoo, K. and Doezema, J. (1998), *Global Sex Workers: Rights, Resistance and Redefinition*, New York: Routledge.

King, L. (2002), "Demographic Trends, Pronatalism, and Nationalist Ideologies in the Late Twentieth Century," *Ethnic and Racial Studies*, 25(3): 367–389.

Krauss, C. (2004), "In Aging Quebec, Town Pays to Keep the Babies Coming," *New York Times*, March 2.

Laslett, B. and Brenner, J. (1989), "Gender and Social Reproduction: Historical

Perspectives," *Annual Review of Sociology*, 15: 381–404.

Lewin, T. (2003), "For More People in 20's and 30's, Home is Where the Parents Are," *New York Times*, December 22: B1, B6.

L'Express (2001) "L'Espagne, nouvel eldorado," *L'Express*, February 22.

Melegh, A. (2002*), East/West Exclusions and Discourses on Population in the 20th Century*, Working Papers on Population, Family and Welfare, 3, Budapest. Hungarian Central Statistical Office, Demographic Research Institute.

Milkman, R., Reese E. and Roth, B. (1998), "The Macrosociology of Paid Domestic Labor," *Work and Occupations*, 25(4): 483–510.

Morgan, S.P. and King, R.B. (2001), "Why Have Children in the 21st Century? Biological Predisposition, Social Coercion, Rational Choice," *European Journal of Population*, 17: 3–20.

Pessar, P.R. and Mahler, S.J. (2003), "Transnational Migration: Bringing Gender In," *International Migration Review*, 37(3): 812–846.

Schoenmaeckers, R.C. and Lodewijckx, E. (1999), "Demographic Behaviour in Europe: Some Results from FFS Country Reports and Suggestions for Further Research," *European Journal of Population*, 15: 207–240.

Szreter, S. (1993), "The Idea of Demographic Transition and the Study of Fertility Change: A Critical Intellectual History," *Population and Development* Review, 19(4): 659–701.

Teitelbaum, M. and Winter, J. (1998), *A Question of Numbers: High Migration, Low Fertility, and the Politics of National Identity*, New York: Hill and Wang.

Van de Kaa, D. (1987), "Europe's Second Demographic Transition," *Population Bulletin*, 42(1): 1–57.

Zelizer, V. (1985), *Pricing the Priceless Child: The Changing Social Value of Children*, New York: Basic Books.

Index